THE CONFEDERATE DEAD IN BROOKLYN

Biographical Sketches
of
513 Confederate
POWs

John F. Walter

HERITAGE BOOKS
2012

HERITAGE BOOKS
AN IMPRINT OF HERITAGE BOOKS, INC.

Books, CDs, and more—Worldwide

For our listing of thousands of titles see our website
at
www.HeritageBooks.com

Published 2012 by
HERITAGE BOOKS, INC.
Publishing Division
100 Railroad Ave. #104
Westminster, Maryland 21157

Copyright © 2003 John F. Walter

All rights reserved. No part of this book may be reproduced or transmitted in any form or by any means, electronic or mechanical, including photocopying, recording or by any information storage and retrieval system without written permission from the author, except for the inclusion of brief quotations in a review.

International Standard Book Numbers
Paperbound: 978-0-7884-2452-6
Clothbound: 978-0-7884-9158-0

This book is dedicated.
to the memory of southern men and
boys who lay far from home in
the earth of New York City
and to my wife, Peg,
without whose help and understanding
this work would never have been completed

John F. Walter,
Middle Village NY
May, 2003

Table of Contents

Introduction	1
Chapter 1 - Cypress Hills National Cemetery	4
Chapter 2 - Identifying the Dead	7
Chapter 3 - Military Biographies of the Dead	14
Appendix I – Checklist	168
Appendix II - Cause of Deaths	196
Appendix III - Units Represented	205
Bibliography	219
Index	221

Introduction

As a native New Yorker who has lived in the Big Apple for more than sixty years, I am always amazed to discover how many of my fellow New Yorkers have no idea that there is a National Cemetery within the city limits. Named Cypress Hills National Cemetery, it straddles the county line between Brooklyn and Queens. For those unfamiliar with New York City, it is composed of five counties - known here as boroughs. New York County is all of Manhattan Island and is probably what most people imagine when they hear of the city. Brooklyn - officially Kings County - and Queens are located on the western end of Long Island. The majority of the people who work on Manhattan live here. The Bronx is north of Manhattan and is the only part of the city on the mainland. Richmond County is better known as Staten Island and is the least urban part of the city. Other smaller islands are clustered around Manhattan, in New York Harbor, in the East River, and in Long Island Sound. It was on these that many of the Confederates were held and died.

Cypress Hills National Cemetery is divided into an old and new section. The old, the subject of this study, is located within a privately owned cemetery also known as Cypress Hills Cemetery.

A detailed map of Brooklyn and Queens shows a belt of cemeteries, many of which are more than one hundred and fifty years old, in the same area as Cypress Hills. In the early 1840's New York State passed the Rural Cemeteries Act which supported the creation of cemeteries in areas removed from city centers. New York City, following up on this Act in 1847, passed an Ordnance stating that no new cemeteries could be created on Manhattan Island. Aware that the passage of this ordnance would in no way stop New Yorkers from dying, enterprising businessmen sought out areas far enough away from New York City (which, at that time, was only Manhattan Island) to be in the country and yet close enough to be within easy travelling distance. There are now almost two dozen cemeteries that fit this definition. Once reached by stage lines leading from ferry slips along the East River, all of them are now within the borders of New York City and are reachable by mass transportation.

In the summer of 1862, in the midst of the Civil War, the Federal Government created National Cemeteries at various locations in the country. New York City, being a hub through which thousands of men passed going to and from the war and a city with a sizeable permanent military garrison as well as numerous military hospitals and camps, was chosen as one of many places where a National Cemetery would be established. A pleasantly hilly section of Cypress Hills Cemetery was purchased and transferred to the Federal Government and named Cypress Hills National Cemetery.

While all of this may be known by some of New York City's residents, the fact that more than five hundred Confederate soldiers are buried there may not be.

Genealogy and history, primarily Civil War History, began as an interest of mine while a high school student. It grew to a passion that turned it from a hobby to an avocation to an occupation as a professional genealogist and historical researcher. So busy had I become in researching Civil War units and details of the careers of individual soldiers that it took the purchase of a book to make me find time to research a subject in my own backyard. The book in question was the 1984 reprint of the *Register of Confederate Soldiers and Sailors Who Died in Federal Prisons and Military Hospital in the North*, compiled in 1912 by the War Department's Commissioner for marking Confederate graves. The reprint bears the much more manageable title of *Confederate P.O.W's* and was published by Ericson Books of Nacogdoches, Texas. The book contains the names of cemeteries from Elmira, New York, to Santa Fe, New Mexico, with dozens of locations between. On page 33 a section begins: "List of Confederate Soldiers who, while prisoners of war, died at David's Island, Hart's Island, Fort Columbus, Willett's Point, Fort Lafayette, Fort Wood, in the State of New York, and at Portsmouth Grove, in the State of Rhode Island, but subsequently removed, either to Cypress Hills National Cemetery, Brooklyn, N. Y. or elsewhere" The next ten pages contain a six long list providing the Name, Rank, Company, Regiment, Date of Death. and Number and Locality of Grave of the men buried there.. The first entry on the list reads William R. D. Abernathy, a Private in Company "H" of the Thirty-Seventh North Carolina Infantry who died on June 18, 1862 at Fort Columbus, and whose grave number is unknown, It ends more than 500 names later with George Zweigler, Private, Company E, Tenth Louisiana Infantry, who died on August 12, 1863, and is buried in grave number 775. The rank of the overwhelming number of the men is Private. They came from every ex-Confederate state except Arkansas, Missouri and Kentucky, including one man, Billy Willis, identified as a Choctaw Indian who served in Company "C" of Deneal's Regiment from the Indian Territory. There are five listed as Unknown, three of whom have a death date and a grave number recorded. The other two

Unknowns have only a grave number. A dozen are listed under their last names only.

Where did they come from? How did they manage to be buried so far from their homes? Who were they? These are all questions I attempted to answer more than five years ago as I became intrigued by the fact that so many southerners were buried in the north.

Chapter 1

There are more than three thousand Federal soldiers buried on the slope of two hills and, across a small road, in a slight valley and back up the slope of a smaller hill. Intermingled among the graves of their former northern foes, the slightly pointed Confederate markers stand out from the rounded tops of the Federal stones. Each tombstone contains the name of the individual buried there and, in most cases, his regiment or the state he was from. I first visited the office of Cypress Hills Cemetery and attempted to learn if they had any additional records besides what I already knew. The had none; in fact, I was told, all of the records of Cypress Hills were kept at the larger, newer National Cemetery at Calverton, in Suffolk County, on the eastern end of Long Island. A phone call there revealed that their records contained less information than the 1912 list. Clearly, if I wanted to know more about these men, I would have to research them myself.

I began my research by identifying each of the places named where the men died.

The first place named is David's Island, or, as it is correctly spelled, Davids Island. This small island, a long narrow stretch of land, with an area of eight acres in site, is located in Long Island Sound, the body of water north of Long Island, that separates Long Island from Connecticut and the southeast corner of mainland New York State. The island lies off New Rochelle, New York. An Army hospital, DeCamp General Hospital, was created there soon after the start of the Civil War and a military hospital was continuously maintained on the island through the Second World War. After it was closed, the buildings stood abandoned and neglected until most were destroyed by a fire in the early 1970's. The island is still U. S. Government property and it cannot be visited without its permission.

DeCamp General Hospital grew from one building at the start of the Civil War to a collection twenty-two wooden buildings divided into various wards and sections. These covered nearly the entire island. Originally Federal sick or injured received treatment there. Later wounded Federal troops arrived. Soon after the battle of Gettysburg wounded Confederates, being sent to prisoner of war camps in the north, also received treatment there. The hospital was designed to accommodate no more than eighteen hundred sick or wounded. Often, however, this number was exceeded and in August, 1864, more than twenty-five hundred were housed in the various wards of DeCamp General Hospital. Since there was no space on the island for a cemetery, most of those who died there, both Federal and Confederate, were buried in Cypress Hills.

Hart Island (almost always referred to as Hart's Island) is considerably larger than Davids Island. It, too, is located in Long Island Sound, slightly south of Davids Island, about twenty miles from the southern tip of Manhattan. It was acquired by the DeLancey family from the British Crown in 1774 and was farmed by a number of families until shortly before the Civil War. The owner at that time leased Hart Island to New York State for use as a military rendezvous, depot and training camp. The state turned it over to the Federal government in late 1861. In the summer of 1863 half of the island was designated as a prisoner of war camp and became, in a short time, one of the prison camps with the highest mortality percentage rates of all northern camps. The original camp was a stockade enclosing four acres and both prisoners and guards were housed in tents. Through the use of many of the arriving prisoners as laborers, wooden barracks were erected by March, 1864, not soon enough, however, for the prisoners to avoid the cold winter winds and storms that swept across the Sound. During the month of April, 1865, more than 3,400 prisoners were crammed into barracks, also called wards, in the camp. Each ward contained a hundred men. There were three rows of bunks and two men to a bunk. Since there were only twenty wards, the crowding must have been even worse than officially admitted. From April to July, 1865, 7% of the total prisoner population died. United States Army Medical Inspector George Lyman reported that "[t]he largest portion of deaths occurred from chronic diarrhea brought with them [by the prisoners], and pneumonia, which began to appear a few days after their arrival....The men being poorly clad, the weather wet and cold, and the barracks provided with no other bedding than such as the prisoners brought with them, the pneumonia cases developed rapidly...increased probably, to some extent by the crowded and unventilated condition of the barracks." A steamboat the "John Romer", manned by the U. S. Army, made regular trips between Manhattan and Hart Island bringing prisoners to the island. Nothing has been found to show how the bodies of those who died there were moved to Long Island, but it is probable that this same steamer performed this task. The dead would be either landed at one of the piers that then stood in Flushing Bay or, more probably, brought back down the East River to the Brooklyn terminus of the Catherine Street ferry for transport to Cypress Hills.

Hart Island was purchased by New York City in 1869 for use as a potter's field. It is now the largest such burial place in the country, containing the remains of more than three quarters of a million individuals.

Fort Columbus was a stone fort built on Governor's Island in New York Harbor, not far from the southern tip of Manhattan. It had been built in the 1830's and 1840's under the name of Fort Jay. At various times during the War, especially in late 1861 and early 1862, it held small numbers of Confederate prisoners.

Willett's Point is a narrow peninsula in the Bronx where the East River flows into Long Island Sound. A pre-Civil War installation, Fort Schuyler, stood there, and it also housed small number of prisoners of war in 1864. Fort Lafayette was a second, smaller stone fort on Governor's Island. Prisoners in both Forts Schuyler and Lafayette were kept in large damp rooms deep inside them, received no regular exercise, and rarely saw daylight while confined there.

Many of the prisoners housed in Fort Lafayette were moved to Fort Wood during the winter of 1862-1863. This star-shaped stone and brick fort stood on Bedloe's Island, in the middle of New York Harbor, almost halfway between Manhattan and Staten Island. Eventually the fort was used only for prisoners with a history of causing problems, political prisoners, and Federal soldiers serving sentences for severe crimes. Much of the fort is now gone but a part has been renovated for another purpose. Even the island's name has been changed. It is now called Liberty Island, and that part of Fort Wood still standing is part of the base of the Statue of Liberty.

Portsmouth Grove, New Hampshire, was the site of a military hospital. A small number of sick or wounded Confederate prisoners were cared for there and the remains of those who died were transferred to Cypress Hills.

Once I learned where all these places which held Confederate P.O.W.'s were, my next task became the most challenging. I would try to bring life to these more than five hundred men on this list by researching their careers as fully as possible.

Chapter 2

Many of those buried in Cypress Hills, I was to learn, are so poorly or incorrectly identified in the cemetery records, that it took considerable effort to ascertain their actual names. Others had careers which showed them to be heroes; the records of others found them to be far from heroic. Two were executed in New York and are buried in unmarked graves. Sadly, because Confederate military records are incomplete, some will never be fully identified.

Alexander Hodges, was tall for a Civil War soldier, standing six feet two inches. William Tilley was a fifty-five year private in the Fourteenth South Carolina Militia. David Amos, First Tennessee Heavy Artillery, was captured at Fort Morgan, Alabama. Alkana McHenry had his right leg amputated after being wounded at Gettysburg. William H Farmer died with sixty cents and a watch in his pockets.

Even as I walked among the headstones at Cypress Hills National Cemeteray reading the simple inscriptions of Names and Unit, I wanted to give "life" to these long dead southernors. Details such as those above were exactly what I was interested in when I began researching the Confederate buried in Cypress Hills National Cemetery.

In order to learn this information, I realized that I would have to consult their compiled service records. Confederate records of this type have been microfilmed and are available at the National Archives in Washington, Family History Centers, the Confederate Research Center in Hillsboro, Texas, and elsewhere. But making an exact identification often proved difficult. The Consolidated Index to Compiled Service Records of Confederate Soldiers (National Archives microform publication M253) contains 535 rolls of film. *The Roster of Confederate Soldiers. 1861-1865*, is a sixteen volume compilation, published by Broadfoot Publishing Co. in 1996, of the same index. Some of the names on the list of the dead at Cypress Hills, however, cannot be found on the index. C M Gice, for instance, is identified as a member of Company B, First Alabama Cavalry who died on April 18, 1865 but there is no entry on the indexes for a man with this name. When I actually examined the service records of the regiment, I could identify no one whose name even remotely resembled this. Cemetery records list an E Prestwood, a member of the Twenty-Sixth North Carolina Infantry. Again, there is no such name in the index but examination of the unit's records succesfully produced an Ervand Preswood. The only person named John Pease on the index was a member of the Third South Carolina Infantry

Battalion but his file gave no indication that he was captured or died in captivity. The only record of him (and a number of others) appears in Microform publication M347, Unfiled Papers and Slips Belonging to Confederate Compiled Service Records. This collection of 442 rolls of microfilm contains papers regarding Confederate soldiers who could not otherwise be identified. And so it was that I discovered that each name of the list had to be checked and double-checked to verify identification. Cemetery records turned out to be misspelled, incorrect, or incomplete. Despite this, positive identification and correction of their records (where necessary) was made for almost all of the men listed. One of the classic examples of errors in the cemetery records concerns the man buried in grave 812. The records give his name as Daniel Nakeep of the Fifty-Seventh North Carolina Infantry. Examination of the unit's files, however, show his was name actually Daniel Kanup who had been wounded at Gettysburg and died at Hart's Island on August 21, 1863, of Chronic Diarrhea.

William B Griffin was a twenty year old Private in the Seventeenth North Carolina Infantry regiment. He enlisted at Plymouth, North Carolina, in May, 1861, and was captured at Fort Hatteras, North Carolina in August, 1861. Taken north, he died at Fort Columbus, New York, on September 28, 1861. He appears to have been the first Confederate soldier to die in New York City.

William D Roberts died on December 13, 1865, long after the war had ended. He was the last to die in New York. A member of the Fifty-Third Tennessee Infantry, Roberts had been captured at Fort Donelson in mid-February, 1862. Exchanged and returned to duty, he was captured in July, 1863, when Port Hudson, Louisiana fell. Exchanged at Vicksburg in early October, 1863, he was captured a third time less than a month later at Connersville, Tennessee. He was held at Fort Delaware for almost a year and was again exchanged. Roberts was wounded in the knee at the Battle of Bentonville, North Carolina, in mid-March, 1865. Sent north and admitted to DeCamp General Hospital on Davids Island, New York, he died there of Phthisis. Few men, Union or Confederate, could equal the number of times he was captured.

Surviving records do not give the ages for most of those who are buried in Cypress Hills. The age of S D Early, of the Fourth Virginia Heavy Artillery, does appear in his records and he may very well have been the oldest. He was 62 when he enlisted, married, a resident of Bedford County, Virginia. He spent much of his career either hospitalized, as a hospital guard, or attached to the Quartermaster's Department. Early was captured at Petersburg, Virginia, on April 3, 1865, and was sent to Hart's Island. He died on June 24, 1865, the cause of his death being given as "old age."

A similar unique cause of death is given for John O Pridgen, a private in McDugald's North Carolina Infantry Battalion. He was detached as a railroad and telegraph guard until late 1864. After being captured in North Carolina on March 20, 1865, he was sent to Hart's Island and hospitalized there suffering from Chronic Bronchitis. On June 4, 1865, he died of "Nostalgia."

William Traitor (also carried on the rolls of the Twentieth Georgia Infantry as William Traytor, W Traiter, W F Trautor, and W W T Traitor) was hospitalized for various ailments so frequently after his enlistment in May, 1861, that he was absent from most of the engagements his regiment fought in. He returned to his unit in early April, 1863, and accompanied it north. At the battle of Gettysburg, Traitor was wounded in the breast, shoulder, thigh, lungs, and eye and was captured when Federal troops occupied the Confederate field hospitals. Despite the number of his wounds, he survived hospitalization at DeCamp General Hospital and was moved to Fort Wood in mid-October, 1863, only to die there a month later.

He was only one of many who died as a result of wounds received at Gettysburg. Among them was Robert Carroll, Third Alabama Infantry, whose effects when he died included a hymn book and an empty pocket book. William G Ivey of the Eleventh North Carolina Infantry was survived by his mother, Eliza, of Chapel Hill. Malachi Statton was a sergeant in the Thirty-Seventh North Carolina Infantry who had survived a wound at Chancellorsville. More than one hundred and twenty-five of those buried in Cypress Hills died between July 15th and August 31st, 1863, almost all as a result of wounds received at Gettysburg.

Despite this, large numbers of men buried at Cypress Hills died of disease. Patrick Burnes, for instance, a private of the Fifteenth Texas Infantry regiment was captured at Cane River, Louisiana, in the spring of 1864. Sent to New Orleans, he was reported hospitalized there suffering from diarrhea. He was readmitted to this facility on May 31, July 27, August 10, and September 29, suffering from the same ailment. Early in October he was transferred to Ship Island, Mississippi, and, from there, to New York City. He appears to have again been stricken on the voyage north and upon his arrival at New York he was placed in the Post Hospital at Fort Columbus. There, on November 19th, he finally died, totally dehydrated by his sickness.

Quite a few of the men sent as prisoners to New York by ship arrived sick. Only one, however, died before the ship arrived in New York. A letter in his file reads: "I have the honor to report that on July 4, 1864, Murdock Jones, Company D, 64 Georgia Regiment, died on the Hospital Transport 'Thomas P. Way'". The letter went on to explain that his personal effects consisted of a "pocket book containing $22.00 Rebel currency, 1 coat, 1 pair pantaloons, 3 letters from his wife [and] 10 postage stamps." The writer of the letter, J B Merwin, Chaplain, U S Army added that '[t]hese things are now in my possession. Jones was buried in grave number 1216 by the Government Undertaker, A J Case.

One of the men buried at Cypress Hill, E M Archibald (cemetery records gives his name as E N Archibald) was captured by the U S Navy. A private in the Seventh Alabama Cavalry, he was captured by a naval shore party at Mobile Point, Alabama. He, too, was held in New Orleans and Ship Island before being transported to Fort Columbus, New York, where he died shortly before Christmas Day, 1864.

The records of many of the men show them to have been good soldiers, some heroic. Richmond Phillips was wounded and captured at Gettysburg. Held in captivity until the spring of 1864, he returned to duty with the Forty-Seventh North Carolina Infantry, was wounded again in the spring of 1864, and was finally captured on April 3, 1865. R F Mattox was also wounded and captured in Pennsylvania in July, 1863. Exchanged, he was so badly injured that he was assigned to the Invalid Corps but was back with his original regiment, the Eighteenth Virginia Infantry. He, too, was re-captured in April, 1865. David Harmon, Twenty-Sixth North Carolina Infantry, was wounded in the face at Chancellorsville and was in and out of hospitals thereafter. He was finally captured at Farmville, Virginia, on April 6, 1865. Ulysses Fisher of the Sixth Louisiana Infantry was wounded in the foot at Antietam and in the thigh at Gettysburg. He died on Davids Island in early September, 1863. Alexander Hodges joined the Thirty-Eighth North Carolina on April 18, 1864. Three weeks later he was wounded at the Wilderness and as late as November was reported to have an "Unhealed gun shot wound on [the] left leg." He was captured on April 3, 1865, and died on July 21, 1865. And the list of men with similar details could go on and on.

Not all of the men buried at Cypress Hills had such meritorious records, however. Jefferson Coindrey, of the Fourteenth Virginia Infantry, for instance, enlisted in May, 1861, and was promoted Corporal by year's end. He was absent without leave in early January and when he returned to the regiment was reduced to the rank of Private. In the summer of 1862 he was again promoted to Corporal only to desert again. He was back with the unit in early 1863 but the rolls of January, 1864, shows that was he under arrest, having been absent without leave for eleven days the previous month. He was court-martialed and lost his pay for two months. On February 2, 1864, he deserted "on the march from Newberne, North Carolina." It is not known when, if ever, he returned to the regiment, only that he died on Davids Island on July 2, 1865.

Since desertion was a huge problem to both Union and Confederate forces, it is not unusual to find the word "deserted" mentioned so frequently in the files of the men buried at Cypress Hills. It appears in the files of more than a tenth of the men buried there.

At least one man, Joshua Byrd (buried under the name of Joshua Bird), of the Third North Carolina Heavy Artillery, appears to have violated an even more serious law.. His file contains references to the fact that he was being held in confinement at Fort Fisher, North Carolina, in July, 1862, and on October 3, 1862, he was "Sentenced to be Shot Dead." General Daniel H Hill commuted his sentence on June 5, 1863 and Bird served at Fort Fisher for the rest of his career. Confederate court martial records are very incomplete, most of them having been destroyed by the Confederate Army itself when Richmond was evacuated, and no record of what his offense was has been found. He was captured on April 1, 1865, having escaped from Fort Fisher when it fell in January of that year. Sent north to Hart's Island, he died there of Typhoid Fever a month and a half later.

The more I researched these men, the more I learned of the little things that made them unique. One of the few identified as being foreign born was George Zweigler, of Germany, Tenth Louisiana Infantry, alphabetically the last name on the cemetery records. Another, Michael McCarty, First Virginia Infantry Battalion, had been hospitalized prior to being captured for treatment of venereal disease. Simon Long was a "Steamboatman" prior to entering the service. Another, James Little, had been company cook for most of his career.

And there is one who served in a Choctaw regiment from the Indian Territory. His name was James P Willis, He served in Deneale's Regiment of Choctaw Warriors during the first six months of 1862, Later that year he was reported in the First Choctaw and Chickasaw Mounted Rifles. No other records are found about him until his name appears on the burial records under the date of May 12., 1863. How he, as a member of a unit that served its entire career in the Indian Territory, Arkansas, and Missouri, ended up buried in Brooklyn, New York, is, perhaps, the greatest mystery of all the Confederate there.

Two men are listed as being buried in Cypress Hills Cemetery "or elsewhere." Both were executed by the United States Army in early 1865. John Yeates Beall was tried for "Violating the Rules of War" and "Acting as a Spy" because of his operations on Lake Erie in attempting to free Confederate prisoners on Johnson's Island, near Sandusky, Ohio, and for subsequently attempting to sabotage the railroad between Buffalo and Dunkirk, New York. Robert C Kennedy was tried as a spy for his part in the setting of numerous fires in New York City in November, 1864. Places burned by him and others (who were never tired) included a number of hotels and Barnum's Museum. They were executed (Beall on February 24, 1865, Kennedy on March 25, 1865) on Governor's Island. Some reports indicate that Beall's body was taken to Green-Wood Cemetery in Brooklyn but there are no records of his being buried there. Kennedy was buried in an unmarked grave on the island in New York Harbor. All of the bodies buried on the island were disinterred in the late 1870's and re-buried in Cypress Hills. It is probable that both he and Beall are buried in unmarked graves in the National Cemetery.

Story after story could be told about the Confederates buried in Brooklyn. Two, however, are so poignant that their inclusion here are imperative.

Jacob Gotte, First South Carolina Artillery, took the Oath of Allegiance on June 17, 1865, at Hart's Island and was to return to his home in Charleston, South Carolina. He made it no further than the Transit Hospital in Manhattan, however. He died there on June 28, 1865.

Finally, a letter in the file of Samuel M Thompson, Twelfth Texas Cavalry, to Federal authorities, reads in part: "My son...was captured by a portion of your forces last September in the state of Louisiana....I wish to ascertain where he is imprisoned in order that I might write to him....My son is a mere boy..." It was signed by Charles W Thompson and dated December 20, 1864. Two days before he penned the letter, however, his son, seventeen years old, died of Chronic Diarrhea at Fort Columbus and was buried in grave number 1817.

They died from causes ranging from Bronchitis to Typhoid Fever, from Pneumonia to Variola, from Gunshot Wounds to Diarrhea. They came from places like Lightwood Hot Springs, South Carolina, Riggsbee's Store, North Carolina, Stone Wall, Mississippi, New Market, Virginia, Tallahassee, Florida, and Wilkinson, Georgia. Some were married. Most were farmers. Quite a few could not sign their own names. Almost none of them appear to have known each other in life; yet, together, they sleep forever in the rolling hills of a cemetery in Brooklyn, New York, their graves intermixed with those of Federal dead.

What follows are brief resumes of the military careers of the Confederate dead in Brooklyn.

Chapter 3

The names shown on the following list are as they appear on the list of Confederate soldiers buried in Cypress Hills National Cemetery as mentioned above. In those cases where research has shown their names as being incorrectly reported, this fact is pointed out in each brief sketch of their careers. Appendex I, at the end of this chapter, lists all those named with both the correct names and alternate spellings.

Almost all Confederate military records are incomplete either because monthly records were destroyed during the war or, in many cases. never prepared. This explains many of the gaps in the records of the men below.

***** ***** *****

ABERNATHY, William R. R. - Abernathy, twenty-seven, enlisted on October 6, 1861, in Company "A", Thirty-Seventh North Carolina Infantry regiment. He was a farmer, native of Gaston County, who stood five feet nine inches tall. Abernathy had black hair, blue eyes, and a sallow complexion. Having originally enlisted for twelve months, his "Enlistment [was] extended 2 years [and] $50 bounty [was] due." On May 27, 1862, he was captured at Hanover Court House, Virginia, and sent to Fort Columbus, New York where he died on June 14, 1862 of Typhoid Fever. His date of death is given as June 18th on burial records, however.

ADAMS, A. B. - He was thirty-four years old when he enlisted, on August 26, 1861, as a Private in Company "K" of the Fourteenth South Carolina Infantry regiment. Information in his consolidated service file shows that he had traveled forty-two miles to enlist at Camp Butler. Incomplete records next show that he was hospitalized at Chimborazo Hospital Number 2, Richmond, Va., diagnosed with Continuous Fever. On the final day of July, 1862, Adams was transferred to Danville, Virginia. It is not known when he returned to the unit but he was present at the battle of Gettysburg, in July, 1863 where he was wounded. When the Army of Northern Virginia retreated from Gettysburg, Adams was among the large number of Confederate soldiers too badly injured to be taken with it. He was captured when Federal troops occupied the Confederate field hospitals at Gettysburg and not long after transferred north, arriving at DeCamp General Hospital, on Davids Island, New York. He died there as a result of his gun shot wound on August 5, 1863. Records indicate that he was buried in grave number 748 at the Cypress Hills National Cemetery.

ALLEN, R. F. - Cemetery records show Allen's name as above, but his service file indicates that his name was Rufus F. Allen. He was born in Johnston, North Carolina and was commissioned First-Lieutenant in Company "C", Thirty-Eighth North Carolina Infantry on October 8, 1861, at Camp Mangum, near Raleigh, North Carolina. At six feet, four inches, he was considerably taller than the average Confederate soldier. His term of enlistment was for the duration of the war. Allen was Absent on Leave from the regiment from January through March, 1862. The rolls of May, 1862, show him Present but records for the unit from July through October, 1862, are missing. He was with the unit in the final two months of 1862. Allen was reported ill in early 1863 and granted a Sick Furlough in February, 1863. He returned to the regiment on March 14, 1863. Allen commanded Company "C" at the Battle of Chancellorsville. At Gettysburg, in early July, Allen was wounded and left at a field hospital, where he was captured. Sent north, he arrived at DeCamp General Hospital on July 17, 1863. Slightly more than a month later, on August 20, 1863, he died there of "Inflammation of Lungs." He is buried in grave number 861, one of a relatively small number of officers buried at Cypress Hills National Cemetery.

ALLEN, Robert H. - A thirty-one year old resident of Anson County, Allen enlisted in Company "I", Forty-Third North Carolina Infantry regiment on May 9, 1862, at Wadesboro. North Carolina. He was six feet tall, had fair complexion, dark hair, and blue eyes. He was reported present with the regiment from his date of enlistment until February, 1865. Allen was never reported sick, absent, or on leave. He was captured on April 2, 1865, when Petersburg, Virginia, fell to Federal forces. Shortly afterwards he was moved with thousands of other captured Confederates to City Point, Virginia. From there he was sent to Hart Island, New York, but the date of his arrival there is not known. Soon after Allen was reported to be suffering from chronic diarrhea. He died as a result of this at the Post Hospital, Hart Island, on June 12, 1865. He is buried in grave 2516.

AMOS, David - David Amos enlisted in the fall of 1863 directly into the Confederate Army and was assigned to the Confederate Ordnance Department at Atlanta, Georgia. In early February, 1864, he accompanied a Sergeant A K Levering to Bristol, Tennessee, where they were placed in charge of an ordnance train with orders to return with it to Atlanta. Later that month Amos received $45.50 for "Expenses incurred" during this movement. On March 6, 1864, he was permitted to transfer to

Company "B" of the First Tennessee Heavy Artillery regiment. He joined his company at Fort Morgan, at the mouth of Mobile Bay, Alabama. Federal forces seized this fortification on August 23, 1864, after a two week siege. He was transferred to New Orleans, Louisiana, but remained there only briefly before being transferred to New York City, arriving there on September 18, 1864. On November 5, 1864, he was admitted to the Post Hospital, Fort Columbus, New York, with "Intermittent fever." Five days later he was released from the Post hospital only to be readmitted on November 28, 1864, suffering from Variola. He died at the Post Hospital on December 10, 1864 and was buried in grave 1937 at Cypress Hills the following day. Burial records, however, give his date of death as December 11, 1864.

  ANDERSON, James - Cemetery records provide no information as to James Anderson's unit and the only information about him is found in the file of Miscellaneous, Unfiled Confederate Records. These show that he was a Lieutenant and that he was received at Fort Lafayette, New York, on November 20, 1863 and that he died there on December 20th, no cause being given. The date of death appears as December 2nd in burial records, however. His grave number is not recorded.

  ANDERSON, Joseph R. - Cypress Hills Cemetery records shows his middle initial as "R" but his consolidated service file shows that his name was actually Joseph K. Anderson. He enlisted in Company "C" of the Eighth Virginia Infantry for a three year term of service in Nelson County, Virginia. Records of the regiment show that he was present with the unit from his enlistment until at least December, 1864. Anderson was captured at Sutherland Station on April 3, 1865. Transferred from City Point, Va. to Hart Island, New York, he died of pneumonia there on May 11, 1865 and was buried in grave 2763 at Cypress Hills.

  ANDERSON, Leroy - Anderson was a Private in Company "F", First Maryland Infantry Battalion. (Cemetery information incorrectly identify his unit as the First Maryland Infantry regiment.) No information on him is found in the files of the National Archives until his name appears on a list of sick and wounded who arrived from Gettysburg, Pa. at DeCamp General Hospital, Davids Island, New York, on July 17, 1863. He had been wounded in the right thigh. Anderson died at DeCamp Hospital of Pyaemia on August 27, 1863. No grave has been located for him but a notation in the Cemetery records state that his remains were "taken to Maryland by his father."

ARCHIBALD, E. N. - Burial records show his name as listed above but his service file shows his name as E M Archibald. His name also is reported at E A Archibald on a small number of records. Archibald, forty-five and married, enlisted in the Seventh Alabama Cavalry in Green County Alabama on August 22, 1863 for the "duration of the war." Records indicate that he provided his own horse when he enlisted and for this he received forty cents a day. Present from enlistment until October 31, 1863, he received $26.80, "Pay due for Horse". After a gap in the unit's records, Archibald is again shown as present from February 29 to May 1, 1864. On July 22, 1864, while on scouting duty at Mobile Point, Alabama, he was captured by a U S Navy shore party. Transported to New Orleans, Louisiana., he was held at Steam Levee Press No. 4 in that city until October 5, 1864. Moved to Ship Island, Mississippi, he remained there a month, from October 7th to November 5th when he was transported to New York City. He arrived at Fort Columbus, New York on November 16, 1864, suffering from diarrhea. He was hospitalized at the post hospital at Fort Columbus three days later. Slightly less than a month after that, on December 17, 1864, he died of Chronic diarrhea. He was buried in grave 1269 at Cypress Hills.

ATTLEBERRY, Charles - Attleberry enlisted, at the age of twenty-three, in Company C, Second Texas Cavalry. His name on the files is also reported as Charles Atteberry, Charles Atleberry, and Charles Atleburg. There are no Confederate records that mention him. Federal records, however, indicate that he was captured at Chickpoage, Louisiana., on April 18, 1864 and was sent to New Orleans, Louisiana. In early June, 1864, he was admitted to St. Louis U S Army General Hospital in New Orleans, suffering from Chronic Diarrhea. On June 13, 1864 he was released from the hospital and returned to captivity. He was once again stricken with the same ailment and he was readmitted to St. Louis General Hospital on September 7, 1864. He spent more than a month in this hospital before being transferred to Ship Island, Mississippi, on October 20, 1864. Transferred to New York City on November 5th, he arrived at Fort Columbus on November 16, 1864, once again ill with diarrhea. Admitted to the General Hospital at Fort Columbus, Attleberry died there on November 25, 1864. A second entry gives his date of death as November 26th. He is buried in grave number 2181.

BAILEY, W. - William R Bailey enlisted on August 26, 1861, in Company "K" of the First (Lawton's/Mercer's/Olmstead's) Georgia Infantry at Savannah for a twelve month term. He was present with his unit from that date until April, 1862. He re-enlisted in late December, 1861, for three years, receiving a $25.00 bounty. Deducted from this was the price of one pair of shoes. Bailey was captured at Fort Pulaski, Georgia, on April 11, 1862. He is next mentioned on May 29, 1862, when he was admitted to the U S Army General Hospital at Hilton Head, South Carolina, no reason being given. He was released from this hospital on June 14, 1862. More than two weeks later, on June 26, 1862, his name appears on a Roll of Prisoners at Fort Columbus, New York. He died there on June 27, 1862 although a second report indicates June 28th. No cause of death is given. Not buried until July 3, 1862, his remains were placed in grave 148.

BAKER, G. D. - His unit is not reported on the cemetery records and nothing has been found about him or his career. The records of more than one hundred Confederate soldiers named Baker with a first name beginning with "G" do not match the little found in cemetery records He died on July 6, 1862 and is buried in grave 158.

BARBURY, J. E. - The records of the Twenty-Eighth North Carolina Infantry regiment show that his name was actually James E Barbee. He enlisted in Company "D" of that regiment in Albermarle County, North Carolina, on July 29, 1861, for a one year term of service. The son of Josiah Barbee, he was single, and nineteen years old when he enlisted. His description shows him six feet, one and a half inches tall, with dark hair, hazel eyes, and dark complexion. He was present with the regiment from his enlistment until late May, 1862. He re-enlisted on February 28, 1862, for an additional two years and was paid a $50.00 bounty. Barbury was captured at Hanover Court House, Virginia, on May 27, 1862. On June 4, 1862 he arrived at Fort Columbus, Governor's Island, New York. Three days later, on June 7, 1862, he died from Febris Typhoides. He was buried in grave 4443 at Cypress Hills. His father applied for his unpaid wages and received them in two installments, September 6, 1862, and May 15, 1863.

BARKER, Killis - Barker, Georgia born. was an eighteen year old farmer from Stone Wall, Mississippi. He enlisted at Fredericksburg, Virginia, on March 16, 1863, and was present with the regiment until early July, 1863. During the second days' fighting at Gettysburg, Pa., Barker was wounded in the lungs and left to be cared for by Federal forces when the Army of Northern Virginia retreated. Sent to DeCamp General Hospital, Davids Island, New York, arriving on July 24, 1863, he died there of a secondary hemorrhage on August 14, 1863. He is buried in grave number 788.

BARNES, James - Burial records show that Barnes died on Nov. 14, 1864 and is buried in grave 1840. He is identified as a Private in Company "A", First Alabama Artillery. No one by this name is found in the regiment, however, and no Confederate soldier named Barnes appears to match the little information known about him.

BARTLEY, Smith - No one by the name of Smith Bartley is found in any Confederate records but a man named Bartley Smith is found in the Unfiled Miscellaneous Confederate Papers. He was shown as a member of "Co. _, Montgomery Guards." This unofficial designation was used for Company "E", Twenty-Second Georgia Artillery Battalion, Company "K", Twentieth Georgia Infantry, Company "F", First Louisiana Infantry, Company "H", Forty-Fourth North Carolina Infantry, Company "C", First Virginia Infantry, and Company "F", Nineteenth Virginia Infantry. No one by this name, however, is found on the rolls of any of these companies. The only information known about him shows that he was admitted to the U S Post Hospital, Fort Columbus, New York, on May 30, 1862. He died there of pneumonia on the same day and is buried in grave number 4452. The date of death in cemetery records is given as May 20th.

BASS, Jethro - Jethroe Bass (as his first name is spelled on most of his service files) was 25 years old when he enlisted in Wayne County, North Carolina in Company "C" of the Second North Carolina Infantry. Illiterate, he signed his name with an "X" when he enlisted for the duration of the war at Camp Mangum on August 21, 1861. He began his career as a Confederate soldier there, one that would last until the end of the war, but saw him ill or absent far more frequently than when he was with the regiment. He was present with the unit from enlistment until October, 1862. There are no regimental records for late 1862 but in January, 1863, he was shown as Absent Without Leave. This record was corrected shortly afterwards when it was noted that he was serving as a nurse at the Confederate hospital in Goldsboro, North Carolina. Sent to rejoin his unit, he was hospitalized at General Hospital #13, Richmond, Virginia, on October 13, 1863, with Bronchitis. On January 9, 1864, he was reported at General Hospital #9 (Receiving and Wayside Hospital.) Still declared unfit for service, he was next reported at Jackson Hospital, Richmond, on February 29, 1864. In March, 1864 he was reported Absent without Leave and was arrested in Richmond later that month and confined at Castle Thunder, Richmond. Once released from Castle Thunder he was again hospitalized until June 29, 1864. On June 29, 1864, Bass finally returned to the Second North Carolina Infantry. Bass was captured at Petersburg, Virginia, April 3, 1865. Sent north, he was held at Hart Island, New York. He died there of Phthisis on June 3, 1865. He is buried in grave 2932.

BEALL, John Yates - Beall was born at Walnut Grove, his family's farm, in Jefferson County, Virginia. on Jan. 1, 1835[1]. He graduated from the Universty of Virginia in 1855, As a member of the Virginia militia, he was present at the execution of John Brown for his raid on Harper's Ferry. At the outbreak of the War, Beall enlisted in Company "G", Second Virginia Infantry regiment. Absent at the Battle of Bull Run, Beall was wounded in the right lung at Falling Waters, West Virginia, on October 15, 1861. He was furloughed and permitted to pass through the lines, moving to Dubuque, Iowa, and Chicago, Illinois. On November 20, 1862, he was living in Dundas, Canada, and, on Jan., 5, 1863, he passed through Cincinnati, Ohio, en route back to the south. Upon returning to Virginia, he was introduced to Stephen Mallory, Confederate Secretary of Navy. Beall was commissioned an Acting Master in the southern navy on March 5, 1863, and was instructed to raid Federal shipping operating in Chesapeake Bay. He proved succesful in these operations but was captured at Tangier Inlet, Virginia, on November 15, 1863, and sent to Fort McHenry, Baltimore, Maryland. He and sixteen other prisoners of war were placed in chains for "piracy." When Confederate authorities learned of this, seventeen U S Marines and two naval officers, held as prisoners in the north, were placed in similar restraints. After being held in chains for forty-two days, Beall was released. In April, 1864, he was moved to Virginia and he was exchanged at City Point, Virginia, on May 5, 1864. After a short furlough, he crossed through the lines again to the Eastern Shore of Virginia. From there he moved to Baltimore, New York City, and back to Canada to put into effect his plan to free the Confederate prisoners held on Johnson's Island, off Sandusky, Ohio, in Lake Erie. On September 14, 1864, he was at Windsor, Canada, and a few days later with twenty men Beale seized the Lake Erie steamer "Philo Parsons" to carry out the plan. Only because the majority of his

---

[1] Information for Beall's biography was obtained primarily from *Memoir of John Yates Beall: His Life; Trial; Correspondence; Diary and Private Manuscript Found Among His Papers, Inclduing His Own Account of the Raid on Lake Erie*, edited by Daniel B Lucas and published by John Lovell, Montreal, in 1865.

crew refused to accompany him in the final phase of this operation did the plan fail. He returned across Lake Erie, scuttled the steamer, and returned to Canada. On December 16, 1864, Beall was captured at Niagara, New York while on board to train to Buffalo. Information in his possession indicated that he was about to raid the railroad line between Buffalo and Dunkirk, New York. Transported to New York City, he was confined at Fort Lafayette. In early January, 1865 he was arraigned there to be tried before a court-martial composed of six Federal officers.[2] His trial began on January 17, 1865, charged with Violating the Laws of War and Acting As a Spy. Found guilty of five of six charges of the first count and three of the second, he was sentenced to be hanged by the neck until dead.[3] After reviews of the case by the commander of the Department of the East, President Lincoln refused to overturn the verdict, Beall was moved to Governor's Island, New York. He was executed there on February 24, 1865. Some reports indicate that his body was claimed by two friends and that he was buried in Green-Wood Cemetery in Brooklyn, New York. There is no record of his remains being buried there, however. Indications are that his remains were buried in an unmarked grave on Governors's Island and then relocated to Cypress Hills. There are no records to indicate where his remains were finally buried.

BEARD, James O. - The records of a number of men buried at Cypress Hills are at odds with their military records. James O Beard, Private, "C", First South Carolina Rifles, is one of these men. He enlisted at Camp Perkins, South Carolina for three years on July 20, 1861. Unit records next show that he was present with the regiment from September, 1861 until February, 1862. Detached for service in the Quartermaster Department, Beard served in this capacity for at least a month. Regimental records for most of 1862 do not exist but in January, 1863, he was reported detached with the Medical Department, serving as an Ambulance Driver until June, 1863. On the 3rd of that month, Beard was admitted to the Farmville, Virginia, General Hospital, where he remained until July 16th. Returned to duty as Ambulance Driver, he served in this capacity until early, 1864. Beard received a "Furlough of Indulgence" in February, 1864. On

---

[2] Brigadier-Generals Fitz Henry Warren and William H Morris, Colonels M S Howe and H Day, Brevet Lieutenant-Colonel R F O'Bierne, and Major G W Wallace.
[3] He was not found guilty of the one charge only because an error in the date on the original indictment invalidated it.

May 11, 1864, he was readmitted to the General Hospital at Farmville after being wounded in the leg. A week later, on May 18, 1864, he was sent home on Wounded Furlough for sixty days. It is not known why, but he did not return to the regiment until September 10, 1864. Beard was among those members of the First South Carolina Rifles at Appomattox Court House on April 9, 1865. There are no records of his being sent north or any reason why he would have been, but cemetery records show that James O Beard of the First South Carolina Rifles was buried on May 23, 1865 in grave number 2861.

BECKMAN, W. H. - Cemetery records show an individual with this name buried at Cypress Hills on May 18, 1865 in grave 2820. He was identified as a Private in Company K, Thirty-Third North Carolina Infantry regiment. No one with this name appears on the rolls of the regiment, however, and records of no man named Beckman match the little known about the man.

BELLSHAW, John - Unfiled miscellaneous records show that John Bellshaw, eighteen, a resident of Petersburg, Virginia, was captured when that city fell in early April, 1865. Bellshaw was listed as a member of the Virginia Militia although no specific unit was given. He died on July 3, 1865, and is buried in grave 3085.

BENNETT, A. W. - Cemetery records identify A W Bennett as a Private of the Tenth Alabama Infantry regiment who was buried in grave 3592 on April 17, 1865. No matching military records for a man with this name, however, have not been located.

BENSON, Jesse W. - Born in Guilford, North Carolina, Jesse Benson was thirty-one years old when he enlisted at Greensboro, North Carolina, on February 27, 1862 for three years or the duration of the war. He was assigned to Company "B", Forty-Fifth North Carolina Infantry. He was a farmer, six feet tall. Benson was present with his unit through June, 1862. He was hospitalized at Petersburg, Virginia, where he remained until September, 1862. Granted a furlough, he did not return to the regiment until March, 1863. At Gettysburg in July, 1863, Benson was severely wounded in the arm. He was one of the many wounded Confederates left at Gettysburg when the Army of Northern Virginia retreated. His arm was amputated soon afterwards and, despite this, he was sent north, arriving at DeCamp General Hospital, Davids Island, New York, on July 19, 1863. Benson died there on July 25, 1863 of Pyaemia and is buried in grave number 688.

BIRD, Josiah - Although cemetery records show his name as above, his service file indicates that his name was actually

Joshua Byrd. He was 26 years old and married when he enlisted in Lenoir County, N. C. on Aug. 1, 1861 as a Private in Company "A", Third North Carolina Heavy Artillery for a twelve month term of service. He appears on no regimental records until Nov., 1861. From then until June, 1862, he was reported present. A letter from his wife, Nancy E Byrd, dated October 8, 1861, explains his absence from any records until November. According to her letter, in which she was attempting to collect her husband's back pay, he was captured at Fort Hatteras on August 29, 1861. There are no records, Federal or Confederate, regarding his capture or confinement at that time, however. Paid a $50.00 bonus in May, 1862, he re-enlisted at that time for an additional three year term. On July 17, 1862, he was placed in arrest at Fort Fisher and placed in confinement. Unfortunately, there are no records of the charges against him or of his subsequent court martial. Whatever the reason, it must have been quite serious as a note on the muster of January, 1863 reads "Sentenced to be Shot Dead, Oct. 3, 1862." An almost maddening silence about the details of he case are increased by an entry in the May-June, 1863 muster: "Released from arrest by order of Maj. Gen. D H Hill, June 5, 1863." He was listed as Present from August 31, 1863 until December 31, 1864. In mid-May, 1864, he was reported on picket duty near Fort Fisher and, in July, 1864, at Confederate States Hospital #3, Greensboro, North Carolina. He was returned to his unit from that hospital on July 20, 1864. Either he was detached from duty at Fort Fisher when that place was captured in January, 1865 or was among the small number who escaped because on March 2, 1865, he was re-admitted to Hospital #3, Greensboro. Two days later he returned to his regiment, members of which, by this point, were serving as infantrymen. Bird was captured at Mosley Hall, North Carolina on either March 31st or April 1st, 1865. He was sent to Newberne and, from there to Hart's Island, New York, arriving there on April 10, 1865. On May 22, 1865, he died of typhoid fever and is buried in grave 2855 at Cypress Hills.

BIRD, W. L. - Bird, an early conscript into the Confederate ranks, was mustered in at Columbia, South Carolina, for a three year term of service on July 10, 1862, He was assigned to Company "G", Second South Carolina Infantry. His service file shows him present until July 2, 1863. Bird was wounded at Gettysburg, Pennsylvania, on July 2, 1863 and was among those left behind when the Army of Northern Virginia retreated. Transferred north, he arrived at DeCamp General Hospital, on

July 23, 1863. He died there as a result of his gun shot wound on August 29, 1863. Bird is buried in grave 830.

BLAKE, A. P. - Blake (also carried on the rolls as E Blake and E C Blake) enlisted at Winchester, Virginia, on March 10, 1862 in Cutshaw's Virginia Artillery Company. Records of this company are incomplete. Shortly after the end of the Maryland Campaign the artillery of the Army of Northern Virginia was reorganized. As a result of this reorganization, Cutshaw's Artillery Company was disbanded and its members assigned to Carpenter's Virginia Artillery Company (also known as the Allegheny Virginia Artillery Company). He was present with that unit until early July, 1863. Blake's arm was fractured at the Battle of Gettysburg and he was captured there when Federal troops occupied the Confederate field hospitals. He was sent to DeCamp General Hospital, Davids Island, New York, arriving there on July 23, 1863. He died there of Pyaemia on August 8, 1863 and is buried in grave 789 at Cypress Hills National Cemetery.

BLANKENSHIP, J. T. - This individual is another of those for whom the cemetery records do not match the military records. A Private James Blankenship of Company "E" of the Thirty-Seventh North Carolina Infantry regiment died on June 13, 1863, at the Confederate General Hospital, Lynchburg, Virginia. A Thomas Blankenship (also listed as Thomas E. Blankenship) was also carried on the rolls of this company. At the age of twenty-four he enlisted at Charlotte, North Carolina, on October 22, 1861 for a one year term of service. A resident of Mecklenburg, North Carolina, he was a farmer, 5' 7" tall, with light hair, light complexion, and light eyes. He was present from January to April, 1862. In the early spring of 1862 he extended his enlistment for an additional two years for which he received a $50.00 bounty. In June, 1862, he was reported as dead but these records were corrected the following month by showing that he had been wounded, shot in the back, and captured at Hanover Court House on May 27, 1862. Three days later Blankenship was admitted to Trippler General Hospital, Fort Monroe, Virginia. His stay there was brief. On July 7, 1862 he was admitted to Portsmouth Grove Hospital, Rhode Island. No date is given but he was transferred to Fort Columbus, New York, where he died on September 23, 1862. Cemetery records give the date as Sept. 24, 1862, however. It is almost certain that the body buried in grave 432 at Cypress Hills is that of Thomas Blankesnhip rather than that of J T Blankenship but is not known why the cemetery records are in error.

BLOCK, C. - No one by the name of C Block served in the Thirty-Eighth North Carolina Infantry, but the files of Duncan Block indicate that he is the man referred to. Duncan enlisted on May 3, 1862, at Fayetteville, Cumberland County, North Carolina, for a three year term of service in Company "K". Soon after enlisting he was reported sick at the Brigade Hospital. He was later moved to the Camp Winder Third Division Hospital, Richmond, Virginia, from which he was furloughed on September 26, 1862. Unit records show that he remained at home until February, 1863. He rejoined the Thirty-Eighth North Carolina Infantry on February 23, 1863. Block was wounded in the knee at Gettysburg, Pennsylvania. Among those who were left at the Confederate Field Hospitals there, Block was sent to DeCamp General Hospital, Davids Island. He arrived there on July 19, 1863 and died the same day. Block is buried in grave 659 at Cypress Hills.

BLOOD, L. W. - Consolidated service files indicate that this soldier's name was Levi William Blount. On May 8, 1861, he enlisted in Company "G" (nicknamed the Dixie Boys), Thirteenth North Carolina Infantry regiment. He was a seventeen year old farmer. His original term of enlistment was for twelve months which he extended for the duration of the War in early 1862. Levi was present with his unit from the date of his enlistment until July, 1863. Blood was wounded and captured at Gettysburg. (It is not know if he was captured during the battle or left at one of the Confederate field hospitals). Sent north, he arrived at DeCamp General Hospital on Davids Island, July 17, 1863. Slightly less than a month later, on August 13, 1863, he died of Pyaemia. He is buried in grave 783, Cypress Hills.

BLOUNT, Hosea - Cemetery records indicate that Blount served in Company "F" of the Seventh North Carolina Infantry regiment. His service file indicates that he was actually a member of Company "F" of the Seventeenth North Carolina Infantry.[4] A resident of Washington County, North Carolina, he was mustered in at Beacon Island, on June 20, 1861. No details are found regarding his capture or being sent north but it is probable that he was taken when Cape Hatteras was seized by Federal forces in

---

[4]There were two North Carolina units numbered First to Tenth created in the spring of 1861. In order to avoid confusion, one set of these was renumbered the Eleventh to Twentieth in the early summer of that year. Despite this renumbering, many instances exist were the original designation continued to be used. This appears to explain the unit "error" in Blount's records.

August, 1861. Blount died at Fort Columbus, Governor's Island, New York, on September 30, 1861 and is buried in grave number 4444 at Cypress Hills, one of those whose remains were transferred to the cemetery when the bodies buried on Governor's Island were moved.

BLUNT, T. H. - Blunt enlisted at Waynesborough, Georgia on April 19, 1861, for twelve months. He is also carried on the regiment's rolls as T. C. C. Blunt. He served in Company "D", Second Georgia Infantry. Regimental records of this unit are very few and nothing is found about Blunt until he was wounded in the shoulder at Gettysburg.. Blunt was left in a Field Hospital at Gettysburg when Lee's army retreated. Sent north, he arrived at Hart Island, New York, on July 23, 1863. He died there of Pyaemia, two weeks later, on August 8, 1863. His body was placed in grave 755.

BOGGS, John D. - Born in Lincoln County, North Carolina, Boggs was twenty-seven years old when he enlisted in Company "C", Fifty-Fifth North Carolina Infantry on March 29, 1862 at Cross Roads, North Carolina. He stood five feet seven inches tall and was a resident of Cleveland, North Carolina. Boggs was mustered in two days later at Camp Mangum, near Raleigh. Regimental records are incomplete and there is no mention of him until May, 1863, when he was reported present. He was wounded and captured at Gettysburg but there are no records of his captivity other than the fact that he was admitted to DeCamp General Hospital in late July, 1863. Paroled or exchanged later (no dates or details are given) he is reported "Absent, Detached Service" in May, 1864. Boggs was present with the regiment at least from September until November, 1864. He was captured at Sutherland Station, Virginia, on April 2, 1865. Sent north, he arrived at Hart Island, New York, on April 7, 1865. Boggs was admitted to the Post Hospital there on June 7, 1865. He died there of smallpox on either June 28th or 29th. The number of his grave is not given in the records.

BOUGHMAN, H. L. - Service records indicate that his name was actually Henry L Baughman. He enlisted on January 27, 1862 at Columbia, S C at a Private in Company "C" in the First (Provisional Army) South Carolina Infantry regiment. He was present until the end of February, 1862. Records from that date until October 31, 1862 include his name but do not show whether he was present or absent, which, more often than not, is an indication of being present. He was hospitalized in late October or early November, 1862 at Winchester, Virginia. Boughman was transferred to Richmond, Virginia, and admitted to Chimborazo Hospital #2 there, suffering from pneumonia. In mid-December (records differ as to whether it was the 16th or the 18th) he was furloughed and sent back to South Carolina. Rejoining the regiment, Boughman was wounded at Gettysburg, Pennsylvania. Obviously not seriously injured, he was brought back with the retreating Army of Northern Virginia and, by August 28, 1863, he was reported in the Episcopal Church Hospital, Williamsburg, Virginia. On September 9, 1863 he was again furloughed, returning to the unit two months later. Wounded again in November, 1863, during the Mine Run Campaign, he was absent from the unit until mid-January, 1864. Boughman was present with the unit for the remainder of 1864. No date or place of his capture is given in the records but he appears to have been taken early in the Appomattox Campaign. He arrived at Hart Island, New York, on April 11, 1865 and died at the Post Hospital there on May 21, 1865 of double pneumonia. He is buried in grave 2844.

BOULDIN, N. H. - Nathaniel H Bouldin, husband of Sally Ann Bouldin, was thirty-three years old when he enlisted in Company "F", Fifty-Seventh Virginia Infantry regiment at Mount Vernon Church for a twelve month term of service. He was a farmer. Bouldin was present with the regiment until the end of 1861. Records for the regiment from that time until the fall of 1862 do not exist. Medical records. however, show that Bouldin was hospitalized at Winchester, Va. on October 6, 1862. Moved to Richmond, he remained hospitalized there until mid-November, 1862. On December 11, 1862, he was rehospitalized at Howard's Grove General Hospital, Richmond, suffering from rheumatism. He next appears on a record as having been captured at Gettysburg and sent to Fort Delaware, Delaware, on July 12, 1863. On October 13, 1863, he was transferred to the prison camp at Point Lookout, Maryland. After not quite six months as a prisoner of war, he was paroled at City Point, Virginia, on March 16, 1864, and granted a thirty day furlough. Bouldin suffered a minor scalp wound in the Battle of the Wilderness and was admitted to Chimborazo Hospital #5, Richmond, on May 10, 1864. Returned to his regiment, he served with it for the remainder of 1864. Bouldin was captured at Five Forks, Virginia, on April 1, 1865. He was sent north to Hart Island, New York, but not long after arriving there was transferred to DeCamp General Hospital, Davids Island. He died there of Chronic Diarrhea on May 1, 1865. He was buried in grave 2677.

BOWINE, James - Cemetery records show a man with this name identified as having been a member of Company "A", Thirteenth Florida Infantry. There was no unit with this designation nor do the records of Confederate soldiers include a man with this name. Whoever he was, he died on July 18, 1863 (indicating that he had probably been captured at Gettysburg) and that he is buried in grave number 651, Cypress Hills.

BOYLE, Stephen - Regimental records show that his name was actually Stephen Boyett, a native of Wilson, North Carolina. He was 18 and signed his name with an "X" when he enlisted at Wilson, North Carolina on October 28, 1863. He was mustered in on November 1, 1863, as a Private in Company "A", Fifty-Fifth North Carolina Infantry regiment. Following his enlistment record, there is no mention of Boyle in the unit's files until March 6, 1864. On that date he was released from Wayside Hospital #9, Richmond, Va. He was present during May and June, 1864 and again in September-October, 1864. He was captured near Petersburg, Va., April 4, 1865, and sent to Hart's Island, New York, April 11, 1865, He died there on June 23, 1865 of Typhoid Pneumonia. He is buried in grave number 3049.

BOZEMAN, M. - Bozeman originally enlisted in the Confederate States Navy but since records on that branch are very sketchy it is not known when or where. His service file shows that he was serving on the ram "Savannah" on July 14, 1864, when, by Special Order, he was permitted to transfer to Company "E" of the Twenty-Second Georgia Heavy Artillery Battalion. Records show that he was thirty-seven and unmarried at the time. Bozeman was present until October, 1864, when he was reported sick at Number 1 Hospital, Savannah. He was again present with the unit during late 1864 and was with the battalion during the siege of Savannah, accompanying it when it abandoned the city. Serving as infantrymen, the unit retreated north ahead of the Federal advance. Bozeman was captured at Cheraw, South Carolina, on March 5, 1865. Originally sent to Newberne, North Carolina, he was eventually moved to Hart's Island, New York, arriving there on April 10th. Bozeman died at the Post Hospital there of diarrhea on April 28, 1865. He is buried in grave 2641 at Cypress Hills.

BRADBURY, Wiley - Bradbury was forty-eight years old, considerably older than the average Confederate enlisted man, married, and a resident of Coweta, Georgia. He was described as being 5'5" tall with dark complexion, light hair, and blue eyes. Nothing is his file tells when or where he enlisted, only that he was captured at Goldsboro, North Carolina, on March 20, 1865, a

Private in Company "A" of the Forty-First Georgia Infantry. He arrived at Hart Island, New York. by way of Newberne, North Carolina, but no date is given. Bradbury took the Oath of Allegiance at New York City on June 14, 1865. Slightly more than a week later, on June 22, 1865, he was admitted to the U. S. Transit Hospital, New York. Sometime afterwards he was moved to DeCamp General Hospital, Davids Island. He died there (no cause given) on July 2, 1865. Bradbury is buried in grave 3080.

  BRADLEY, _____ - No first name or unit is given for this individual and he cannot he located in the Unfiled Miscellaneous File. Hundreds of men with this surname served in the Confederate military and of those checked, none match the small amount of information known about the man. Cemetery records show only that he died on July 14, 1862 and that he is buried in gave number 199.

  BRADSHAW, J. P. - James P Bradshaw, a twenty-five year old carpenter and a resident of Alamance County, enrolled at Goshen, North Carolina on May 8, 1861. He enlisted on the 16th of May at Garysburg as a member of Company "E", Thirteenth North Carolina. No regimental records mention him for a year but on May 1, 1862, he was promoted to the rank of Corporal. Bradshaw was present with the unit from then until July, 1863 with the exception of a brief stay in Moore General Hospital (General Hospital #24) in late June and early July, 1862, Bradshaw was promoted to the rank of Fourth Sergeant, September 25, 1862, Third Sergeant, November 17, 1862, and Second Sergeant, May 3, 1863. At the battle of Gettysburg he was wounded and captured. He arrived at DeCamp General Hospital, Davids Island, New York, on July 19, 1863. He died there of Pyaemia on August 9, 1863 and is buried in grave 772.

  BRANHAM, W. - No enlistment date appears in William Branham's service file. It is known that he received an extra fifty cents a day pay from December 17 to 31, 1861 while he was on detached service at White Sulphur Springs, Virginia, but the nature of that service is unknown. Branham was a Private in Company "I", Forty-Sixth Virginia Infantry. Most members of this unit, Branham included, were captured at Roanoke Island, North Carolina, on February 8, 1862. He was paroled at Elizabeth City, North Carolina, on February 21st. On July 5, 1862 he re-enlisted at Albermarle, Virginia. He was marked Absent, "On Parole", in August, 1862 and Absent Without Leave in September and October, 1862. There are no records of him during late 1862 but in January, 1863, he was listed as present until May 7, 1863. On that date he was admitted to Howard Grove General Hospital, Richmond. Branham was returned to duty on June 8, 1863 but on September 14, 1863, he was admitted to Chimborozo Hospital, a victim of Typhoid Fever. In a little more than a month he returned to active service and remained with the unit until January 2, 1864. He was, on that date, granted a 30 day furlough. Records show that Branham was present with his regiment through the remainder of 1864. Captured at Petersburg, Virginia, on April 3, 1865, he was sent north and arrived at Hart Island, New York, on April 11, 1865. Branham died there on May 22, 1865 of Typhoid Fever and is buried in grave 2854.

BROWN, _____ - The file of Miscellaneous Unfiled Confederate Papers shows this individual, with no first name and no unit. His entry reads that he was a "Prisoner of War: admitted to the U S Post Hospital, Fort Columbus, New York, on October 4, 1861, suffering from Rubeola. He died there of Typhoid Fever on October 26, 1861. No grave number is provided in the cemetery records.

BROWN, Elisha - Elisha Brown (also carried on regimental rolls as E B Brown) enlisted on May 5, 1862 for three years or the duration of the War at Riggsbee's Store, North Carolina, in Company "D", Fifteenth North Carolina Infantry. The son of May B Brown, he was a resident of Chatham, North Carolina, thirty, and single. There are no records of his activities until January, 1863 when he was reported present until October, 1864. He signed a clothing receipt in late December, 1863. Brown was captured at Hatcher's Run, Virginia, April 2, 1865. He arrived at Hart Island, New York, on April 7, 1865. A month later, on May 10, 1865, Brown was admitted to the Post Hospital there. On July 18, 1865, he was transferred to DeCamp General Hospital, Davids Island, New York and he died there, July 21, 1865, of Chronic Diarrhea. He is buried in grave number 3122. When he died his effects consisted of one blouse, one pair of trousers, one pair of bootees, and one part of socks. These were sold for thirty cents on April 4, 1866, and the proceeds turned over to the Paymaster of the Army, General Benjamin Alvord.

BROWN, H. E. - Harrington E Brown enlisted (no date given) at Camp Johnson, Spartanburg, South Carolina in Company "B", Thirteenth South Carolina Infantry. His term of service was for three years or the war. Brown was present with the unit from September, 1861 until July 10, 1862 when he was admitted to Camp Winder General Hospital, suffering from debilitis. He returned to service on July 19th. Brown was wounded at the Battle of Groveton, Virginia, August 29, 1862. The nature of his wound in not mentioned in the records but he appears to have been hospitalized until November, 1862. Sent home on furlough, Brown was listed as Absent until March, 1863, rejoining the regiment at that time. He was wounded there and was among those left behind when the Army of Northern Virginia retreated. He arrived at DeCamp General Hospital, Davids Island, on July 19, 1863. Records show that he died there on October 12, 1863 and is buried in grave 898.

BROWN, Henry - Records show that Brown was a private in Birdsall's Louisiana Artillery Company when he was captured at Petersburg, Virginia, on April 2, 1865. He was sent north and arrived at Hart's Island, New York, on April 7th. He died there of diarrhea on April 27, 1865, and is buried in grave 2615. No other details of his career are found in his file.

BROWN, J. J. - Brown enlisted in the Sixth South Carolina Cavalry, Company "I", on February 20, 1863, shortly after the regiment was organized. Immediately after he enlisted at Ranloe, South Carolina, he was "sent home for a horse." He returned not long afterwards and was present with the unit from March 1863 to February, 1864. No regimental records exist from February until the summer of 1864. He is next shown as present in July, 1864. By this time the regiment had been moved north, serving with the Army of Northern Virginia. Brown was reported serving with the "dismounted battalion" of the unit until October, 1864. There are no details showing where and when he was captured but he arrived at DeCamp General Hospital, Davids Island, on April 15, 1865. He died there on May 5, 1865 of Chronic Diarrhea and was buried in grave 2686.

BROWN, John - Brown enlisted in Company "H", Thirty-Fourth North Carolina Infantry regiment on September 1, 1864, at Camp Holmes, North Carolina. Not long afterwards he was "sent home, sick" but returned to the regiment in early November, 1864. He signed a clothing receipt on November 5th (signing his name as "X") and again on December 13th and the 23rd. Brown was captured on April 2, 1865, at the South Side Railroad. A week later, on April 7, 1865, he arrived at Hart Island, New York. He died at the Post Hospital there, of Typhoid Pneumonia, on June 3, 1865 and is buried in grave 2938.

BRYAN, John J - Bryan (also carried on unit rolls as J J Bryant) was thirty years old when he enlisted in the Second Mississippi Infantry Battalion on August 13, 1861, at Port Gibson, Mississippi. Despite the fact that he was a resident of Bluckers,

Cumberland County, North Carolina, he served in a Mississippi unit for his entire career. Bryan was unmarried. Not long after being mustered into service, the battalion was ordered north to Virginia. Bryan was listed as present until December 29, 1861 when he was assigned to the Quartermaster's Department as a Teamster. He performed this duty until February, 1862 and then returned to active duty with the battalion. Bryan was again assigned to extra duty as a Teamster in November, 1862. By this time the battalion's strength had grown to nine companies. A tenth was added and the unit was remustered as the Forty-Eighth Mississippi Infantry regiment. Bryan was sick in camp in January, 1863 and was then transferred to Ladies Hospital, Richmond, Va., suffering from Hemorrhoids. He returned to active service in May, 1863, taking part in the Gettysburg Campaign. The rolls of September, 1863, show him again sick in camp and on October 8, 1863, he was once more detailed as a Teamster to the Quartermaster's Department, serving in that manner until mid-February, 1864. On February 13th he was granted a furlough "As indulgence to go to North Carolina" for 18 days. Bryan returned to the regiment in March, 1864, and was present with it as late as January, 15, 1865. It is not known if he was again furloughed, detached, detailed, or whether he deserted but the records show that he was captured at Fayetteville, North Carolina, on March 16, 1865 while his regiment was still in Virginia. He was sent to Newberne, North Carolina, and from there to New York City. He arrived at DeCamp General Hospital on April 10, 1865 and died there on August 23, 1865 of Chronic Bronchitis. He was buried on that date in grave 3513. (A second report, in error, lists his date of death as July 1, 1865 of Chronic Diarrhea.) Bryan's disposable effects consisted of a dress coat and $1.01 in United States currency. His coat was sold on April 4, 1866 for forty cents and this, plus the U. S. currency, was turned over to the Paymaster's Department at that time.

BULLIS, David W. - David W Bullis, twenty-one years old, enlisted at Wadesboro, North Carolina, on April 28, 1862, in Company "F", Fifty-Second North Carolina Infantry regiment. His term of service was for three years. Incomplete information available for the regiment shows that he was Absent with Leave during May and June, 1862. Bullis was wounded and left at Gettysburg, Pennsylvania. Sent to Hart Island, New York, arriving there on July 9, 1863, he died on August 3, 1863 and his remains placed in grave number 742 at Cypress Hills National Cemetery.[5]

BULLIS, Simeon - A resident of Wilkes County, North Carolina, Simeon Bullis enlisted at Wilkesboro, North Carolina, June 12, 1861, in Company "C", Twenty-Sixth North Carolina Infantry regiment. He was twenty-five years old and his original term of enlistment was for one year. Bullis was present with his regiment through December, 1861. No unit records exist for the first two months of 1862 but he was reported present in March and April, 1862 . Once again there is a gap in regimental records and Bullis' name is not mentioned again until he was admitted to the General Hospital, Petersburg, Va., suffering from Debilitis. He returned to duty on September 13, 1862. He is next mentioned as having been wounded and left at Gettysburg when the Army of Northern Virginia retreated from that battle. Sent to New York, he arrived at DeCamp General Hospital, Davids Island, New York. He died there on September 2, 1863 as a result of his gunshot wound. Bullis is buried in grave number 847.[6]

BURDICK, E. W. C. - The soldier's name, according to his consolidated service file, was Edward C Barwick. There is no record of his date or place of enlistment and he does not appear on a unit record until March, 1863. At that time he is shown as a Private in Company "G", Fourteenth South Carolina Infantry, and was marked as Present from March through June, 1863. Burdick was reported hospitalized in Richmond (no reason given) and returned to the unit in September, 1863. From then until February, 1864, he was present with the regiment. He was reported as home on sick furlough in April, 1864. On June 30, 1864, Burdick was hospitalized at Richmond with Chronic Diarrhea. Two months later, on August 31, 1864, he was admitted to Wayside Hospital #9, Richmond, Virginia, but appears to have reported back to his unit the same day. He was present with the regiment for the remainder of the year. On April 2, 1865, Burdick was captured at Sutherland Station, Virginia, April 2, 1865. He arrived at Hart Island, New York on April 23, 1865, and died there on the same day on pneumonia. He is buried in grave number 2591.

BURMINGHAM, John - Burmingham enrolled in Company "D", Eleventh Mississippi Infantry at Philadelphia,

---

[5] It is not known if he is any relation to Simeon Bullis, shown below.

[6] It is not known if he is any relation to David Bullis, shown above.

Mississippi on March 1, 1862. His term of enlistment was "for the war." He was present with the unit until being admitted to the General Hospital at Charlottesville, Va. on June 24, 1862 with a diagnosis of Acute Diarrhea. He returned to duty on July 8, 1862. The next record of him shows that he was wounded and left at Gettysburg, Pa. in July, 1863. Sent to DeCamp General Hospital, Davids Island, New York, arriving on July 23, 1863, he died there of Pyaemia on July 25th. He is buried in grave 686. One medical record in his file, however, states that he died at Chester, Pa. on July 15, 1863. His burial at Cypress Hills would indicate that this record is in error.

BURNES, Patrick - Burnes enlisted on October 14, 1861 at Tyler, Texas in the Thirteenth Texas Infantry regiment. He was 20 years old. Mustered in on November 14, 1861, he was present with the unit until February 28, 1862. A month later, on March 28, 1862, he transferred to Company "B", Fifteenth Texas Infantry regiment at Velasco, Texas. He was shown present with the regiment through the fall of 1862. No records bear his name until May, 1863, when he was reported present with the unit during the summer of that year. There are no unit records for the fall of 1863 but he is again shown as present from January to March 24, 1864. On that date he was captured at Cane River, Louisiana. He was sent to New Orleans and arrived there on May 7th where he was hospitalized at St. Louis General Hospital. Four days later he was released from this hospital only to be rehospitalized at St. Louis General Hospital a short time later, suffering from Chronic Diarrhea. A list dated May 31, 1864 bearing his name includes this notation, "Deserter wants to take the Oath." Returned to custody July 7th, Burnes was once more stricken with diarrhea and rehospitalized at the same hospital on July 27, 1864. Burnes was again returned to custody on August 10,1864. Six weeks later, on September 29, 1864, he was again placed in a hospital in New Orleans but on this occasion the hospital is not named. He was transferred to Ship Island, Mississippi, on October 5, 1864 and remained there for a month. On November 5th he was one of a shipment of prisoners sent north. Whether he was again laid low by diarrhea or whether he never fully recovered is not known but, on his arrival at Fort Columbus, New York, on November 16, 1864, he was immediately placed in the Post Hospital. Burnes lost his battle against the chronic diarrhea that had plagued him since the spring of 1864 when he died there on November 19, 1864. He is buried in grave number 1353.

BURNETT, William T - A private in Company "E", Thirteenth South Carolina Infantry regiment, Burnett was captured at the South Side Railroad on April 2, 1865. There are no earlier records of his activities. Sent to Hart Island by way of City Point, Va., he died there on May 11, 1865 of Typhoid Pneumonia. He is buried in grave 2750 at Cypress Hills National Cemetery.

BUSHING, _____ - No records of any kind have been found regarding this individual who died on July 6, 1862, and is buried in grave number 132. Only four men with this surname served in the Confederate army and none of these match the little known of this man.

CAMDEN, J. S. - Also carried on regimental rolls at Joseph Camdon, this soldier enlisted at Lexington, Virginia, on July 15, 1861, for a one year term of service in Company "H", Twenty-Seventh Virginia Infantry regiment. He was present with the unit from that time until captured in July, 1863. On April 17, 1862 he had extended his enlistment for two additional years and was paid a $50.00 bounty for having done so. He was promoted to the rank of Corporal on October 1, 1862 but was reduced to the rank of Private by order of the regimental commander, Colonel James K Edmundsen, on November 26, 1862. No reason has been found why this action was taken. Camden was wounded in the thigh at Culp's Hill, Gettysburg, Pa., and left there when the Confederate Army withdrew. He arrived at DeCamp General Hospital, Davids Island, New York, on July 23, 1863. He died there as a result of the gun shot wound on August 31, 1863 and his remains were placed in grave number 832.

CAMHILL, Charles - The file of Miscellaneous and Unfiled Confederate records lists this man as being a member of the First South Carolina Infantry regiment. Which of the three regiments bearing this designation he was a member of, however, is not indicated.[7] The only information found shows that he was admitted to the U. S. Transit Hospital, New York City, on June 26, 1865 and that he died there on the same date. No cause of death appears in the records. He was buried in grave number 3062.

---

[7] The First (Provisional Army) South Carolina Infantry, the First (Regulars) South Carolina Infantry - which served almost exclusively as a Heavy Artillery unit - and the First (Volunteers) South Carolina Infantry, as identified in the *Official Records of the Union and Confederate Armies in the War of the Rebellion*. The same units at the National Archives are identified as the First (McCreary's) South Carolina Infantry, the First (Butler's) South Carolina Infantry, and the First (Hagood's) South Carolina Infantry regiments.

CAMP, James - Cemetery records show that a man with this name, belonging to Company "A", Sixth South Carolina Cavalry, was buried on May 5, 1865 in grave number 2708. No one with this name is found in the regiment's records, however, and none of the Confederate soldiers named Camp match the little information known about him.

CAMPBELL, E. - Although cemetery records show that he was a member of Company "A", Sixteenth South Carolina Infantry, military records indicate that he was actually a member of Company "A" of the Fifteenth South Carolina Infantry regiment. He enlisted on February 12, 1862 at Camp Greenville, South Carolina for a one year term of service with the rank of Sergeant. He was present with the unit until June, 1863, with that rank. In July, 1863, he was shown as a present but his rank was reported as private. Nothing has been found to show why he had been reduced to the ranks, On August 31, 1863, Campbell was reported as Absent Without Leave and was carried in this manner on subsequent rolls until January, 1864. His name does not appear in any record thereafter until September, 1864, He was, at this time, reported as being absent on detached service. The nature of this and how long he had been so detached is not shown and it is possible that all or part of his absence could be explained by his being detached combined with poor record keeping. This was not an uncommon situation in Confederate military records. Nothing has been found to show where or when he was captured but he was admitted to the Hart Island Post Hospital, New York, on May 5, 1865. He died there a day later of Chronic Diarrhea. A note in his file states that his effects were considered worthless. Campbell's remains were placed in grave 2729.

CAMPBELL, R. J. - R J Campbell enlisted on June 9, 1864 at Darlington, South Carolina, in the Pee Dee South Carolina Artillery Company (Zimmerman's South Carolina Battery). He was present with the unit through the remainder of 1864. A month after he enrolled, his pay was stopped for fifteen days. Nothing has been found why this step was taken and there is no additional information on him in the company's files. Cemetery records, however, identifying him as a member of the Fourth South Carolina Artillery[8], show that a man with this name was buried in grave number 2571 on April 19, 1865.

---

[8] There was no unit officially or unofficially referred to by this designation.

CAMPBELL, Robert - Consolidated service records show that Robert Campbell enlisted in the First (Provisional Army) Infantry at Sullivan's Island, South Carolina, on November 26, 1863. He was assigned to Company "H" and he was present with his unit from enlistment through February, 1864. During the following two months he was reported as "Sick in quarters," but returned to his regiment in the summer of 1864. Records show that Campbell was captured at the Bentonville, North Carolina, on March 22, 1865. Transported to Hart Island, New York, by way of Newberne, North Carolina, he arrived there on April 10, 1865. He died there as a result of Chronic Diarrhea on May 18, 1865, and is buried in grave number 2814.

CANNON, John - Cannon was 28 years old when he enlisted in Mooty's Florida Independent Infantry Company on July 28, 1863. Not long afterwards this company became Company "F" of the Sixth Florida Infantry Battalion. He was described as five feet eleven inches tall with dark complexion, blue eyes, and brown hair. He was present with the battalion during the summer of 1864. He next appears on the rolls of April, 1864, shown as present. The battalion was ordered north to Virginia in mid-May, 1864 and, in early June, 1864, it was consolidated with three Florida Infantry companies and remustered as the Ninth Florida Infantry regiment. In the summer of 1864 he was assigned as an Orderly at Receiving and Wayside Hospital #9, Richmond, Virginia, There is no information in his file regarding his capture but, on January 23, 1865, he was reported to have taken the Oath of Allegiance and was transported north. A week later, on January 30, 1865, he was admitted to the Convalescent Barracks, Fort Wood, Bedloe's Island, New York. His file contains no information about his death. Cemetery records, however, show that he died on February 20, 1865, and was buried in grave 2302.

CARLTON, James C. - Carlton enrolled on August 31, 1862 at Jacksonville, Florida, in Company "B" of the Sixth Florida Infantry Battalion. He was 30 years old at the time and enlisted for the duration of the war. There is no additional mention of him in any records until May, 1864, when he was reported present. During that month the battalion was ordered to Virginia and there, having been consolidated with three Florida infantry companies, it was remustered as the Ninth Florida Infantry regiment. Records show him present with the unit from May through August, 1864. His name is next found on two lists dated February 25, 1865. One of these is entitled "List of Refugees and Rebel Deserters Turned over to the Provost Marshall General,

Washington, DC" and the other "Prisoners of War Disposed of by the Provost Marshall, Army of the Potomac, and sent to New York.." There is no additional information about him in the military files. Cemetery records show that he was buried in grave number 2334 at Cypress Hills. No date of death or burial is given.

CARROLL, John - He was a 33 year old conscript from Johnston County, North Carolina. He enrolled at Camp Holmes, on July 18, 1863, for the duration of the war in Company "E", Fourteenth North Carolina Infantry regiment. Available rolls show him present from his enlistment until December, 1863. He was next shown present during the spring of 1864 and from August, 1864, to the end of that year. Carroll was captured at Petersburg, Va., on April 3, 1865. Sent to City Point, Virginia, he arrived there on April 7, 1865. No records have been found showing when he was sent to New York but he died at DeCamp General Hospital, Davids Island, of Chronic Diarrhea on May 20, 1865. His remains were buried in grave 2715.

CARROLL, Robert A. - Robert Carroll, single and nineteen, enlisted on April 26, 1861, in Company "A", Third Alabama Infantry regiment at Montgomery, Alabama. His original term of enlistment was for twelve months but he extended this for an additional two years in early 1862. Regimental rolls show him present with the unit through January, 1862. He is next shown on the muster of September, 1862. Here it is reported that he had been captured at Boonsboro, Maryland, on September 14th according to one report and at Hagerstown, Maryland, on September 15th according to another. Carroll was paroled at Aiken's Landing, Virginia, less than two weeks later. Admitted to Winder Hospital No. 5, Richmond, Virginia, he returned to duty on November 28, 1862 and was present with the regiment thereafter until early July, 1863, when he was wounded at the Battle of Gettysburg. Medical reports state that he was wounded "[b]y a cannon ball, producing a slight flesh wound on the right leg." Carroll was one of the many wounded Confederate soldiers left at Gettysburg when the Army of Northern Virginia retreated after that battle. He was sent to DeCamp General Hospital, Davids Island, New York, but the exact date of his arrival there is not given. On November 29, 1863, his right leg was amputated "by double flaps lower third of femur." He never recovered from surgery and he died at DeCamp on February 17, 1864 of Pyaemia. He was buried the same date in grave 1027. His effects were listed as one haversack, one canteen, one cap, one hat, one flannel shirt, one uniform coat, one pair of boots, one pair of shoes, one pocket knife, a hymn book, and a pocket book (which was reported to be empty). These effects were sold on April 4, 1866 for seventy-five cents and the proceeds turned over to the U S Army Paymaster.

CARTER, Timothy - A native of Tennessee, Carter enrolled on May 9, 1861, at Nashville, Tennessee, in the First South Carolina (Regular Army) Infantry. He was thirty years old. Although this unit was designated as an infantry unit, it served as a heavy artillery regiment during almost all of its career. Sent to Sullivan's Island, South Carolina, he was mustered in there on May 24, 1861, but transferred to Company "H" the following month. Records show that Carter was present with the regiment until the spring of 1865. In the spring of 1862 he was assigned as cook for the unit's non-commissioned staff. Nothing in the file shows that he was ever absent from the unit. The regiment served in the area around Charleston for almost the entire war, with detachments manning Fort Sumter, and on Morris Island, James Island, Sullivan's Island and other locations in the region. In February, 1865, Charleston was evacuated by Confederate forces and Carter joined it in the retreat north, the unit's members finally serving as infantry. He was captured near Bentonville, North Carolina, on March 16, 1865 and sent to Hart Island, New York, by way of Newberne, North Carolina. He arrived in New York on April 10, 1865 and died there of Typhoid Fever on May 19, 1865. He is buried in grave 2819.

CARTLAND, Francis - Cemetery records show that a man by this name was buried in grave 2900 on May 28, 1865. He was listed as a member of Company "C" of the Tenth North Carolina regiment (First North Carolina Heavy Artillery.) There are no records of anyone with this or a similar name in this unit, however.

CARVER, Lewis C. - On February 4, 1864, Lewis Carver enlisted in Sturdivant's Virginia Artillery Company at Camp Sturdivant (near Petersburg, Virginia) for the duration of the War. He was present with the unit as late as February, 1865. There are no details concerning his capture or death in military records but cemetery records show that he died on May 8, 1865 and is buried in grave 2742. These records identify his unit as Company "A", Sixteenth Virginia Artillery Battalion. There was no battalion with this designation but Sturdivant's Company was Company "A" of the Twelfth Virginia Artillery Battalion.

CASEY, A. M. - Casey enlisted in the Marion South Carolina Artillery Company on November 23, 1862 at Charleston, South Carolina. The unit served there and nearby for its entire career. Records show him present with the unit from enlistment through June, 1863. In July, 1863, while his company was involved in the operations on Morris Island, he was reported Absent Without Leave. Casey was reported back with the company in early 1864. Incomplete unit records show him present with the unit through the summer of that year. An entry in his file states that he was returned to duty as a deserter, on September 25, 1864. An entry dated October 20, 1864 reads "Deserted. Escaped from Battery Marshall." No other information in found in his service file regarding his desertion, when he returned to the regiment, and where or when he was captured and sent north. Cemetery records, however, shows that he was buried at Cypress Hills on May 8, 1865, in grave 2605.

CASH, Peter - Cash enlisted in Company "G", Forty-Eighth Alabama Infantry regiment at Hendrixville, DeKalb County, Alabama, on April 12, 1862. His term of enlistment was for three years or the war. He appears on no other regimental records until May, 1863. At that time he is reported as present in Company "E". Cash was wounded in the leg on July 2, 1863, and left at Gettysburg when the Confederate Army retreated from there. Sent north, he was admitted to DeCamp General Hospital, Davids Island, New York (no date given). One report show that he died there as a result of this wound on August 31, 1863 and another on September 1, 1863. He was buried on the latter date in grave number 833.

CHAMBERS, G. W. - George W Chambers was a Private in Company F, Thirty-Third North Carolina Infantry regiment. A resident of Tyrell County, he enrolled on April 9, 1861 for twelve months. He reenlisted for the duration of the War on September 9, 1861, and was present until captured at Newberne, North Carolina, on March 14, 1862. It is not known when he was sent north or arrived at New York, but he was admitted to the Post Hospital, Fort Columbus, New York, on July 12, 1862, suffering from Phthisis Pulmonatis. He died there of this ailment on July 16, 1862. and was buried in grave 215.

CHAMBERS, Harvey R. - At the age of 29, Chambers enlisted at Gadsden, Alabama on May 10, 1862, in Company "G", Forty-Eighth Alabama "for the war." There are no regimental records until May, 1863. Listed as present at that time, he was wounded, receiving a "Ball in knee" at Gettysburg, Pennsylvania. Captured there when Federal troops occupied the Confederate field hospitals, Chambers was transported north and admitted to

DeCamp General Hospital on Davids Island (no date given) where he died on August 2, 1863 and was buried in grave 729.

CHAMPION, William - Champion was a resident of Guilford County, North Carolina, described as being 5' 7" tall with dark complexion, light hair, and blue eyes. He was unable to sign his own name. He enlisted at Raleigh, North Carolina on May 1, 1861 in Company "F" of the Second North Carolina Infantry and was present with that unit from that date until October 1, 1861. Very few records exist for the regiment and he does not reappear in them until June, 1864. On the 25th of that month he was reported "Absent Without Leave." There is no record of when he returned to the unit but he was captured on April 3, 1865 at Petersburg, Virginia. Sent north, he arrived at Hart Island, by way of City Point, Va., arriving there on April 7th. He died of phthisis on June 17, 1865, and is buried in grave 3020.

CLARK, Joseph W. - Clark enlisted for a one year term of service at Hicksford, Virginia, on May 4, 1861 in the Fifth Virginia Infantry Battalion. He is also carried on various rolls at Joseph W Clarke and James W Clarke. On September 25, 1862 he was transferred to Company "K", Fifty-Third Virginia Infantry. and was present from the regiment from that date until October 9. 1864. On that date he was admitted to Chimborozo Hospital #4, Richmond, Virginia, (no reason given) and was furloughed from there in November, 1864, for sixty days "to return home." Nothing is found in his file to show exactly when he returned to the unit but it is known that he was captured at Five Forks, Virginia, on April 1, 1865. He arrived at Hart Island, New York, on April 7, 1865. He died there of Chronic Diarrhea on June 14, 1865 and it buried in grave 2948.

CLARK, W. F. - Burial records indicate Clark's name as listed here but military service files show that his name was actually William T Clark. He enlisted in Pegram's Virginia Artillery Company at Campbell, Virginia, on January 10, 1863, for the duration of the War. Cemetery records identify the unit as Coit's Virginia Battery. Records show him present with the company through the late summer of 1863. On January 6, 1864, he was appointed to the rank of Sergeant but resigned this rank, returning to a Private on June 1, 1864. Incomplete military records show him present through October, 1864. Clark was captured at Petersburg, Va. on April 2, 1865 and sent to Hart Island, New York, where he arrived on April 7, 1865. He died there May 7, 1865, of Chronic Diarrhea and is buried in grave 2740

CLIFTON, George - He enlisted at Franklin, North Carolina, on February 17, 1864 as a member of Company "B", Forty-Seventh North Carolina Infantry regiment. According to regimental returns he was present with the unit from that time until June, 1864.. On July 29, 1864 he was admitted to Moore General Hospital #8, Richmond, Virginia, suffering from acute diarrhea. He was granted a furlough in August, 1864 (exact length of time not given) and he returned to his home. Back with the regiment by mid-September, 1864, Clifton was marked present until the end of the year. Clothing receipts he signed on August, 1864, and November 6, 1864 indicate that he could not write his name and signed with an "X". He was captured at the Appomattox River, Virginia, April 2, 1865, and was transferred north, arriving at Hart Island on April 11th. On the 28th of that month he was admitted to the Post Hospital at Hart Island where he died of Typhoid fever on the following day. He is buried in grave 2663.

COFFEY, J. G. - Coffey enlisted in Company "B" of the Twenty-Sixth North Carolina Infantry regiment at Lenoir, North Carolina, on July 15, 1861, for a twelve month term of service but he was not mustered in until a month later, on August 12th. A native of Caldwell County, he was twenty-two years old and single when he entered the service. He was present with the unit until the end of 1861. He appears on no records for the unit during all of 1862. An entry dated January 16, 1863, mentions that he was released from the Confederate States General Hospital, Petersburg, Virginia, on that date. It is not known why he had been hospitalized or for how long. Coffey was then present with the regiment until wounded in the first day's fighting at Gettysburg, Pa. Among those left at Gettysburg when the Army of Northern Virginia, he was captured by Federal forces and sent north, arriving at DeCamp General Hospital, Davids Island, on July 19, 1863. Shortly after arriving there his left arm was amputated. He died there, as a result of this operation, on August 24, 1863 and was buried in grave number 2663. On Feb. 11, his father (whose name does not appear in the records) applied for a settlement of his back pay through an attorney, T P Dula, of Lenoir, North Carolina.

COLEMAN, Hazel - Service records show the spelling of his name as Hazel Colman and a small number of records list his first name as Azel. On October 4, 1861, he enlisted at Raleigh, North Carolina, in Company "D", Thirty-Third North Carolina Infantry regiment. He was a nineteen year old native of Wilkes County, a farmer, 5'7" tall. He was present with the unit from, enlistment until mid-May, 1863. On May 11, 1863, he was reported to have "deserted from Camp Gregg, Va.," near Fredericksburg. By June, 1863, he had returned to the regiment and served with it until wounded on May 6, 1864, at the Battle of the Wilderness. Because of this wound he was absent from the unit until August, 1864. Records then show that he was present with the regiment until February, 1865. Coleman was captured on April 3, 1865, at Petersburg, Virginia. Transferred north by way of City Point, Virginia, he arrived at Hart Island, New York, on April 7, 1865. He died there on May 17, 1865 of Double Pneumonia and was buried in grave number 2812.

COLLINS, James - Collins appears only in the Miscellaneous file of Confederate Unfiled records. The entry in the file shows him as a Prisoner of War who was admitted to the U S Post Hospital, Fort Columbus, New York, on August 15, 1862, and that he died there five days later, on August 20, 1862 of Febrious Typhoides. He was buried in grave 345.

CONDREY, Jefferson - Three different names are found in this individual's service file, none of which match the name on his burial records. Most records list his name as James Condrey but he is also shown as Jefferson Condry and J L Condrey. He was a 23 year old farmer, a resident of Chesterfield County, Virginia, when he enlisted in Company "D" of the Fourteenth Virginia Infantry regiment on May 11, 1861. He was present with the unit from his date of enlistment until the end of 1861. Sometime during this period he was promoted from his original rank (Private) to Second Corporal and on November 24, 1861, he was promoted to the rank of Third Corporal in his company. Records show that he was Absent without Leave from January 9th to 17th, 1862 and he was reduced to the rank of Private to date from January 13th. Once again present with the unit from mid-January, 1862, the rolls carry him this way until June, 1862. On May 5, 1862, he was again promoted to the rank of Corporal, this time being assigned as the company's First Corporal. The company muster of July/August, 1862 shows that on August 19, 1862, he was "[s]ent home on sick leave from Louisa Court House." For some reason not explained in the records he had again been reduced to the rank of Private on August 1, 1862. With the rank of Private, Condrey served with the regiment until the end of December, 1863. The muster of January/February 1864 shows that he was present, under arrest, for being absent without leave for eleven days in December, 1863. He was court-martialed in January, 1864 and two months pay was stopped as a result. On February 2, 1864,

Condrey "[d]eserted on the March from Newberne, North Carolina." There are no additional records of when he returned to the regiment or when he was captured. The only remaining information shows that he died at DeCamp General Hospital, Davids Island, on July 2, 1865. No cause was given. His effects were listed as a blanket, a uniform coat, one pair of trousers, a shirt and jacket, and a pair of boots. He is buried in grave 3096.

CONETRIAN, J. - No one with this name has been found for anyone in military records. Cemetery records, however, show that a man with this name was buried on July 16, 1862 and was buried in grave number 211.

COOK, Samuel F. - At the age of 40, Cook enlisted on August 13, 1863, at Macon, Georgia, in Company "E" of the Twenty-Eighth Georgia Heavy Artillery Battalion. Surviving battalion records show him present from that date until October, 1864. He is reported as having been captured at Goldsboro, North Carolina, on March 28, 1865. A second, contradictory report, undated, shows that he was admitted to the Second Division, XX Corps Hospital as a "Confederate Deserter." Sent north. he was admitted to the Hart Island Post Hospital on May 4, 1865. He died there on the following day of Chronic Diarrhea. His effects were reported as "Worthless" and destroyed Cook was buried in grave number 2710.

COSART, Lewis - Miscellaneous Confederate records show his name as Lewis Cussart and that he was a member of Company "C", Thirty-Fifth North Carolina Infantry regiment. He died at DeCamp General Hospital, Davids Island, on June 24, 1864, no reason being given. Cemetery records show that he was buried on June 29th in grave 1266.

COSTELLE, Lewis - Cemetery records show that a man with this name, a member of Lee's Virginia Battery, died on August 16, 1863 and that his body was subsequently taken by his brother to Jersey City, New Jersey. No one with this name, however, has been found in any Confederate records.

COUSINS, James - Also carried on the rolls of his unit (Company "C", Forty-First Virginia Infantry) as James Cozzens, this man enlisted on September 3, 1864 at Camp Lee, Petersburg, Virginia. Less than two months later, on October 27, 1864, he was captured at Boydton Plank Road, Virginia. He was sent to Point Lookout, Maryland, on October 31st, and was exchanged on March 28, 1865. Less than a week later, on April 2, 1865 Cousins was recaptured at Petersburg, Virginia. He arrived at Hart Island,

New York, on April 7, 1865. He died there on Chronic Diarrhea on June 9, 1865, and was buried in grave number 2969.

COVINGTON, Elijah - Covington enlisted in Company "D", First South Carolina Heavy Artillery on July 8, 1864 at Columbia, South Carolina for a three year term. Existing records show him as present with the unit through the fall of 1864. In February, 1865, the First South Carolina Heavy Artillery evacuated Charleston and retreated north in the face of Sherman's advance through the Carolinas. Covington was captured in the Marlborough District of South Carolina but no date is given. He arrived at Hart's Island, New York, by way of Newberne, North Carolina, on April 10, 1865. He died there on Chronic Diarrhea on May 24, 1865.

COWARD, N. M. - Sketchy information shows that he was a member of Company "B", Fourteenth South Carolina Militia. He was captured at Lynch's Creek, South Carolina, on February 28, 1865, and was sent north to Hart Island, New York. He died there of Chronic Diarrhea on May 10, 1865. His grave number is not given in the cemetery records.

COX, Leander - Cox enlisted in Company "A", Thirty-Seventh North Carolina Infantry on November 30, 1861. A native of Ashe County, North Carolina, his term of enlistment was for twelve months. In March, 1862, he reenlisted for two additional years. Cox was shot in the thigh at Hanover Court House, Virginia, May 27, 1862, and captured. He was admitted to Trippler Hospital, Fortress Monroe, Virginia but no date is given. His stay there was brief and he was transported to Portsmouth Grove, Rhode Island. He died there on July 8, 1862, one of a small number of men who died there and is buried at Cypress Hills. The cause of death was Typhoid Fever. He is buried in grave number 3331.

CRAWFORD, E. P. - Service records show that his correct name was A D Cranford. A 40 year old conscript of Montgomery County, North Carolina, he was mustered into Company "G", Fourth North Carolina Infantry regiment on September 12, 1863 at Camp Holmes, Raleigh, North Carolina. He was described as being 5'10" tall with a dark complexion. He next appears on the roster of March, 1864. A note there states that he was on Detached Service since January, 1864. The exact nature of this duty is not given.. Very few regimental records exist but a clothing receipt he signed on August 31, 1864 bears the notation "Detailed by command of General Lee, Special Order No. 67, January 19, 1864." He was captured at Petersburg, Virginia on April 3, 1865 and sent to Hart Island, New York, by way of City Point, Virginia, arriving there on April 7, 1865. Records show that he took the Oath of Allegiance on June 19, 1865 while confined in the Post Hospital. He died there on June 27, 1865, of Dropsy, and was buried in grave number 3003. Cemetery records give the date as June 21, 1865. however.

CROUDER, William - According to regimental records, his name was actually William Crowder. He enlisted in Company "C", Fifteenth South Carolina Heavy Artillery Battalion at Battery Means, South Carolina, on November 28, 1862, and was present with the unit through February, 1864. From March through August, 1864, he was reported on detached service at Fort Ripley, Charleston, South Carolina. The nature of this service is not revealed in the records. In September, 1864, he returned to duty with the battalion. Crouder was captured on March 16, 1865, at Smith's Farm, North Carolina, during the Confederate retreat from Charleston, South Carolina. He arrived at Hart Island, New York, on April 10, 1865, and died of Pneumonia there on May 11, 1865. He was buried in grave 2764.

CUBBAGE, J. - Cubbage enlisted at Centreville, Virginia, on April 6, 1861, for a one year term of service. There are almost no regimental reports for the unit (Company "D", Fifty-Third Virginia Infantry regiment) and he appears only on the roster of July/August, 1861 as being present. He signed clothing receipts on November 30th and December 31st, 1864. None of the details of his career over this long period are known. He was captured at Five Forks, Virginia, on April 1, 1865. Transferred north, he arrived at Hart Island, New York, on April 7, 1865. He died there of Chronic Diarrhea on June 6, 1865 and is buried in grave number 2954.

DARROLD, J. L. - Burial records give his name as above but his consolidated service file shows that it was James C Darnold. (A small number of records also give his name as J S Darnold.) He enlisted in Company K, Eleventh North Carolina Infantry on August 19, 1862, at Wilmington, North Carolina for three years or the duration of the war. One record shows that he enlisted at Swannanoa, North Carolina. He was a resident of Buncombe County. On July 1, 1863, he was wounded and captured at Gettysburg, Pa. Sent to DeCamp General Hospital on Davids Island, New York, he arrived there on July 26, 1863. He died there later that same day as a result of the gunshot wound. He was buried in grave 679.

DAVENPORT, M. C. - In addition to the name shown above, various records also identify him as Mac C Davenport, McCarey Davenport, and McKaney Davenport. He was the 19 year old son of Randolph Davenport, a farmer of Pitt County. He stood 5' 4 3/4" tall. Davenport enlisted on July 31, 1861 (no place is given in his record) in Company "B", Thirty-Third North Carolina regiment was present with the unit until captured at Newberne, North Carolina on March 14, 1862, Sent north, he was admitted to the U S Post Hospital, Fort Columbus, New York, on May 15, 1862. He was released from the hospital on May 26th only to be readmitted on July 12, 1862. Davenport died there on July 25, 1862 of Phthisis Pulmanitus. He was buried in grave number 261.

DAVIDSON, Lewis - Also carried on unit rolls as Louis Davidson, he enlisted at Hertford County, North Carolina, in Company "F", Eleventh North Carolina Infantry regiment. He was forty years old when he enlisted. A month after enlisting he was reported "Absent at Seaman's Hospital, Wilmington, North Carolina." The roster of June/July, 1862, shows him hospitalized at C S A General Hospital #4, Wilmington, suffering from "Colica." Davidson returned to active service on August 8, 1862, and was present with the unit thereafter until the Battle of Gettysburg. Wounded there, he was among the many Confederate casualties left behind when the Army of Northern Virginia retreated. He was moved north to DeCamp General Hospital, Davids Island, arriving on July 19, 1863. He died there, as a result of the gunshot wound, on July 27, 1863. Davidson was buried in grave number 693.

DAVIDSON, William T. - Nothing is known about Davidson's enlistment or career until his capture at Columbia, South Carolina on February 17, 1865, as a Private in Company "G", Ninth Alabama Cavalry. He was sent, by way of Newberne, North Carolina, to Hart Island, New York, where he arrived on April 10, 1865. Davidson died there of Typhoid Fever on May 2, 1865. He was buried in grave number 2681.

DAVIS, A. - Allen Davis enlisted in Company "E", First North Carolina Light Artillery Battalion, on March 21, 1863. He was present with the company until July, 1863, when he was reported hospitalized at Richmond, Virginia, no reason being given. Returned to the company in early September, 1863, he was marked present until the end of 1863. No company records exist until May, 1864. At that time he is reported "Absent, Detailed Service." He appears on no other records until he was reported captured at Petersburg, Virginia, on April 3, 1865. Davis arrived at Hart Island, New York, on April 11, 1865, and he died there on

June 5, 1865 of Chronic Diarrhea. Cemetery records show that he was buried in grave number 2949.

DAVIS, J. R. - Davis enlisted at Greenville, South Carolina on February 3, 1864, in Company "K", Seventh South Carolina Cavalry. Records show that he was present with the regiment through August, 1864. Davis was reported sick (no reason given) in the fall of 1864. A letter in his file dated November 12, 1864, is reprinted here.

> Infirmary, 7th S.C. Cav.
> Nov. 12, 1864
>
> I certify that I have carefully examined that J. R. Davis, private, Company K, 7th Regt. S. C. Cav. and find that he suffers from diarrheaa of two months duration by reason of which he is unfit for duty.
>
> I further declare my belief that he will not be able to assume his duties in a less period than 40 days, for which time I respectfully recommend that a furlough be given to him.
>
> F. L. Frost,
> Surgeon

His regiment remained on duty in Virginia but Davis was captured in the Kershaw District, South Carolina, on February 25, 1865. No date is given in the files but he arrived at Hart Island, New York, by way of City Point, Virginia. Davis died at Hart Island of Chronic Diarrhea on May 11, 1865 and was buried in grave number 2759.

DAVIS, Sampson - Sampson Davis enlisted in Coffee County, Alabama, on August 19, 1862, in Company "E" of the First Alabama Artillery Battalion for the duration of the war. He was 31 years old. Serving as a member of the garrison and defenses of Mobile, Alabama, he remained with the unit from enlistment until February 29, 1864. Rolls for the period of February 29th to April 30, 1864 shows him present but a second, contradictory, set of records show him as "Absent. On extra duty in Ordnance Department, Selma, Alabama, since April 13, 1864." He was captured when Fort Morgan, Alabama, was captured by Federal forces on August 23, 1864. Davis was moved to New Orleans, Louisiana, and, from there, on September 18, 1864, to New York, where he arrived ten days later. On December 5, 1864 he was reported "Sick in Hospital at Fort Columbus since Dec. 1, 1864." Davis died on February 10, 1865, at Fort Columbus, of Chronic Diarrhea. He was buried in grave 2294.

DE BAR, L. W. - Service records show this soldier's name in six different ways: Lewis W Debard, L W Debava, L W Debara, L W DeBard, L W Debard, and L D Dubard. He enlisted on August 3, 1864 at Greenville Court House, South Carolina, for the duration of the War, in Company "F", Fourteenth South Carolina Infantry regiment. DeBar was admitted to Jackson Hospital, Richmond, on September 23, 1864 suffering from Rubeola. He was furloughed for thirty days on October 7, 1864 and returned to duty in early November, 1864. He was captured at Dix Road, Virginia, April 2, 1865 and transferred to north to Hart Island, New York (no date being given). He died there on June 1, 1865 of pneumonia and was buried in grave number 2568.

DE BRADY, DeYoung - No records have been found for a man named DeYoung DeBrady (nor for a DeBrady DeYoung) in any Confederate file. Cemetery records show that an individual of this name was buried in grave 2713. No date of death is given.

DEE, Patrick - No date or details of enlistment have been found for this soldier, only that he was a private in Company "L", Twenty-Second North Carolina Infantry regiment. Clothing receipts dated November 23rd, November 28th, and December 24th, 1864, bear his signature. Dee was captured at Petersburg, Virginia, on April 3, 1865 and sent north, arriving at Hart Island, New York, on April 7th. He died there of "Pericarditis" on May 22nd and was buried in grave 2856.

DIXON, J. J. - John J Dixon was a Private in Norwood's Florida Home Guards when he was "Captured by a portion of Federal troops under command of Brigadier-General Asboth on the late raid into the interior of Western Florida - Captured at Marianna, Florida, on September 27, 1864." Transported to New Orleans, Louisiana, on the steamer "Clinton", he arrived there on October 12, 1864. Slightly more than a week later, on October 20th, he was moved to Ship Island, Mississippi. On November 5, 1864, Dixon was moved to New York City. He arrived at Fort Columbus on November 16, 1864 and died there on Chronic Diarrhea on December 16th. Cemetery records gave his date of death as December 15th. He was buried in grave number 1465.

DRUMMON, James - His service file shows his last name as Drummond. He was a private in Company "B", Fourteenth South Carolina Infantry. There are no records of where or when he enlisted. He was captured at Lynch's Creek, South Carolina, on

February 25, 1865 and was sent to Newberne, North Carolina, and from there to Hart Island, New York (no dates given). He died there of Diarrhea on May 21, 1865 and was buried in grave 2471.

DUDLEY, J. - The records of none of the men found in the various Confederate files with the last name Dudley appear to refer this individual. All that is known is that a man of this name is buried in grave 725, having died on August 8, 1863.

DUFF, B. R. - Duff enlisted in Sturdivant's Virginia Artillery Company on April 11, 1862. He was present with the unit until June, 1863 although one record shows that he was Absent With Leave sometime in June, 1862. His name does not appear again on unit records until December, 1863. He was present with the company until October, 1864. His name appears on a clothing receipt dated August 24, 1864. Duff was again shown as present in January/February, 1865 and was captured at Petersburg, Virginia, on April 3, 1865. Transferred to Hart's Island New York by way of City Point, Virginia, he arrived there on April 7, 1865. Duff died of dysentery on April 28, 1865, and was buried in grave 2783.

DUFF, James A. - At the age of 27, Duff enlisted in Company "D", Fourth Virginia Artillery (also known as Deen's Virginia Heavy Artillery Company). He was mustered in on May 25, 1861 at Madison Court House, Virginia, for a one year term. He was present until August 30, 1861, when he was granted a seven day leave of absence. He appears on no further records until March, 1862 when was shown present until June, 1862. In July/August, 1862, he was reported sick in camp during which time he reenlisted for three years or the war. Records show him present with the company, but sick in camp until December, 1862. From January to April, 1863, he was on detached service at the Brigade Hospital. Duff was then shown as Present with the company until August, 1863. He was then detached for service in the Brigade Quartermaster's Department, serving there for a month. The regiment was sent south to aid in the defense of Charleston, South Carolina, and he was reported hospitalized there. He received a thirty day sick furlough on November 8, 1864. During this period the regiment was official redesignated as the Thirty-Fourth Virginia Infantry regiment. Duff was again reported sick in May and June, 1864, and, in July, 1864, he was marked "Absent, Detached Service," being employed at the Division Commissary Department as a teamster. Duff was admitted to Chimborazo Hospital #4, Richmond, Virginia in early November, 1864, suffering from Syphilis and Dyspepsia. He once again returned to his unit on November 26, 1864, and was captured at

Petersburg, Virginia, on April 3, 1865. Sent north, he arrived at Hart Island, New York, on April 7, 1865. He died there of Double Pneumonia on May 14, 1865, and was buried in grave 2783.

DUGGANS, J. R. - Although his name is spelled as above on cemetery records, his service file shows his name as J R Duggins. He was a 22 year old conscript, native of Stokes County, North Carolina, who was mustered into Company "M", Twenty-First North Carolina Infantry on August 8, 1862 at Raleigh. He appears only on records dated January to July, 1863, being shown as Present. He was wounded at Gettysburg, Pa. and left behind when the Army of Northern Virginia retreated. Moved to DeCamp General Hospital, Davids Island, New York, Duggans arrived there on July 23, 1863. He died there of Pyaemia on October 15, 1863. He was buried in grave number 900.

DUGGINS, Robert - Duggins enlisted in Company "F", Ninth Virginia Infantry on August 14, 1863, in Isle of Wight County, Virginia, He was present with the regiment until Christmas Eve, 1863, at which time he was reported hospitalized. A report dated February 1, 1864 shows that he had deserted on that date. He rejoined his regiment on April 18, 1864, and was confined in Castle Thunder, Richmond. On April 22, 1864 Duggins was reported is General Hospital #13, Richmond, returning to confinement at Castle Thunder on April 27th. Clothing receipts dated November 30 and December 31, 1864 bear his signature. He was captured at Five Forks, Virginia, on April 1, 1865 and moved to Hart Island, New York, where he arrived on April 7th. He was admitted to the Post Hospital there on April 21, 1865 and released on April 27th. Records show that Duggins was re-admitted to the Post Hospital on June 23, 1865 and he died there of Chronic Diarrhea on June 24th and was buried in grave number 3052,

DULLINS, P. E. L. - Burial records show that a man by this name, a private in Company "L", First South Carolina Infantry, died on July 30, 1863, and was buried in grave number 2712. No one by this name, however, has been found in the records of any of the units known as the First South Carolina Infantry or in any other Confederate unit.

DUNLAP, J. S. - Dunlap, 26 years old, enlisted August 26, 1861, as a Private in Company "E", Twelfth South Carolina Infantry. He was a resident of Lancaster, South Carolina, and was married to Nancy Dunlap. Records show he enlisted at Lancaster Court House, South Carolina, for the war and was present until January, 1862, when he was reported Present, sick. Dunlap was again marked present until November, 1862, when he was hospitalized (no reason given). He returned to the regiment and was present until January 24, 1863. On that date he was admitted to the C S General Hospital, Charlottesville, Virginia, suffering from Debilitis. Dunlap was wounded and captured at Gettysburg, Pennsylvania. Moved to DeCamp General Hospital, he died there on September 6, 1863 (no cause given). He was buried in grave 841. His widow received four months and six days back pay ($46.20) and clothing allowance ($70.76), total $111.96, on October 26, 1863.

DURISCOE, C. L. - At the age of 23 Duriscoe enlisted in Company "D", Fourteenth South Carolina Infantry on August 10, 1861. He was mustered in on September 10th and was present with the regiment until August 15, 1862, when he was reported sick at Orange Court House, Virginia. He was present with the unit from January to July, 1863. Duriscoe was wounded at Gettysburg, Pa. and captured when Federal troops occupied the Confederate field hospitals. Transferred to DeCamp General Hospital, arriving on July 9, 1863, he died there on July 23, 1863, the cause being given as "Amputation of thigh." He was buried in grave 664.

DURN, Perry - An individual with this name was buried in grave 3089 on July 3, 1865. Cemetery records show him as a Private in the First South Carolina Heavy Artillery regiment. No one with this name is found on the records of any soldiers who served in Confederate units, however.

EARLY, H. F. - Early, a 20 year old farmer, born in Cherokee County, North Carolina, enlisted in Company "E", Eleventh Georgia Infantry regiment at Atlanta, Georgia, on July 3, 1861. He was described as having blue eyes, light hair, and a fair complexion. The regimental roster for July and August, 1861, shows him as "Sick" while those of September through December, 1861, show him as Present. His name does not appear in the files again until a report stating that he was captured (place and date not given) and paroled at Keedysville, Maryland, September 2, 1862, The regimental special roster of October 7, 1862 shows him present with the unit. On November 17, 1862 he was arrested at Winchester, Virginia, as a deserter and returned to his regiment. Despite this mark on his records (there is no report of any disciplinary action taken against him) his rank in January, 1863 is reported as Corporal and he still held this rank when wounded in the thigh at Gettysburg, Pa. in July, 1863. He was captured when Federal troops occupied the Confederate field hospitals there. Sent to New York, Early arrived at DeCamp General Hospital, Davids

Island, New York, on July 18, 1863. His thigh wound had been originally described as a flesh wound but the cause of his death on July 23, 1863 is given as caused by this wound. He was buried in grave 673.

EARLY, S. D. - The age of all Confederate soldiers buried at Cypress Hills National Cemetery is not known. Even if they were, however, it is doubtful if any of these men were older than S D Early who, on April 10, 1862, enlisted in the Fourth Virginia Heavy Artillery at the age of 62. He was married, a resident of Bedford, Virginia, with a dark complexion, dark eyes, and gray hair. He stood 6'1" tall. Early was present with the regiment (which subsequently redesignated the Thirty-Fourth Virginia Infantry) until June 10, 1862. On that date he was granted a thirty day sick furlough, The unit roster from September, 1862, through February, 1863, shows his present. He re-enlisted for the duration of the War in July, 1863. Reports show that he was sick in camp on September 13, 1863, and soon thereafter admitted to Chimborazo Hospital #9, Richmond, Virginia, suffering from rheumatism. On November 3, 1863, Early was furloughed for sixty days. His name does not appear on any unit records again until April 1, 1864. On that date he was admitted to Liberty Hospital, Richmond. In May, 1864, he was assigned to the Quartermaster's Department for special duty as a guard. He served in this capacity until at least October, 1864. Early was captured at Petersburg, Virginia, on April 3, 1865, and sent north to Hart Island, New York. The date of his arrival there is not mentioned. He died at the Post Hospital there on June 24, 1865, the cause being given as "old age". He was buried in grave 3031.

ECKARD, Cyrus - Also identified on the unit rolls as Cyrus Eckhardt, C Eckard, and Cyrus Eckart, he was 24 years old when he enlisted in Company "C", Twenty-Eighth North Carolina Infantry on August 13, 1861. A native of Catawba County, he was 5'10" tall, had dark hair, dark eyes, and a pale complexion. He was present with the until December 31, 1861. Records show that he re-enlisted on March 1, 1862 for two additional years and received a $50.00 bounty. Eckard was captured at Hanover Court House, Virginia, May 28, 1862 and was sent north to Fort Columbus, New York Harbor, where he was admitted to the Post Hospital on June 20, 1862, He died there two days later of Febris Typhoides. His grave number is not mentioned in the records. In February, 1863, his father, David Eckard, received his back pay and clothing allowance at White Sulphur Springs, North Carolina.

EDWARDS, J. H. - John H Edward was 18 years old, a resident of Johnson County, North Carolina, when he enlisted in Company "F", Sixteenth North Carolina Infantry at Raleigh on September 30, 1861. He was present with the regiment until April 1, 1862 at the General Hospital, Petersburg, Virginia, suffering from Bronchitis. He returned to duty with the regiment on June 9, 1862, being shown as present until June, 1863. On June 12, 1863, he was admitted to Chimborazo Hospital #3, Richmond, suffering from chronic diarrhea. He was then listed as present with the regiment through October, 1864, and records show that he signed clothing receipts on November 5th and 23rd, 1864. Edwards was captured at Petersburg, Virginia, April 3, 1865. Sent north, he was received at Hart Island, New York, on April 7, 1865. He died there of typhoid fever on June 6, 1865. He was buried in grave 2950.

EDWARDS, T. D. - The file of Miscellaneous and Unfiled Confederate papers show that he was a member of Company "D", First Confederate States Infantry Battalion. He signed for rations while on special duty (the nature of which is not given) for the period of January 19 - 22, 1863, and February 19 - 22, 1863. A report dated August, 1864, show that he was reported as part of the Guard Mount of the Confederate States Military Prison in Richmond, Virginia. There are no reports of his being captured, his transfer north, nor his death. Cemetery records, however, show that he was buried in grave 1643 on August 14, 1864.

ELDRIDGE, D. - There is no record of when he enlisted in Company H, Thirty-Seventh North Carolina Infantry regiment. Some unit musters show his name as David Eldreth. Born in Grayson County, he was thirty-five years old, a resident of Ashe County. He was 5' 8 1/2" tall, had dark hair, blue eyes, and a dark complexion. Eldridge was captured at Hanover Court House, Virginia, on May 27, 1862. Transferred north, he was admitted to the U S Post Hospital, Fort Columbus, New York, on July 1, 1862 and died there, July 9, 1862 of "Pneumonia and Diarrhea following measles." He is buried in grave number 182.

ELLIOTT, Joseph T. - Elliott enlisted in Orange County, North Carolina, in Private "B", Twenty-Second North Carolina Infantry regiment on February 22, 1864 for a three year term of service. He was shown as present until July, 1864. For the next month he was reported, Absent Sick, but listed as present from September to December, 1864. Elliott was captured at "Hatch Run" [sic], Virginia on April 2, 1865. Moved to City Point, Virginia, and then Hart Island, New York. He died there of typhoid pneumonia on May 21, 1865. He was buried in grave 2845.

ELLIS, John - Records show his that name appeared, in addition to the above, as J W Ellis and J M Ellis or unit rolls. He enlisted on March 25, 1862, on Company "H". Fourth Texas Infantry regiment, one of the units Hood's Texas Brigade of the Army of Northern Virginia. On May 25, 1862 he was sent to Richmond, Virginia, sick, but was back with the regiment in July, 1862. On September 1, 1862 he was reported at the Episcopal General Hospital, Williamsburg, Virginia, suffering from pleurisy. Ellis returned to duty in November, 1862, and served with the regiment until wounded at Gettysburg, Pennsylvania, on July 2, 1863. He was among the Confederate wounded left at Gettysburg and was sent north, arriving at DeCamp General Hospital, Davids Island, New York, July 17, 1863. Ellis died there of his gunshot wound on July 30, 1863. He was buried in grave 703 at Cypress Hills.

ELLMORE, Jonas - Ellmore, a conscript, was enrolled in Company "C", Fifty-Fifth North Carolina Infantry regiment on October 25, 1864. He was a resident of Cleveland County with dark complexion, dark hair, and dark eyes. He stood 5'10" tall. He signed a clothing receipt in November, 1864, as Jonas Elmore. Captured at Petersburg, Virginia, on April 3, 1865 he was sent north, arriving at Hart's Island, New York, April 11, 1865. Admitted to the Post Hospital there on June 24, 1865, he died three days later of Chronic Diarrhea. His effects were listed as "Worthless." He was buried in grave number 3066.

EMERSON, John R. - Emerson (also carried on rolls as J R Emerson and J B Emerson) was 22 years old when he enlisted in Company "E", Twenty-Sixth North Carolina Infantry at Cornersville, Chatham County, North Carolina, on May 28, 1861. He was mustered in with the rank of Second-Corporal and served with that rank until December, 1861. On April 21, 1862, he was elected to the rank of Second-Lieutenant and on September 15, 1862, was promoted to the rank of First-Lieutenant. He was present with the unit until June 7, 1863. On that date he was admitted to General Hospital #4, Richmond, Virginia, but was returned to duty on June 10, 1863. Emerson was wounded less than a month later at Gettysburg, Pennsylvania, and was left there when the Army of Northern Virginia retreated. Sent north, he arrived at DeCamp General Hospital, Davids Island, New York, on July 18, 1863. He died there of Pyaemia in August 11, 1863. He was buried in grave number 773.

ENSTER, Samuel - There are no records showing when Enster enlisted in Company "M", Twenty-Third North Carolina

Infantry regiment. His file contains information showing only that he was captured at Petersburg, Virginia, on April 2, 1865. He was moved north to Hart Island, New York, by way of City Point, Virginia. He died of Chronic Diarrhea on May 14, 1865. He is buried in grave 2784.

ESTIS, J. M. - Estis enlisted for a one year term of service in Company "A", Twenty-Second North Carolina Infantry on April 30, 1861. He was a native of Caldwell County, North Carolina, He was present with the unit until November, 1861, and was then assigned as a Hospital Steward at the regimental hospital. In July, 1862, he was reported as absent, having been wounded. Estis does not appear again in regimental records until the summer of 1864. Reported present at that time, records show him as such until at least October, 1864. Captured at "Hatch Run" [sic], Virginia, on April 2, 1865, he was sent to City Point, Virginia, and, from there, to Hart Island, New York where he died on May 14, 1865 of Chronic Diarrhea. He was buried in grave number 2785.

EVANS, Jay - A resident of Darlington, South Carolina, Evans was forty-four years old when he enlisted in Private "G", Twenty-First South Carolina Infantry regiment. He was unmarried. No date is given for his enlistment. Evans was wounded and captured at "Wells Railroad"[9], Virginia, on August 21, 1864. He arrived at DeCamp General Hospital on September 8, 1864, suffering from a gun shot wound in the left shoulder. He died there the following day as a result of "Secondary hemorrhage from gun shot wound of left side". He was buried in grave number 1841.

FARMER, J. L. - Nothing exists in the records to show when or where J L Farmer enlisted. It is known, however, that he was a Private in Company "D", First South Carolina (Regular) Infantry regiment who was captured at Cumberland Ferry, South Carolina, on January 29, 1865. He arrived at Hart Island, New York (no date given) by way of Newberne, North Carolina. He died of Phlebitis there on June 4, 1865, and was buried in grave 2941.

FARMER, William M. - Farmer enlisted in Company "H", Twenty-Fourth Georgia Infantry regiment on August 24, 1861. Unmarried, he was mustered in at Habersham County, Georgia with the rank of Corporal. He is listed as present until the end of October, 1861. He appears on no other records until September 8, 1862. On that date he was elected Second-Lieutenant. In

---

[9] Weldon Railroad

November, 1862, the roles show that he was Absent (Wounded) and on furlough. In December 1862 he was reported as having been admitted to General Hospital #4, Richmond, and transferred from there to Atlanta, Georga, suffering from a gun shot wound. Once again there is a long period in which he appears on no records. An entry dated June, 1864, states, in error, that he was "Killed, June 1, 1864, at Cold Harbor, Va." He had been, in fact, wounded and captured. Sent to DeCamp General Hospital, Davids Island, New York, later that month, he died there on September 7, 1864, of Chronic Diarrhea. He was buried in grave 1838. His effects were identified as one hat, a blanket, a uniform coat, a watch, and sixty cents in Confederate money. The total value was placed at $6.15. These were sold on April 23, 1866, and the proceeds turned over to the U. S. Army Paymaster.

FERGUSON, G. N. - Nothing has been found in the various Confederate personnel or miscellaneous files to identify this individual. All that is known is that a man with this name was buried on July 16, 1862, in grave 210 at Cypress Hills National Cemetery.

FEW, M. D. - It is not known when or where Few joined the Twenty-Fifth North Carolina Infantry regiment. It is known that, as a member of Company "E who was captured in Sampson County, North Carolina, on March 16, 1865. Sent north to New York by way of Newberne, North Carolina, he arrived at Hart Island on April 10, 1865 where he died at the Post Hospital on April 26, 1865 of Typhoid Fever. He was buried in grave number 2616.

FISHER, Ulysses W. - Fisher enlisted on March 3, 1861 in St Landry Parish, Louisiana, in Company C, Sixth Louisiana Infantry. He was single, a native of St Landry Parish, and a farmer, who resided near Big Cane Post Office, Louisiana. His name is shown on various rolls as V W Fisher, U W Fisher, W W Fisher, V W Fischer, W A Fisher, and W W Fischer. He was mustered in at Camp Moore, Louisiana, on June 4, 1861 and was present from enlistment until the end of October, 1861. No records exist from that date until the spring of 1862 when he shown as present from May through September, 1862. Fisher was captured at Antietam, Maryland, on September 17, 1862 and sent to Fort McHenry, Baltimore, Maryland. Because he had been wounded in the foot at Antietam he was transferred from there to U S General Hospital #5, Frederick, Maryland. A list of wounded men paroled in October, 1862 (exact date not given) contains his name and, on October 24, 1862, he was admitted to Chimborazo Hospital #4,

Richmond, Virginia. Fisher returned to duty on December 14, 1862. On January 1, 1863, he was promoted to the rank of Corporal. He was again wounded and captured on July 2, 1863, and Gettysburg, Pennsylvania. Transferred north, he was admitted to DeCamp General Hospital, Davids Island, New York, on July 17, 1863. He died there as a result of a "gun shot wound of thigh" on September 6, 1863. He was buried in grave number 843.

FLEMMING, John E. - Information in his consolidated service file shows that Flemming enlisted in Company "I", Fifty-Ninth Alabama Infantry regiment on February 8, 1864, at Greenville, Florida. (His name is spelled as Fleming on a small number of records.) There are no details on his career until an entry of June 18, 1864, showing that he had been admitted to the Episcopal Church Hospital, Williamsburg, Virginia, with dysentery. He was present with the unit in early 1865 and was captured at the South Side R. R. on April 2, 1865. Sent north to Hart Island, New York, by way of City Point, Virginia (no date given). Flemming died there of Chronic Diarrhea on June 8, 1865, and was buried in grave 2960.

FLETCHER, Charles - A resident of Leesburg, Virginia, Fletcher, single and 26 years old, enlisted in Company "K", Eighth Virginia Infantry regiment on July 30, 1861 at Warrenton, Virginia. He was reported present until January, 1862 when a notation indicated that he was sick and hospitalized. He is next mentioned in an entry stating that he had been Absent without Leave since September 15, 1862. Fletcher does not appear in any other records until he was captured at Petersburg, Virginia, on April 3, 1865. Moved north, he arrived at Hart Island on April 7, 1865, On July 1, 1865 he was transferred to DeCamp General Hospital where he died on July 4, 1865. Two reports give his cause of death, one as Chronic Bronchitis and the other as Chronic Diarrhea. He was buried in grave 3083.

FLOWERS, Franklin - According to his service records, his complete name was Benjamin Franklin Flowers. He was a private in Company "A", First Tennessee Heavy Artillery but it is not known when or where he enlisted. He was captured at Fort Morgan, Alabama, on August 23, 1864, and sent to New Orleans, Louisiana. On September 18, 1864, he was transferred to New York. Admitted to the Post Hospital, Fort Columbus, New York, on December 2, 1864 Flowers died there on December 18th of Chronic Diarrhea. He was buried in grave number 2125.

FOUST, Jacob - Jacob Foust enlisted in Company "B", Twenty-Seventh North Carolina Infantry regiment on February 5,

1863 at Camp Stokes, North Carolina. Company records do not mention him thereafter. A Federal record indicates that he was captured at Petersburg, Virginia, on April 2, 1865. On April 7, 1865 he was moved to City Point, Virginia, and sometime thereafter he was sent north to Hart Island, New York. The exact date of his arrival there is not known nor is the date of his admission to the U S Post Hospital at the Draft rendezvous on Hart Island given. What is known is that he died there on April 26, 1865 a victim of Typhoid Fever. He is buried in grave 2612.

FOWLER, S. B. - Records reveal that Fowler enlisted at Spottsylvania Court House, Virginia, but no date is given. He was a private in Company "E", Fifty-Seventh Virginia Infantry. Contradictory records provide different ages, one stating his was 23 and the other 33. Both agree that he was single. There are no details of his capture but he was admitted to DeCamp General Hospital, Davids Island, on April 29, 1865. He died there of Chronic Diarrhea on May 7, 1865 and is buried in grave 2703.

FOWLER, T. - A resident of Fayette, Virginia, Fowler was a Private in Company "D", Fifty-Third Virginia Infantry regiment. All that is known is that he was captured at Petersburg, Virginia, on April 2, 1865 and sent to City Point, Virginia, and then Hart Island, New York. An entry in his file, crossed-out, indicates that he was released by General Orders June 6, 1865. Cemetery records show, however, the he died on Hart's Island and was buried on May 5, 1865. No grave number appears in the records.

FOX, James F. - Fox was a 22 year old resident of Buncombe County, North Carolina, when he enlisted on May 23, 1861, in Company "F", Fourteenth North Carolina Infantry. Regimental records show him present with the unit until July, 1863. He was promoted to the rank of Second-Sergeant in February, 1863. Fox was shot "through lung and thigh." at the Battle of Gettysburg and was among the numerous Confederate wounded left at Gettysburg. He arrived at DeCamp General Hospital on July 23, 1863. He died there of Pyaemia on July 30, 1863 and is buried in grave number 704.

FRANKLIN, R. L. - A private in Company "K", Thirteenth South Carolina Infantry, Franklin enlisted on September 3, 1861. He was a resident of Lexington District, South Carolina. Descriptive information showed him to be 6' 1/2" tall with a dark complexion, dark eyes, and gray hair. He was present with the unit from enlistment until the end of 1862. Franklin was reported Absent without Leave on March 17, 1863 (a second record gives the dates as March 18th), but was back with the unit, Present, in

May and June, 1863. He was reported "Sick in Hospital" from July, 1863 until the end of the year, no reason given. Clothing receipts bearing his signature are found for July, 1864, and the Second Quarter of 1864. He was taken prisoner at the South Side Railroad on April 2, 1865 and was received at Hart Island, New York, on April 7, 1865. He took the Oath of Allegiance there on June 16, 1865 but was reported admitted to the Post Hospital on June 22, 1865. Franklin died there on the same day of Chronic Diarrhea. Cemetery records show that he was buried at 8 a.m., June 23, 1865, in grave 3051.

FREEMAN, John - Freeman enlisted on February 17, 1862 in Company "K", First South Carolina (Regular) Infantry, which, despite its designation, served as a heavy artillery unit during most of its career.. (Cemetery records identify his unit as the Third South Caroalina Artillery but there was no unit with this designation.) He was mustered in for three years or the duration of the war at Walterboro, South Carolina. Records show that he was unable to sign his name and made his mark with an "X". He was present with the unit from enlistment until September, 1864, and was promoted Corporal in July or August, 1864. The unit was stationed at or near Charleston, South Carolina, throughout this period. On September 25, 1864, he was returned to the rank of Private (no reason being given) and remained present with the unit until the end of 1864. When Charleston was evacuated in February, 1865, the regiment finally served as infantry and on the retreat north, many members could not keep up or bear the hardships of field service. Freeman was captured at the Battle of Bentonville, North Carolina, on March 22, 1865. Sent to Newberne, North Carolina, he was transferred north and arrived at Hart Island, New York, on April 10, 1865. He died there of Chronic Diarrhea on June 17, 1865. Cemetery records indicate that he had died ten days earlier. He is buried in grave 2952.

FULK, J. W. -His correct name, according to regimental records, was John W Fulke. He was a private in Company "I", Twenty-Second North Carolina Infantry regiment who enlisted at Camp Holmes, North Carolina, on June 22, 1864. He was present with the regiment until late September, 1864. On the 29th of that month he was reported "Absent, sick." It is not known when he returned to duty with the unit but he was captured at Hatcher's Run, Virginia, on April 2, 1865, He was received at Hart Island, New York, by way of City Point, Virginia, on April 7, 1865. On

May 12, 1865 he died of Chronic Diarrhea. He was buried in grave 2772.

GAMMON, H. J. - Gammon enlisted in Pittsylvania County, Virginia, on October 14, 1864, and was assigned as a Private in Company "H", Thirty-Eighth Virginia Infantry. He was present with the unit on company muster rolls until February 28, 1865. Gammon was captured at Five Forks, Virginia, on April 1, 1865. He was next reported at Hart Island as present but no date is provided. He died there on Chronic Diarrhea on June 18, 1865. He was buried in grave number 2961.

GARDNER, F. M. - His name appears as F Marion Gardner on the rosters of Company "E", Twelfth South Carolina Infantry regiment with the rank of Private. He enlisted in the Lancaster District of South Carolina on February 17, 1863 "during the war" [10] He was reported present with the regiment through April, 1863. Company rosters for May/June, 1863 do not indicate whether he was present or absent (which, more often than not, is an indication of being present). Gardner was wounded and left at Gettysburg, Pa. when the Army of Northern Virginia retreated from there. He was received at DeCamp General Hospital on July 19, 1863, and died there on July 23rd, a victim of the gun shot wound he had received. He was buried in grave 668.

GARRETT, James - Garrett enlisted in Taylor County, Georgia, on May 8, 1862, for three years or the duration of the war. He was mustered in as Corporal of Company "C", Fifty-Ninth Georgia Infantry regiment. His name also appears as J Garrot on one roll. He was present with the unit from enlistment until August, 1862. He was next reported on sick furlough during September and October, 1862 but back with regiment in November. Garrett was reported present until April, 1863. On the 27th of that month, he was shown as present at the C. S. General Hospital, Farmville, Virginia, suffering from the "Effects of Vaccination." He returned to duty on May 19, 1863. Garrett was wounded at the Battle of Gettysburg, and like many others, was left behind when the Confederate army retreated from there, He arrived at DeCamp General Hospital on Davids Island, New York, on July 21, 1863, and died there of the gunshot wound. No date is given for his death but he was buried on July 25th in grave 683 at Cypress Hills. On March 20, 1865, a claim was filed for his back pay by an attorney, William A Walton, acting on behalf of

---

[10] instead of the usual "for the war"

Garrett's father. His father's name is not given in the records and although nothing is shown to indicate whether the claim was settled it is probable that it was not in lieu of the end of the War.

GAY, N. -It is probable that the individual buried under this name in grave 304 on June 23, 1865 was Nathaniel Gay, a private in Company "B", Forty-Seventh North Carolina Infantry. Nothing appears in his file showing where or when he enlisted but it is know that he was a resident of Edgecombe County with light complexion, brown hair, and blue eyes. He was 5' 8 1/2" tall. His signature appears on a clothing receipt dated November 25, 1864. Gay was captured at the South Side Railroad, Virginia, on April 2, 1865 and was received at Hart Island, New York, on April 7, 1865. His name appears on a list of men released from there on June 17, 1865, but his entry on the list is crossed out. Nothing further is known about him or his death.

GEISLER, James - James Geisler (also carried on some rolls as James H Geisler) enlisted on July 1, 1863 at Tyner's Station, Tennessee, for the duration of the war. He was present with the unit from enlistment until August, 1864. Geisler was shot in the back and captured at Bentonville, North Carolina, on March 19, 1865. He was treated at the XX U S Army Field Hospital, "using simple dressing" and transferred to the U S General Hospital, Newberne, North Carolina, on April 3, 1865. Geisler was admitted to DeCamp General Hospital, Davids Island, New York, on May 19, 1865, and died there on June 30, 1865. No cause is given. He is buried in grave 3071.

GIBBS, George F. - Cemetery records show that a private with this name was buried in grave 2503 on April 11, 1865. His unit was given as Pegram's Virginia Artillery Company. No one by this name is found in remaining company records, however, nor do any of the records of Confederate soldiers named Gibbs match the little that is known of him.

GICE, C. M. - This individual was listed as a member of Company "M", First Alabama Cavalry, Unit records, however, list no such individual nor does the name Gice appear on any index of all Confederate soldiers. He was buried in grave 2542 on April 18, 1865.

GILDER, J. A. - An examination of this soldier's service file shows that his name was G A Gilder but a small numbers of records refer to him as Gilford A Gildon and J A Gildon. He was a private, Company "B", Fourteenth South Carolina Infantry who enrolled at Camp Butler, South Carolina on August 12, 1861 and was mustered in on September 10, 1861. Conflicting records give his age as 20 and 25. He was present with the regiment through the end of February, 1862, and next appears on a record dated August 7, 1862, At that time he was admitted to Livingston Hospital, Winchester, Va, where he remained until October, 1862. No reason for his hospitalization is given. He was present with the regiment again until early May, 1863. On May 6, 1863, he was admitted to Wayside Hospital (General Hospital #9), Richmond, Va., suffering from a slight gunshot wound to the head. Gilder was transferred to Chimborazo Hospital #5, Richmond, on May 7th and was discharged from there on May 17th. Returned to active duty, he was again wounded at Gettysburg, Pa. and was left behind when southern forces retreated. Gilder arrived at DeCamp General Hospital, Davids Island, New York, on July 19, 1863 and died from a gunshot wound on August 2, 1863. He was buried in grave 731. His effects (which are not listed) were sent to his mother Martha A Gilder, through the lines, on February 1, 1864.

GILES, Richard - Richard Giles enlisted on February 10, 1863, at Bedford, Virginia, for the war. He was mustered into Company "C", First Virginia Infantry and was present from enlistment until July, 1863. At the Battle of Gettysburg, he was shot in the left breast and captured. Sent north, he was admitted to DeCamp General Hospital, Davids Island, New York, on July 23, 1863, He died there also a month later, on August 21, 1863, as a result of a "shell wound." Giles was buried in grave 815 at Cypress Hills.

GILLILAND, Abner - Gilliland enlisted for a 3 year term of service on January 1, 1863, at Charleston, South Carolina. He was mustered in as a Private in Company "C", Eighteenth South Carolina Infantry regiment. His name next appears on the roster dated September, 1863. An entry on that date indicates that he was Absent, on sick furlough, since July 6, 1863. It is not known exactly when he returned to the regiment but the roster of November, 1863 shows him Present as does that of December. After a brief absence from the rolls he again is marked present on the rolls of March, 1864, and appears thus until October, 1864. On January 19, 1865, Gilliland was promoted to the rank of Sergeant. There are no details regarding where or when he was captured. He is reported to have been admitted to the U S Transit Hospital, New York, New York, on July 21, 1865 and to have died there on July 23, 1865. No cause of death is given. He was buried in grave 3042.

GILMORE, Henry J. - This soldier's name appears as shown above on some records and as Henry H Gilmore on others.

He enlisted for the war in Company "H", Fourth Virginia Infantry regiment, on October 28, 1864, at Lexington, Virginia. He was shown as present until the end of 1864. On March 30, 1865, he was wounded in the head and captured near Petersburg, Virginia. Sent north, he was admitted to De Camp General Hospital on April, 1865. He died there of his head wound on May 2, 1865. Burial records give the date as May 10, 1865. Records indicate that his body was removed from Cypress Hills Cemetery but no date is shown nor where his remains were transferred or by whom.

GLASGOW, J. N. - James N Glasgow was 25 years old when he enlisted on August 17, 1861 at Lightwood Hot Springs, South Carolina. He was mustered in to Company "G", Fourteenth South Carolina Infantry at Camp Butler, South Carolina, on September 10, 1861 for the duration of the war and was carried as present until February, 1862. Unit records are incomplete until January, 1863. At this time he was again shown as being present and as such until June, 1863. The following month, Glasgow was attached to the division pontoon train as a teamster and served in this manner until September, 1864, He was then temporarily assigned to the First Confederate States Engineers as a Teamster. It is not known where he returned to his original regiment, but on April 3, 1865, he was captured at Petersburg, Virginia. Transferred to Hart Island, New York, he died there of chronic diarrhea on June 13, 1865 and is buried in grave number 2998.

GLOVER, John R. - Glover enlisted at Columbia, South Carolina, on July 19, 1861. He was mustered in as a Private in Company "C", First (Provisional Army) South Carolina Infantry regiment on August 30, 1861, at Richmond, Virginia. Glover was present from August, 1861, until October, 1862. Sometime in October, 1862, he was detailed to the "Infirmary Corps" but was shown Present once again with his regiment in November, 1862 through October, 1863. On October 10, 1863, he was admitted to the C S General Hospital, Charlottesville, Virginia, suffering from Catarrh. He returned to his unit on October 23rd. Records then show his present with the regiment from November, 1863, until the end of 1864. Glover was captured at Petersburg, Virginia, on April 3, 1865. Transferred to Hart Island, New York, by way of City Point, Virginia, he died there of Double Pneumonia on May 20, 1865. He is buried in grave number 2838.

GOOD, A. H. - Albert H Good is one of a small number of Confederate officers buried in Cypress Hills National Cemetery. He was eighteen years old, a Virginia-born farmer, standing six feet tall when he enlisted on June 3, 1861 at Whitehall, Virginia, in Company I, Seventh Virginia Infantry. He had auburn hair, blue eyes, and a fair complexion. Good was mustered in for a one year term of service with the rank of Private. On July 19, 1861 he was admitted to the General Hospital at Charlottesville, Virginia, but returned to service on August 9, 1861. In December, 1861, he re-enlisted for three years and received a $50.00 bonus, Good was captured at Frazier's Farm, Virginia, on June 30, 1862, and was sent to Fort Columbus, New York Harbor. Transferred to Fort Delaware on July 9, 1862, he was exchanged at Aiken's Landing, Virginia, on August 5, 1862, and returned to duty with the unit. On February 14, 1863, he was elected Second-Lieutenant of his company. Good was wounded at the Battle of Gettysburg, Pennsylvania, in July, 1863, and was among the Confederate wounded left there when the Confederate Army withdrew. He was received at DeCamp General Hospital, Davids Island, New York, on July 9, 1863, and died there on August 29, 1863, after his left leg was amputated. His body was transferred to Brady's Receiving Tomb, Second Avenue, New York City, and was buried in grave number 1114 in early September according to his consolidated service file. Cemetery records, however, list his date of burial as August 29th, the date of his death.

GOODING, Thomas - Gooding, a resident of Beaufort County, South Carolina, enlisted at McPhersonville, South Carolina, on September 7, 1863. His term of service was for a three year term. He was often listed as T Gooding on the regimental returns as a Private in Company D, Eleventh South Carolina Infantry. He was present with the regiment until December, 1863, and was then reported as "Detached" on James Island, South Carolina. The reason for his being detached is not given in the records. Returned to duty in March, 1864, he was present with the unit through the summer of that year, On October 3, 1864, he was admitted to Episcopal Hospital, Williamsburg, Virginia, with Chronic Diarrhea. On November 18, 1864, he was transferred to Pettigrew General Hospital, Raleigh, North Carolina. There is nothing in his file to indicate where and when he was captured but he arrived at Hart Island, New York, on April 10, 1865 and was admitted to the Post Hospital on April 13th. Gooding died on April 23rd of dysentery, He is buried in grave number 2589.

GORDON, J Harvey - Gordon was conscripted into the Thirty-Fifth North Carolina Infantry and assigned to Company "F" on November 1, 1864. Regimental records show him present in January and February, 1865. He was captured at Five Forks, Virginia, on April 1, 1865, and was sent to Hart Island, New York, from City Point, Virginia. He died there of Typhoid Fever on May 16, 1865. He is buried in grave number 2796.

GOTTE, Jacob - Jacob Gotte enlisted at Fort Sumter, South Carolina, on January 18, 1862[11], in Company D. First South Carolina Artillery. Gotte was five feet, one inch tall, had a dark complexion, and dark hair. He was present with the regiment from that date until August, 1863. A note on the roster of that date shows that he was Absent but a note explained that he had been "detached at Battery Ramsey. A member of company was left behind when the Captain and First Lieutenant with 40 men were ordered to report to Lt. Col. Elliott for duty at Fort Sumter." He was then shown as present with the regiment until October, 1864. Gotte was captured at Rockingham, South Carolina, on March 9, 1865, and moved to Newberne, North Carolina. He was transported to Hart Island, New York, but no date is given. On June 17, 1865, Gotte took the Oath of Allegiance at Hart Island and a note states that he was to return to Charleston. Instead, he was admitted to the U S Transit Hospital, New York City, on June 23, 1865, and died there on June 28, 1865, no cause being given. He was buried in grave 3064.

GOUGH, Charles A. - This soldier, a private in the Third Company, Washington Louisiana Artillery Battalion, is also carried on unit muster rolls under the names of S G Gouch and S A Gouch. Born in New York, he was a resident of New Orleans in the spring of 1861 when he joined the Chasseurs a Pied Louisiana Infantry Company. This short-term unit was released from service in March, 1862 and Gough was paid $22.00 for his services in it on March 13th. Records show that he re-enlisted on October 12, 1862, at Winchester, Virginia, joining the Washington Artillery Battalion. Wounded and captured at the Battle of Gettysburg on July 3, 1863, he was sent north and arrived at Davids Island, New York, on July 17, 1863. He died at DeCamp General Hospital on July 19, 1863, of Typhoid Fever and was buried in grave number 700.

GRADY, C. M. - Cemetery records show that a man with this name, identified as a Sergeant in Company C, Twenty-First South Carolina Infantry, was buried in grave 3021 on June 17, 1865. Nothing has been found on him, however, in Confederate military records.

---

[11] A second record gives the date as January 28, 1862 at Charleston, South Carolina

GRADY, W. S. - Grady was a Private in Company I, First North Carolina Cavalry regiment. He enlisted on July 4, 1861, at Kenansville, North Carolina, for the war. He was a 36 year old resident of Duplin County, five feet seven inches tall, with light hair, and blue eyes. He was reported present with his regiment until captured on the Virginia Peninsula on June 29, 1862. He was sent from Harrison's Landing, Virginia, to Fort Delaware, Delaware. Grady was exchanged at Aiken's Landing, Virginia, on August 5, 1862. He then served with the regiment until the end of 1862. In January, 1863, Grady was reported on Detached Service and, in March, 1863, he was reported as Absent, Sick, in Campbell County, Virginia. Records of the regiment are incomplete during 1863 and no rolls bearing his name are found until the fall of that year. He is then shown as present until the spring of 1864. He was reported to have been captured at Snow Hill, North Carolina on March 29, 1864 but there are no Federal records of this and he signed a clothing receipt in the second quarter of 1864 and on November 28, 1864. He had, in the meantime, been wounded on August 22, 1864, and hospitalized in Petersburg, Virginia. No date is given but Grady was reported captured again in the spring of 1865 and was received at Hart Island, New York, by way of Newberne, North Carolina. He died at Hart Island of Typhoid Fever on April 25, 1865. He is buried in grave number 2480.

GREEN, B. M. - Green enlisted on July 12, 1861 for a one year term of service and was assigned to Company G of the Fifth Texas Infantry. When mustered in he was given the rank of Third Sergeant. Green was a resident of Milam County, Texas. He was present from his enlistment until the summer of 1862 and on August 7, 1862 he was reported sick in camp. After returning to the regiment a month later, he was hospitalized in Richmond, Virginia, in late 1862. In early 1863 it was reported that he had been reduced to the rank of Private, no reason being given. Green was wounded in the right lung at Gettysburg, Pennsylvania. He was one of the many Confederate wounded soldiers who were captured at Gettysburg when Federal forces occupied the Confederate field hospitals. He was sent to DeCamp General Hospital, Davids Island, New York. On October 24, 1863 he was transferred to Fort Wood, Bedloe's Island, New York. He is next reported to have been admitted to the Post Hospital there on December 3, 1864. On February 12, 1865, he died at the Post

Hospital, Fort Columbus, the cause of death being given as "gun shot wound."[12] He was buried in grave number 1933.

    GREEN, Maston - A native of Montgomery County, North Carolina, Green enlisted on March 1, 1864 at Goldsboro, North Carolina. He was assigned to Company H, Forty-Fourth North Carolina Infantry regiment. Green deserted from his regiment in the fall of 1864 near Orange Court House, Virginia, and, not long afterward, was reported to be under arrest. Nothing in his record shows whether he was court-martialed or when he returned to his unit. Green was captured on April 2, 1865, at South Side Railroad, Virginia. Sent to Hart Island, New York, by way of City Point, Virginia. He died there on Chronic Diarrhea on May 7, 1865. He was buried in grave 2737.

    GREGORY, _____ - The only information located for this individual is found in the file of Miscellaneous Papers of Confederate soldiers. His record reads that he was a "Prisoner of War" who was admitted to the U S Post Hospital, Fort Columbus on October 16, 1861. He died there the following day of Typhoid Fever. No grave number is given in his records.

    GRIFFIN, D. T. - David T Griffin was an eighteen year old resident of Cleveland County, North Carolina. He enlisted on February 23, 1863 and was assigned to Company C, Fifty-Fifth North Carolina Infantry regiment. Wounded at Gettysburg, Pennsylvania, he was among those left there when Confederate troops withdrew. Griffin was received at DeCamp General Hospital, Davids Island, New York, on July 22, 1863. He died there on Typhoid Fever on January 20, 1864, and is buried in grave number 990.

    GRIFFIN, Silas - Although this individual is buried under the name shown above, his military records reveals that his name was actually William B Griffin, a Private in Company A, Fourteenth South Carolina Militia. He was captured at Lynch's Creek, South Carolina, on March 1, 1865, and was received at Hart Island, New York, by way of Newberne, Norh Carolina. He died at Hart Island on June 4, 1865, of chronic diarrhea and was buried in grave number 2935.

    GRIFFIN, William B - William B Griffin was twenty years old when he was mustered into the Seventeenth (First Organization) North Carolina Infantry regiment at Beacon Island,

---

[12] Unless part of Green's career is undocumented it seems unusual that a wound received in July, 1863, could be the cause of his death a year and a half later.

North Carolina on June 20, 1861. He had enrolled at Plymouth, North Carolina, on May 3, 1861. Griffin was captured at Fort Hatteras, North Carolina. He died at Fort Columbus, New York (no cause given) on September 28, 1861.

GRIFFITHS, F. O. - Griffiths was a Sergeant in Company A, Sixty-Third Georgia Infantry. He died at DeCamp General Hospital, Davids Island, New York, on August 20, 1863, and is buried in grave 802, Cypress Hills National Cemetery. No other information is found in his consolidated service file.

GRIGG, William - This soldier enlisted in Cleveland County, North Carolina, on December 28, 1863, for a three year term of service. He was assigned to Company F, Thirty-Eighth North Carolina Infantry regiment, and reported to the unit on March 27, 1863. Grigg was wounded and left at Gettysburg, Pennsylvania. Sent to DeCamp General Hospital, Davids Island, New York, he arrived there on July 19, 1863. Grigg died of Pyaemia on July 21, 1863 and is buried in grave number 656.

GRUMBLES, Perry B. - Grumbles enlisted in Company B, Fourth Texas Infantry, on July 11, 1861, at Camp Clark, Texas, for the duration of the war. He was promoted to the rank of Sergeant in the summer of 1862. On July 2, 1863, he was wounded in the shoulder at the Battle of Gettysburg and was among the Confederates left at Gettysburg when the Confederate army withdrew. Sent to DeCamp General Hospital, Davids Island, New York, he died there as a result of this wound on July 14, 1863. He is buried in grave number 803 at Cypress Hills National Cemetery.

HAIR, W. J. - Born in Barnwell, South Carolina, W J Hair enrolled on August 10, 1861 at Williston, Barnwell District. He was assigned to Company I, First South Carolina (Provisional Army) Infantry. Records show that he was present with his unit until the spring of 1862, when he was reported absent, sick at Richmond, Virginia. He was subsequently furloughed but no date is given for when it began and when he returned to his unit. In early 1863 he was reported back with the unit. Hair was wounded at Gettysburg, Pennsylvania, and was captured when Federal forces occupied the Confederate field hospitals there. Sent north to Hart Island, New York, arriving on July 23, 1863, and died there on September 14, 1863 as a result of Chronic Diarrhea. He was buried in grave 858.

HALL, Joseph T. -A Private in Company A, Forty-Seventh North Carolina Infantry, Hall signed clothing receipts on November 25th, December 1st, and December 19th, 1864. He was captured at Garrett's Station, Virginia, on April 2, 1865, and was received at Hart Island, New York, from City Point, Virginia, on April 7th. On May 27, 1865, he died there on Typhoid fever and Pneumonia. He was buried in grave 2899.

HALL, P. P. - Hall was a private in Company K, Twelfth South Carolina Infantry regiment. He was thirty-one years old when he enlisted at Walhalla, Pickens District, South Carolina, on August 23, 1861. He was among the wounded who were captured at Gettysburg, Pennsylvania, when Confederate troops withdrew after that battle. Hall was received at DeCamp General Hospital on July 19, 1863, and died there on August 5, 1863. No cause is given. He was buried in grave number 745 at Cypress Hills National Cemetery.

HAMMILL, A. - Records show that his full name was A R Hamel but he was also carried on regimental rolls at A Harmel, A H Hamel, and A Hammel. A resident of Mecklenburg County, North Carolina, he was a conscript, who, at the age of thirty-three, was assigned to Company H, Thirty-Eighth North Carolina Infantry regiment with the rank of Private. Cemetery records, however, incorrectly indicate that he was a member of Company H, Eleventh North Carolina Infantry. Hamill joined the regiment in November, 1862. He was wounded and captured at Gettysburg, Pennsylvania. Sent north, he was received at DeCamp General Hospital, Davids Island, New York, where he died on August 28, 1863, of Chronic Diarrhea. He was buried in grave number 829.

HAMMOCK, J. H. - Joseph H Hammock enlisted in June 12, 1862 at Chaffin's, Virginia. His name is also shown on regimental records as J H Hammocks and J H Hamocks. He was assigned to the Fifty-Ninth Virginia Infantry, Company B, with the rank of Private. Hammock was present with the regiment until early 1863. He was then reported sick until June, 1863. For at least a part of this time he was at the Wise Brigade Hospital. In July, 1863, he was furloughed for thirty days, Returned to the regiment, he was with it until May 10, 1864. Hammock was admitted to the Confederate States Hospital at Petersburg, Virginia, but returned to duty on May 19th. He was promoted to the rank of Sergeant in September, 1864 and was present with the regiment until captured at Chester Station, Virginia, on April 3, 1865. He arrived at Hart's Island, New York, from City Point, Virginia, on April 7, 1865. He died there of consumption on June 13, 1865. He was buried in grave number 2995.

HANNAH, E. B. - No enlistment or muster information is found in Hannah's file. As a Private in Company G, Forty-Fifth Georgia Infantry, he was wounded and captured at Gettysburg,

Pennsylvania. Sent north, he arrived at DeCamp General Hospital, Davids Island on July 7, 1863, He died there on July 27, 1863, the cause given being "Amputation of thigh." He was buried in grave number 680.

HARMON, David - Although cemetery records show that Harmon was a member of Company C, Twenty-Sixth North Carolina Infantry regiment, his consolidated service file shows that he was a member of Company D, Fifty-Seventh North Carolina Infantry regiment. At the age of 28 (a second source says that he was 30 at the time) he enlisted at Salisbury, North Carolina, on July 7, 1862, for a three year term of service. A native of Forsythe County, he stood five feet ten inches tall, with a fair complexion, light hair, and blue eyes. He was present with his regiment until the end of 1862. After a brief period of hospitalization in early 1863, he returned to the regiment. On May 4, 1863, at Chancellorsville, Virginia, he was wounded slightly in the face and head. He was sent to the Episcopal Hospital, Williamsburg, Virginia, arriving there on June 22, 1863. On September 11, 1863, he was transferred to the General Hospital at Farmville, Virginia. Harman finally returned to duty on September 28, 1863 and was present with the until the summer of 1864. On July 26, 1864, he was reported at the Confederate States General Hospital, Charlottesville, Virginia, for debility. He returned to his regiment in September, 1864 and was captured at Farmville, Virginia, on April 6, 1865. There is no record of his being sent north but he died at Hart Island on June 15, 1865, and is buried in grave number 3007.

HARRIS, E. J. - A private in Company D, Sixth South Carolina Reserve Infantry Battalion, Harris was captured on March 19, 1865, at Smithville, North Carolina. Records show that he was eighteen years old and was a native of Edgefield, South Carolina. He was received at DeCamp General Hospital, Davids Island on April 29, 1865, suffering from "frost bite both feet".Nothing has been found to show how he could have been so diagnosed at this time of the year. He died there on June 3, 1865, as a result of Chronic Diarrhea He had no personal effects. He was buried in grave 2936.

HARTFORD, John - Hartford was a sixteen year old member of the Florida Home Guards who was admitted to the U S General Hospital, Fort Columbus, New York, on November 18, 1864. He was ordered to be returned to confinement at Fort Columbus on December 22, 1864. He died on February 18, 1865, and is buried in grave 2303. There are no other details concerning his enlistment, career, capture, or cause of death in his service file.

HARVEY, A. J. - A. Jeffers Harvey enlisted on January 22, 1862 for a three year term of service on January 2, 1862 at Camp Lee, Virginia. His name also appears on regimental rolls as A J Harvey, A G Harvey, and Jefferson Harvey. He was present with his unit, Company G, Seventeenth South Carolina Infantry regiment, until February, 1863 and then on no additional unit records until September, 1863, when he was reported "Present. On guard." On October 31, 1863, Harvey was found guilty by a Court Martial and sentenced to forfeit twenty-one days pay. Nothing has been found to show why he was court-martialed, however. Present with the unit from November, 1863 until October, 1864, an entry dated November, 1864, states that he has deserted while he was guarding private property. He appears to have returned to duty before the end of the year and it is not known if he was court martialed for this offense. On March 3, 1865, he "Deserted to U S Lines" and a week later, on March 10th, he was received at Washington, DC. He took the Oath of Allegiance on March 22, 1865, and was given permission to return to Charleston, South Carolina. Records show that Harvey died at the U S Transit Hospital, New York City, however, on March 25, 1865. No cause of death is given. He was buried in grave number 2511.

HARVILLE, William - Private William Harville, Company I, Thirty-Third North Carolina Infantry, was a forty-five year old resident of Yadkin County, North Carolina. He enlisted at Pfafftown, North Carolina on July 8, 1862. His service file indicates that he was married but his wife's first name is not mentioned. He was present with the regiment until March 15, 1863. On that date he was reported to have deserted and he did not return to the unit until November, 1863. He served with his regiment until February, 1865 except for a brief period in November, 1864, when was furloughed. The reason he received a furlough, especially since he had once been absent from the regiment, is not shown in the records. Harville was captured at Garrett's Station, Virginia, on April 2, 1865. He was transported north to Hart Island, New York, and on July 1, 1865, he was transferred to DeCamp General Hospital. He died there on July 21, 1865 and was buried in grave number 3128. The cause of his death was Erysipelas. His effects, one pair of trousers, one pair of bootees, and a uniform jacket, were sold on April 4, 1866 for fifty cents and the proceeds turned over to the Paymaster of the United States Army.

HASSEL, _____ - The file of Miscellaneous Unfiled records shows that a man with this name (with no first name mentioned) died at the U S Post Hospital, Fort Columbus, New York, on October 9, 1861. The cause of death was Typhoid Fever. No grave number is given in the file or in cemetery records.

HASSELL, John W. - A private in Company I, Thirty-Eighth North Carolina Infantry, Hassell signed clothing receipts on November 4th and December 22nd, 1864. There is nothing else in his file concerning his enlistment or earlier career. He was captured at the South Side R R on April 2, 1865. Sent to Hart Island, New York (where he arrived on April 7, 1865), he died there on Double Pneumonia on June 11, 1865 and was buried in grave number 2927.

HAZLEGROVE, A. S. - Information in his service file shows that the correct spelling of his surname was Hazelgrove. He enlisted on September 26, 1864, at Chesterfield, Virginia, in Company I, Fifteenth Virginia Infantry. Captured at Five Forks, Virginia, on April 1, 1865, he arrived at Hart Island, New York, by way of City Point, Virginia. He died there of Consumption on May 23, 1865. No grave number is mentioned in his file or in cemetery records.

HELM, A. J. - Helm was a private in Company F, Forty-Eighth North Carolina Infantry regiment. A resident of Union County, he enlisted on February 2, 1864. He was briefly hospitalized at Camp Winder, Richmond, Virginia, and was furloughed to return to Charlotte, North Carolina on September 17, 1864. He returned to his regiment prior to November 30, 1864 when he signed a Clothing Receipt. He was captured at "Hatch Run [sic]", Virginia. on April 2, 1865, and was sent to Hart Island, New York, where he died of Typhoid fever on June 20, 1865. He was buried in grave number 3033.

HELTON, Alfred - Carried on the rolls of Company A, Twenty-Third North Carolina Infantry as Alfred F Helton, he enlisted at Fredericksburg, Virginia on February 28, 1863, for a three year term of service. He was a resident of Catawba, North Carolina. Helton was captured at Gettysburg, Pennsylvania, and was sent to Fort McHenry, Baltimore, Maryland, and from then to Fort Delaware, Delaware. On October 18, 1863, he was moved to Point Lookout, Maryland. He died there on July 30, 1864. There is no record of his remains being sent to New York yet cemetery records show that he was buried in grave 2901 on May 28, 1865 almost a year after his death.

HENSON, W. B. - The only data found concerning Henson is found in the Unfiled and Miscellaneous records. There are no records of when W B Henson enlisted as a Private in Company I, Sixty-Second North Carolina Infantry regiment. Clothing receipts with his mark dated the Second Quarter 1864, October 10, 1864, and the Fourth Quarter, 1864, are found in his service file. There are no details regarding his capture or imprisonment but cemetery records show that he was buried in grave number 699 on July 28, 1865.

HILL, J. H. - Hill was a private in Company C, First South Carolina Rifles. Nothing it known regarding his enlistment, career, or capture. Information on him is found only in the Miscellaneous Unfiled files. Hill died at DeCamp General Hospital, Davids Island, New York, on April 28, 1865. No cause is given. He was buried in grave number 2647.

HILL, Jesse - He enlisted on November 17, 1864, at Camp Stokes, North Carolina. Hill was assigned to Company G, Thirty-Second North Carolina Infantry regiment. In January, 1865, he was reported under arrest and as late as April 1, 1865 he was listed "In Arrest at Division Provost Guard." He was discharged by Special Order Number 78, Paragraph 10, Adjutant and Inspector General's Office, April 1, 1865 but was captured on April 3, 1865 at Petersburg, Virginia. Sent to Hart Island, New York, by way of City Point, Virginia, he was transferred to the Post Hospital in May, 1865. He died there on May 24, 1865 of Pneumonia. He was buried in grave number 2876.

HODGES, Alexander - Hodges enlisted on April 5, 1864 at Rockingham, North Carolina, for a three year term of service. He was taller than the average soldier of the time at six feet two and one half inches. He had a dark complexion, dark hair, and gray eyes. Hodges joined his regiment, the Thirty-Eighth North Carolina Infantry, in the field on April 18, 1864, and was wounded at the Battle of the Wilderness on May 6, 1864, less than a month later. Hodges was absent from his regiment as a result of this wound until November 6, 1864, During at least part of this time he was at General Hospital Number 4, Wilmington, North Carolina. His condition was described as "Unhealed gun shot wound of left leg." He returned to his regiment in early November, 1864, and signed a clothing receipt on December 23, 1864. Hodges was captured at the Appomattox River, on April 3, 1865 and was sent to Hart's Island, New York. He took the Oath of Allegiance there and was released on June 19, 1865. Records show that he was admitted to the New York Transit Hospital on June 26, 1865. On

July 1, 1865 he was admitted to DeCamp General Hospital where he died on July 21st, Chronic Diarrhea being the cause. He was buried in grave number 3124.

HOFFMAN, _____ - Cemetery records show that a man with this name was buried on July 6, 1862 in grave number 156. No first name or unit is mentioned in the cemetery records and it has been impossible to further identify him.

HOGAN, W. P. - Walker P Hogan was a Private in Company A, Fifty-Third Virginia Infantry regiment. There is no record of when he enlisted but his file shows that he signed a clothing receipt on December 31, 1864, at Chester, Virginia. He was captured at Five Forks, Virginia, on April 1, 1865 and was received at Hart Island, New York, on April 7th Hogan died there of Consumption, on May 20, 1865. No grave number appears in either military or cemetery records.

HOLLERFIELD, Jacob - Although cemetery records show his name as above, his service file shows that it was actually Jacob Hollingfield. He was a Private in Company "G" of the First (Regular) South Carolina Infantry regiment. He was twenty-four when he enlisted, unable to sign his name, the son of Preston Hollingfield. He enlisted on January 28, 1862 for three years or the war at Cleveland, South Carolina and was present with his unit thereafter until late 1864. In November, 1862, by sentence of Court Martial, his pay was stopped for six months. On January 1, 1863, his sentence was remitted by orders of General Beauregard. It is now known why he was court martialed but the following letter is found in his file.

> Fort Moultrie,
> March 3, 1863
>
> Brig. Gen. Thomas Jordan,
> AAG & Chief of Staff:
> GEN.: I have the honor most respectfully to request that the Sentence of the Court in the case of Private Jacob Hollingfield of Company "G", 1 S.C. Infantry be remitted for the remaining time and that he be restored to his company.
>
> Private Hollingfield's conduct previous to the offence for which he is now undergoing punishment [and] his conduct since the confinement affords ample ground for belief that he will hence forth [sic] fulfill the obligations of the Soldier.

Very respectfully,
Your Ob'd Serv't.
E. A. Erwin,
Lieut. Comm. Co. G

This would seem to suggest that, in addition to his loss of pay, he was also place in confinement. In August, 1863, he was assigned as a woodchopper at Fort Moultrie. Hollingfield was captured at Chester Station, Virginia. He was received at Hart Island, New York on April 10, 1865, and died there of Chronic Diarrhea on May 8, 1865, He was buried in grave number 2735

HOLLIBINTON, A. J. -Service records show that his name was actually J J Halliburton, he was a Private in Company F, Eighth South Carolina Infantry regiment. He enlisted on April 13, 1861 by "The Executive of the State of South Carolina" for twelve months. He was present through August, 1861. His file contains information showing the he was "slightly wounded at Bull Run in left arm by spent ball." On February 28, 1862 he re-enlisted for an additional two years of service at Manassas, Virginia. He was transferred to Company M in the fall of 1862. Wounded and captured at Gettysburg, Pennsylvania, when Confederate troops withdrew from that field, he arrived at DeCamp General Hospital on July 23, 1863, and died there of his gun shot wound on September 5, 1863 and is buried in grave number 842 according to cemetery records and grave 826 according to his service file. [13]

HOLLINGSWORTH, William J. - He enlisted in Company I, Fifteenth Georgia Infantry regiment on July 15, 1861. He was present with the unit until early in September, 1862. At that time he was admitted to the General Hospital at Charlottevsille, Virginia. From there Hollingsworth was moved to the General Hospital at Lynchburg, Virginia. Returned to his unit, he was promoted to the rank of First-Sergeant on April 4, 1863. Hollingsworth was wounded on July 3, 1863 at Gettysburg, Pennsylvania and left at the Field Hospital at Plank's Farm. Sent to New York, he was admitted to DeCamp General Hospital, Davids Island, New York. He died there on July 31, 1863, and is buried in grave number 712.

HORTON, Noah C. - Born in Spartanburg, South Carolina, Horton enlisted as a Private in Company C, First Alabama Artillery Battalion at Fort Morgan, Alabama, on

---

[13] Visual examination at the cemetery verifes the cemetery record.

September 6, 1862. He was five feet, three and a half inches tall with black hair, black eyes, and a dark complexion. He was present from the date of his enlistment until April 30, 1864. Horton was captured at Fort Morgan, Alabama, on August 23, 1864. First sent to New Orleans, Louisiana, he was transferred to New York on September 18, 1864. He arrived at Fort Columbus, New York, ten days later. On November 30, 1864, Horton was admitted to the post hospital suffering from variola. He was released on January 11, 1865 but was readmitted on January 31, 1865. He died there the same day of variola and was buried in grave 2254.

HOWARD, J. C. - He enlisted at Pittsboro, North Carolina, on July 14, 1864 and was assigned to Captain Lilly's Company of North Carolina Supporting Force. This unit subsequently became Company H, Sixth North Carolina Senior Reserves. No other information is found in his consolidated service file. Burial records, however, show that a man with this name and unit was buried in grave number 2709 of May 5, 1865.

HOWELL, Harvey R. - Miscellaneous and Unfiled records show that Howell was an unassigned recruit who died at DeCamp General Hospital, Davids Island, New York, on April 25. 1865 at the age of nineteen of Chronic Diarrhea. He was buried in grave number 2602.

HOWELL, Koder - Howell was a forty-two year old farmer who enlisted in Company F, First North Carolina Artillery, at Goldsboro, North Carolina on July 9, 1861. His term of enlistment was for the duration of the war. He was a resident of Wayne County who stood five feet eleven inches tall (a second entry states his height was six feet tall). He had dark complexion, dark hair, and dark eyes. Howell was captured at Fort Macon, North Carolina, on April 26, 1862 but was paroled the same day. Incomplete unit records show that he was present from May, 1862 until August, 1862, and from May to June, 1863. Hospitalized at Smithville, Virginia, during the summer of 1863, he returned to his company in September, 1863, and was present with the regiment until February, 1864. He was next reported sick at the Marine Hospital, Williamsburg, Virginia for about a month and was then sent to Wayne County, North Carolina, rejoining the regiment in July, 1864. At some unspecified date Howell was admitted to the General Hospital, Goldsboro, North Carolina and he was returned to duty on March 11, 1865. Howell was captured at Goldsboro on March 28, 1865 and was moved to Hart Island, New York, by way of Newberne, North Carolina, arriving there on

April 10, 1865. He was admitted to DeCamp General Hospital, Davids Island, New York, on July 1, 1865. He died there on July 9, 1865 of consumption and is buried in grave 3100.

HUDSPETH, James J. - Also carried on company rolls as J J Hedgpeth, he was born in Georgia and was twenty-six years old when he enlisted in Company I, Forty-Second Mississippi Infantry regiment on May 14, 1862 at Grenada, Mississippi. A second record gives his age as twenty-seven. His file shows that he was a married farmer, a resident of Pleasant Mount, Mississippi. Hudspeth was present from enlistment until he was wounded at the Battle of Gettysburg, Pennsylvania. Captured when Federal forces occupied the Confederate field hospitals, Hudspeth was sent to New York and was admitted to DeCamp General Hospital on July 22, 1863. He died there of his gunshot wound on July 31, 1863. He was buried in grave number 705.

HUFHAM, William F. - He enlisted on August 15, 1861 for a one year term of service in Company E, Eighteenth North Carolina Infantry regiment. Regimental rolls show that his name was also spelled Huffham. He was a twenty-four year old farmer, born in New Hanover County, North Carolina who stood five feet eleven inches tall. Hufham was present with his unit until October 31, 1861. Unit records are incomplete and he is next shown, on April 30, 1862, detailed as a guard at Camp Winder Hospital, Richmond, Virginia. While here he was temporarily assigned to Tabb's Company of Camp Guards. On November 28, 1862 he was admitted to General Hospital Number 5, Richmond. He returned to duty with Tabb's Company in December, 1863, but was readmitted to Camp Winder General Hospital on February 28, 1863 suffering from chronic rheumatism. On February 26, 1863, Hufham returned to his duties as a Guard. In November, 1863, he was again reported in Camp Winder General Hospital, suffering from Cattarhus. On April 12, 1864, he was granted a Surgeon's Certificate furlough and did not return to Virginia until early July, 1864. Reassigned to guard duty at that time, he finally rejoined his regiment three months later, on October 26, 1864. Hufman was captured at the Appomattox River, Virginia, on April 4, 1865. Sent north from City Point, Virginia, he arrived at Hart Island, New York, on April 11, 1865. He died there of Typhoid Fever on May 1, 1865 and was buried in grave number 2670.

HUGHES, John - Conflicting information is found in the records of many Confederate soldiers. Hughes' file appears to contain information on two different individuals which somehow have become interfiled. The majority of the information shows that

Hughes enlisted on March 20, 1862 at Laurens, South Carolina in the First (Provisional Army) South Carolina Infantry. Incomplete records next show him present from January until August, 1864. On October 1, 1864 he was admitted to Jackson Hospital, Richmond, Virginia, with dysentery, he returned to duty on November 13, 1864 and was captured at Cox Road, Virginia, April 2, 1865. Transferred to Hart Island, New York, he died there of Typhoid Fever on May 28, 1865, He was buried in grave number 2898.[14]

HULSEY, Henry - Hulsey enlisted on July 3, 1861 at Atlanta, Georgia in Company G, Eleventh Georgia Infantry but was reassigned to Company E on the same date. Born in Walker County, Georgia, he was twenty-two when he enlisted. A farmer, Hulsey had gray eyes, black hair, and a dark complexion. He was admitted to the General Hospital, Petersburg, Virginia, on October 16, 1861, suffering from Rubeola. He was next present with the regiment from November, 1861, until February, 1862. Incomplete company records show that he was present at Winchester, Virginia, on October 6, 1862. Hulsey was wounded in the foot at Gettysburg, Pennsylvania and was among the Confederates captured when Federal troops occupied the Confederate field hospitals. Sent north, he was admitted to DeCamp General Hospital, Davids Island, New York, on July 17, 1863. He died there three days later but was not buried in Cypress Hills National Cemetery until July 26th. He was buried in grave number 681.

HUMPHREYS, J. J. - He enlisted on February 25, 1864, at Big Island, Virginia and was assigned to Company C, Fifty-Eighth Virginia Infantry regiment. An entry in his file reads "Wounded near the Mechanicksville [sic] Turnpike, June 6, 1864. Now at Home." On June 9, 1864 it was reported that his left forefinger had been amputated. The next item in his file is dated in late 1864 and shows that he had deserted but was back with the regiment in early 1865. Humphreys was captured at Petersburg, Virginia, on April 3, 1865. He arrived at Hart Island, New York on April 7,

---

[14] Information in his file also mentions an individual who was present with the Fourteenth South Carolina Infantry from April 26, 1864 until October 6, 1864. At that time he was admitted to the Confederate Hospital, Jackson, Mississippi, suffering from Vulnus Sclopet. An item dated October 14, 1864 states that he was transferred to the First (Provisional Army) South Carolina Infantry on October 14, 1864, but a second report states that he was transferred to the Confederate Invalid Corps on the same date. No other information about this man is found in the file.

1865 and he died there on April 15th of Typhoid Pneumonia. He was buried in grave number 2529.

HURLEY, C. C. - No records have been found about Hurley in Confederate military files but burial records show that a man with this name, a Private in Company C of the Fourteenth South Carolina Infantry, was buried in grave number 3029 on June 19, 1865.

HUTTO, Charles - A resident of the Barnwell District, South Carolina, Hutto enlisted on December 9, 1861 at Camp Hampton, South Carolina in Company F, Seventeenth South Carolina Infantry regiment for a twelve month term of service. He stood five feet six inches tall, had a dark complexion, dark hair, and blue eyes. He was wounded "slightly" in the hand on August 31, 1862 at Manassas, Virginia, and was admitted to the General Hospital at Charlottesville, Virginia, on September 4, 1862. He was returned to his regiment the next day. Unit records show that he was present with the regiment until October 23, 1863. He was then reported hospitalized at Charleston, South Carolina, and, five days later, at Summerville, South Carolina. He rejoined the regiment in early 1864 and was present with it throughout that year. On January 7, 1865, Hutto was admitted to Jackson Hospital, Richmond, Virginia and was granted a furlough on February 11, 1865. On February 24th he was admitted to General Hospital Number 11, Charlotte, North Carolina, suffering from chronic diarrhea. Hutto returned to duty on March 20, 1865 and was captured at Petersburg, Virginia, on April 3, 1865. Sent north, he was received at Hart's Island, New York, on April 11, 1865. He took the Oath of Allegiance there on May 14, 1865. More than a month later, on June 22, 1865, he was admitted to the U S Transit Hospital in New York City. He died there the following day with no cause of his death being given. He was buried in grave number 3041.

HUTTO, John -Miscellaneous Unfiled records show that John Hutto was a Private in Company A, Fourteenth South Carolina Infantry regiment. Cemetery records identify his unit as the Thirteenth South Carolina Infantry, however. He died at DeCamp General Hospital, Davids Island, New York, on April 27, 1865, no cause being given.

INGRAHAM, James - Ingraham enlisted at Greenville, Alabama, on September 1, 1862 for a three year term of service. He was assigned to Company I, Fifty-Ninth Alabama Infantry regiment. He was twenty-four years old and single. Incomplete regimental records show that he was hospitalized at Dalton,

Georgia, on November 11, 1863 and at Howard's Grove General Hospital, Richmond, Virginia, in May, 1864. Wounded in the left shoulder on June 17, 1864 and captured at Petersburg, Virginia, he was sent to City Point, Virginia and was hospitalized there on June 28, 1864. Transported north, he was hospitalized at Grant General Hospital, Willett's Point, New York, on July 4, 1864. Ingraham died there three days later. His effects included one haversack, a hat, a knapsack, and a pocketbook containing twenty-five cents Federal currency. No grave number is given in the records. He was survived by his mother, Rachel Ingraham.

IRBINET, Archibald - Cemetery records show that a Private in Company A, First South Carolina Militia, with this name was buried in grave 2918 on May 29, 1865. No other records of a man with this name has been found in any Confederate files.

IRVING, A. - Irving was shown as a Private in Company D, Thirty-Ninth North Carolina Infantry regiment when he was buried on July 6, 1862 in grave number 3319. No information regarding his enlistment, career, or capture has been found in any other files, however.

IVEY, W. G. - Military records show that his full name was William G Ivey. He enlisted on February 26, 1862 at Chapel Hill, North Carolina, for a three year term of service. Ivey was assigned to Company G, Eleventh North Carolina Infantry, with the rank of Corporal. Ivey was wounded and "left in the hands of the enemy" at Gettysburg, Pennsylvania. Sent north, he was admitted to DeCamp General Hospital, Davids Island, New York, on July 23, 1863. He died there as a result of his wound on August 8, 1863 and was buried in grave 756. He was survived by his mother, Eliza Ivey, who petitioned the Confederate War Department for his back pay on December 23, 1863. Nothing has been found to indicate whether or not this claim was ever satisfied.

JENKINS, Charles - Buried under this name, Jenkins' military records show that his name was actually Craven Jenkins. He enlisted on May 10, 1861 at Rutherford, North Carolina and was assigned to Company D, Sixteenth North Carolina Infantry regiment. Available records show him present from May to August, 1861, and from March 1862 until January, 1863. He was captured at Falling Waters, Maryland, on July 13, 1863, and held as a Prisoner of War at Point Lookout, Maryland. On this prison camp's records, his name is given as Charles Jiggins. He was paroled at City Point, Virginia, on March 16, 1864. In April, 1864, he was reported absent, detailed, in Richmond, Virginia, but his specific duty is not mentioned. Records show him present through

October, 1864. He signed clothing receipts on March 22nd, October 15th, November 5th, November 28th, and December 23rd, 1864. On March 9, 1865, Jenkins was admitted to Receiving and Wayside Hospital (General Hospital Number 9), Richmond and, on the following day, to Jackson Hospital, Richmond, suffering from debilitas. On April 2, 1865 he was captured at Garrett Station, Virginia. Moved from City Point, Virginia, to Hart Island New York, he died there on chronic diarrhea on May 19, 1865 and was buried in grave 2826.

    JENNINGS, _____ - The file of Miscellaneous Confederate records show that a man with this name was admitted to the U S Hospital at Fort Columbus, New York, on March 7, 1862 where he died on Typhoid Fever on March 11th. Burial records show that he was buried in grave number 4451. No record has been found of his unit or career.

    JENNINGS, W. - His consolidated service file shows that his name was S W Jennings but that he was also carried on regimental rolls as W Jennings, J W Jennings, and G W Jennings. He was fifty years old when he enlisted on March 8, 1862, as a Private in Company I, Twenty-Eighth North Carolina Infantry regiment. Married to Elizabeth G Jennings, he was five feet four inches tall with gray hair, blue eyes, and light complexion. After enlisting at Yadkinville, North Carolina, for a two year term of service, he served with the regiment until late May, 1862. On the 28th of that month, he was captured at Hanover Court House, Virginia. Transferred north, he was admitted to the Post Hospital, Fort Columbus, Governor's Island, New York. Jennings died there of "fever" on June 28, 1862. He was buried in grave number 147. His wife applied to the Confederate War Department on September 14, 1863, for his back pay and received settlement on February 20, 1864.

    JOHNSON, Fleet - Fleet Johnson was a Private in Company D, Second North Carolina Infantry Battalion. He was captured at Fayetteville, North Carolina, on March 12, 1865. Sent north, Johnson died at Hart's Island, New York, of meningitis on May 29, 1865. He was buried in grave number 2914.

    JOHNSON, M. D. - Records of Company A, First (Regular) South Carolina Infantry regiment, of which Johnson was a member, show his full name as Murdock D Johnson. He enlisted in July, 1863, and was present with the regiment until he was captured on March 31, 1865, in the Darlington District, South Carolina. Received at Hart Island, New York, via Newberne,

North Carolina on April 10, 1865. He died at the Post Hospital there on May 24, 1865, and is buried in grave number 2873.

JOHNSON, Stephen - He enlisted as a Private in Company G, Twenty-Sixth North Carolina Infantry regiment on February 14, 1865, at Raleigh, North Carolina. On April 2, 1865 he was captured at Petersburg, Virginia, and was sent to Hart Island, New York, arriving there on April 7, 1865. Johnson died of pneumonia at the Post Hospital there on June 9, 1865. He is buried in grave 2973.

JOHNSON, T. A. - Cemetery records show that a man with this name, a Private in Company E, Ninth Virginia Infantry, was buried in grave 2907 on June 12, 1865. No other information have been found regarding his career in regimental records.

JOHNSTON, John B. - Johnston, thirty-one years old, enlisted on May 24, 1862, for a three year term of service in Company A, First Alabama Artillery Battalion. He was present at Fort Morgan, Alabama, from enlistment until April 30, 1864 but was "Absent Sick" in Ross Hospital, Mobile, Alabama, from June 23 to July 19, 1864, suffering from dysentery. Johnston was captured on August 23, 1864 when Fort Morgan fell to Federal forces. Sent north from New Orleans, Louisiana, to New York, on September 18, 1864, he arrived there on September 28, 1864, Admitted to the post Hospital, Fort Columbus, New York, on November 30, 1864, he died there on January 11, 1865. He was buried in grave number 2207.

JOLLY, _____ - Miscellaneous Confederate records show that a man with this name was admitted to the Post Hospital, Fort Columbus, New York, on October 30, 1861. He died there on November 6, 1861 of Typhoid Fever. No additional information, including his grave number, has been located.

JONES, F. M. - Cemetery records show that a man with this name was buried in grave 2510 on April 13, 1865. He was identified as a Private in Company C, Seventeenth South Carolina Infantry regiment. No other details have been found concerning him or his career.

JONES, J. W. - Cemetery records show his name as above but his consolidated service file shows his names was actually Wesley Jowers. He was carried on some rolls as J W Jowers. A resident of Anson County, North Carolina, he enlisted at Petersburg, Virginia, on July 18, 1862. An entry in his file shows that he was "Received as Substitute for his father." He was present with his regiment until the end of 1862. He returned to his regiment on January 13, 1863. Jones was wounded and left at

Gettysburg when Confederate forces withdrew from that field. He arrived at DeCamp General Hospital, Davids Island, New York, and died there on September 18, 1863 as a result of his gunshot wound. He was buried in grave number 860.

JONES, Murdock - Jones enlisted on March 15, 1863, at Albany, Georgia, in Company D, Sixty-Fourth Georgia Infantry regiment. Unit records show that he was a substitute for a man named S. Atkinson. Jones was present with the unit until August, 1863. He signed a clothing receipt on May 9, 1864 and he was wounded and captured at Petersburg, Virginia, on June 17, 1864. He was admitted to the Fourth Division, V Corps, Army of the Potomac Hospital, on July 1, 1864, with a Minie ball wound. On the following day he was moved to City Point, Virginia, and from there, to New York. The following letter is found in his file:

Medical Director's Office
New York, July 30, 1864

SIR: I have the honor to report that on July 4, 1864, Murdock Jones, Company D, 64 Georgia Regiment, died on the Hospital Transport "Thomas P. Way" while being taken to the Grant General Hospital at Willett's Point, New York Harbor.

His effects consist of:
1 pocket book containig $22.00 Rebel currency
1 coat
1 pair pantaloons
3 letters from his wife
10 Rebel postage stamps

These things are now in my possession and I await your instructions as to their disposition.

You will doubtless remember that as the Medical Director of Transportation was Absent on duty at the time - you accompanied this detachment of men to the hospital. He was buried by the Government Undertaker, Mr. A. J. Case, at Cypress Hils Cemetery, Brooklyn, N. Y. No. grave - 1216.

I have the honor to remain,
Very respectfully,
Your Ob't Serv.
J. B. Merwin,

Hospital Chaplain, U.S.A.

There is no additional material about him found in military or cemetery records.

JONES, W. G. - Although cemetery records show his name as listed here, military records show that his name was Giles W Jones. A Private in Company I, Thirteenth North Carolina Infantry regiment, Jones was a twenty year old cooper from Rockingham County, North Carolina when he enlisted on May 13, 1861 at Wentworth, North Carolina. He was mustered in at Garysburg, North Carolina, having traveled two hundred and eight miles to his place of muster. He was present with the regiment until February, 1862. He was then reported "In Confinement. Court Martialed. Forfeit [of] his pay for February." The reason for his court martial is not given in his file. Jones was present with the regiment until June, 1862. A note in his records states that he served as Acting Teamster. On June 27, 1862 he was promoted to the rank of Color Sergeant. Jones was wounded in October, 1862, and was absent in Richmond, Virginia, until January, 1863. He returned to the unit at that time and, on June 27, 1863, was reduced in rank to Private, no reason being given. At the Battle of Gettysburg he was wounded and captured. On July 19, 1863 he arrived at DeCamp General Hospital, Davids Island, New York. He died there as a result of the amputation of his left leg on August 8, 1863. He was buried in grave 818.

JONES, Wilson - The small number of records found regarding Jones' career show that he was also carried on the rolls under the name of Wesley Jones. He was a private in Company B, Thirty-Eighth North Carolina Infantry regiment when he was captured at Petersburg, Virginia, on April 3, 1865. Sent to Hart Island (no date given), he died there of Chronic Diarrhea on April 29, 1865, and is buried in grave 2662.

JORDAN, J. J. -Military records show that his full name was John S Jordan. He enlisted on September 3, 1861 in Company H of the First (Olmstead's) Georgia Infantry regiment. Unit records show him present until January, 1862. Nothing has been found to show when and where he was captured but on May 29, 1862, he was admitted to the U S General Hospital at Hilton Head, South Carolina suffering from bronchitis. On June 14, 1862 he was released from the hospital and transported north. Jordan died at the U S Post Hospital, Fort Columbus, New York, on July 5, 1862 of Phthisis Pulmonalis. Cemetery records give his date of death as

July 6th. On January 21, 1863 his back pay was awarded to his widow, Mary J Jordan.

JOWERS, J. W. - Jowers was a resident of Thomas Cross Roads, South Carolina. He enlisted in Company A, Twenty-Third South Carolina Infantry, on February 1, 1864, at Georgetown, South Carolina. Records show that he was furloughed soon after enlisting and that he did not rejoin the regiment until March 3, 1864. On May 22, 1864 he was admitted to General Hospital #4, Wilmington, North Carolina, suffering from remittent fever. His file shows that two days later, on May 24, 1864, he was "sent to other hospital." Jowers was captured in the Chesterfield District, South Carolina, on February 25, 1865. Moved north, he was received at Hart Island, New York, on April 10, 1865. He died there on May 29, 1865, of Chronic Diarrhea and he was buried in grave number 2897.

JOYCE, Sullivan - A native of Rockingham County, North Carolina, Joyce enlisted on May 6, 1862 at Ayresville, North Carolina for a three year term of service. He was assigned to Company A, Forty-Fifth North Carolina Infantry. He was present with the regiment until June, 1863 except for the period of September 13th to 20th, 1862, when he was reported hospitalized at Petersburg, Virginia. He was wounded and captured at Gettysburg. Sent to Hart's Island, New York, Joyce was admitted to DeCamp General Hospital, Davids Island, on July 23, 1863. He died there, no cause being given, on August 31, 1863 and was buried in grave 708.

KAY, Robert M. - Kay enlisted on July 20, 1861 at Camp Pickens, South Carolina in Company K, First South Carolina Rifles. He was present with the regiment until April 20, 1862. Kay was hospitalized at Livingston Hospital, Winchester, Virginia, from August 4 to 20, 1862 and was reported at General Hospital Number 17, Richmond, Virginia from September 1 to October 2, 1862, and at Winder Hospital Number 2, Richmond, from November 1 to 28, 1862. Incomplete regimental records show him present from January 1863 to October, 1863 and from October 1863 until February, 1864, Absent Sick. No records have been found to show when and where he was captured. Cemetery records, however, indicate that he was buried in grave number 2836 on May 20, 1865.

KEENEY, Simpson - Regimental records show that his name was Simpson Kiney. He enlisted on December 1, 1863 in Randolph County, North Carolina in Company E, Fifty-Eighth North Carolina Infantry regiment. Incomplete records show him present through February, 1864, and that he deserted near Dalton, Georgia, on June 10, 1864. Although there is nothing in the records to indicate it, he returned to the unit sometime thereafter. He was captured at Orangeburg, South Carolina, on February 14, 1865. Sent north, he arrived at Hart Island, New York, on April 10, 1865, and died of Pneumonia there on April 20, 1865. He is buried in grave number 2569.

KEEP, Erwin H. - Records show that a man by this name, a Private in Pegram's Virginia Artillery Company, was buried in grave number 2966. These records also give his date of death at June 8, 1865. No additional information has been located on him or his career, however..

KEGLEY, W. - William Kegley was a native of Wythe County, Virginia. He had dark hair, dark complexion, dark eyes, and stood five feet, ten inches tall. Nothing has been found regarding his enlistment or career except that he was a Private in Company K, First Virginia Infantry who was captured at Dinwiddie Court House, Virginia, on April 6, 1865. He was sent to Hart Island, New York but no date is given for his arrival there. Kegley died there on June 10, 1865 of "Inflammation of [the] Brain." and was buried in grave 3032.

KEISLER, G. A. - He enlisted in Company K, Thirteenth South Carolina Infantry regiment on September 3, 1861, at Lexington Court House, South Carolina. Incomplete records show him present from September to December 1861, from November to December, 1862, and from March to June, 1863. Keisler was wounded and left at Gettysburg, Pennsylvania. Transported north to Hart Island, New York, he arrived there on July 19, 1863. He died there on July 28, 1863 of Hemorrhage and was buried in grave number 694. On October 29, 1864, his wife, Martha A D Keisler, received a settlement to the amount of $81.47 from the Confederate War Department. Her address was given as Locust Grove Post Office, Lexington District, South Carolina.

KELLY, John J. - Various rolls show his name listed as J J Kelly, John J Kelley, and John Kelly. He enlisted at Tallahassee, Florida, on August 29, 1862, for a three year term in Company D, Fifth Florida Infantry. On November 17, 1862 he was reported hospitalized at Winchester, Virginia, having been wounded. Nothing in his records indicate where or when he had been wounded nor the nature of the wound. On December 2, 1862, he was reported on a thirty day furlough, returning on December 31, 1862. He was present until August 10, 1863, when he was admitted to the General Hospital at Farmville, Virginia, suffering from Intermittent Fever. Kelly returned to his regiment on June 10, 1863, and remained with it until August, 1864. At this time he was detached to the Pioneer Corps, serving with it until at least October, 1864. Kelly was captured at Chester Station, Virginia, on April 3, 1865. Sent to Hart Island, New York, (no date given) he died there on June 6, 1865, of Double Pneumonia. He was buried in grave number 2951.

  KENNEDY, Patrick - Kennedy enlisted as a Private in Company C, Fifty-Ninth Georgia Infantry in Butler County, Georgia, on May 10, 1862. Existing regimental records show him present until June 1862 and from September 1862 until June, 1863. He was wounded ("Ball in thigh") at Gettysburg, Pennsylvania, Transported north, he was admitted to DeCamp General Hospital, Davids Island, New York, on July 22, 1863. He died there on August 23, 1863. The cause of death is identified as "Amputation of thigh." Kennedy was buried in grave number 821.

  KENNEDY, Robert C. - Cemetery records identify this man as a "Citizen" who died at Fort Lafayette on March 25, 1865. The truth is, however, that he had been executed as a spy of March 25, 1865, and his body placed in an unmarked grave. His military service file shows his name as Robert Cobb Kennedy[15]. A native of Louisiana, he enlisted in the First Louisiana (Regular) Infantry in August, 1861, and was comissioned Captain. Kennedy was present with the regiment until his capture at the Battle of Shiloh, Tennessee, in the spring of 1862. Kennedy somehow managed to escape from captivity at Camp Douglas, Chicago, Illinois. His activities thereafter are unclear but he eventually was contacted by the Confederate Secret Service in Canada. In November, 1864, he was one of the principal agents in the plot to burn down the city of New York by placing incendiary devices at various hotels and places of enterianment, including Barnum's Museum. A number of fires were started by him and others in New York but, overall, the plot fell far short of creating the havoc planned. Members of the plot scattered and Kennedy was apprehended at Detroit, Michigan, early in 1865. Although the identities of many of the other men involved in the plot subsequently became known, none were arrest or tried. Transported to New York City, he was charged with a two count indictment of "Waging irregular warfare" and "Setting fires in

---

[15] The first mention of him and his trial found in the New York "Times" of Fab. 28, 1865, incorrectly gives his name as Howell Cobb Kennedy and claimed that he was a close relation to Howell Cobb of Georgia.

company with others to hotels and places of amusement which were crowded with men, women, and children."[16] On March 14, 1865 he was found guilty of these charges and sentenced to be hanged by the neck. His sentence was approved by General Dix, commander of the Department of the East and President Abraham Lincoln refused to review the proceedings. Kennedy was exacuted at Fort Lafayette on March 25, 1865, and either buried there or at Cypress Hills. All of the bodies buried at Fort Lafayette were subsequently removed to Cypress Hills and no grave numbers recorded for them.

KEYSER, W. L. - No information has been found other than cemetery records. These provide only his name, date of death, and grave number. These show that a man by this name was buried in grave number 201 on July 14, 1862.

KING, John C. - King enlisted on January 16, 1862 in Company C, Thirty-Eighth North Carolina Infantry regiment, and was given the rank of Fourth-Sergeant. He was a seventeen year old farmer, standing five feet, seven inches tall. King was reported absent, sick and hospitalized at Petersburg, Virginia, during March and April, 1862.He appears to have been reduced in rank to Private sometime during this period and on April 20, 1862, an entry in his file reads "Promoted from Private to Third Corporal." He was rehospitalized because of illness from November 1862 until February 1863 and was present from March 1863 until June, 1863. He had been promoted to Fourth-Corporal on April 8, 1863. King was wounded at the Battle of Gettysburg and was among those left behind when Confederate forces retreated from the area. He was admitted to DeCamp General Hospital on July 19, 1863. He died there of Pyaemia on August 18, 1863. He was buried in grave number 787.

KING, M. - He enlisted on March 4, 1862 in Fayette County, Georgia for three years or the war. King was assigned to Company G, Forty-Fourth Georgia Infantry. He was admitted to Chimborazo Hospital Number 3 at Richmond, suffering from fever, on June 23, 1862, and was transferred to the Confederate Hospital at Lynchburg, Virginia, three days later. On September 1, 1862 he was reported sick at General Hospital Number 13, Richmond, Virginia, suffering from diarrhea. Records show he was admitted

---

[16] The officers presiding at his trial were Brig. Gen. Henry Warren (President), Brig. Gen. William H Morris, Colonels M S Howe, Third U S Cavalry and H Day, U S Art, Brevet Lieutenant-Colonel R F O'Beirne Fourteenth U S Infantry, and Major John A Boiles, U S Volunteers.

to the Fourth Division General Hospital, Camp Winder, Richmond, Virginia, on September 24, 1862. He was shot in the cheek and captured at Gettysburg, Pennsylvania. Sent north, he was admitted to DeCamp General Hospital, Davids Island, New York, on July 23, 1863. King died there on August 24, 1863 and was buried in grave number 814. Cemetery records give his date of death as August 21, 1863.

  KING, Thomas J. - King enlisted at Fort Gaines, Alabama, on February 20, 1861, in Company A, Gee's Alabama Artillery Battalion. This unit was subsequently renamed the First Alabama Artillery Battalion. A resident of Eufaula County, Alabama, he was thirty years old when he enlisted. Records show him present from enlistment until February 29, 1864, when he re-enlisted for the duration of the War. His rank at this time was shown as Fourth Corporal. On April 30, 1864 his rank was reported at Third Corporal. King was captured at Fort Morgan, Alabama, on August 23, 1864. Sent to New York from New Orleans, Louisiana, on September 18, 1864, he arrived at Fort Columbus on September 28th, He died at the Post Hospital there on November 30, 1864 of Pneumonia. He was buried in grave number 2142.

  KITE, Stephen - Kite enlisted on May 10, 1861 in Company G, Seventeenth North Carolina Infantry on May 10, 1861, at Hamilton, North Carolina. He was mustered in at Camp Hatteras, North Carolina, on July 27, 1861. Nothing has been found to show when or where he was captured. Cemetery records show that he died on October 27, 1861, and is buried in grave 4447.

  KNIGHT, T. H. - Knight was an eighteen year old conscript, a resident of Halifax County, North Carolina. He enrolled as a Private in Company E, Thirtieth North Carolina Infantry, on June 29, 1863. On August 5, 1863 he was detailed as a shoemaker in Richmond, Virginia, serving in that capacity until August, 1864, having been briefly hospitalized at Receiving and Wayside Hospital (General Hospital Number 9), Richmond, in mid-September, 1863. He was captured at Clover Hill, Virginia, on April 5, 1865, and sent north. Nothing has been found to show when he arrived but he died at the Post Hospital, Hart's Island, New York, of Scurvy, on June 5, 1865. He was buried in grave number 2947.

  KORN, J. A. - Records of his unit, Company E, Fourteenth South Carolina Militia, show that his name was actually J A Horn. He was captured at Lynch's Creek, South Carolina, on February 25, 1865 and was received at Hart's Island, New York, on April 10,

1865, and died there on April 28, 1865, of Diarrhea. He was buried in grave number 2640.

LAMBRA, Paul - Many of the names found on the cemetery records differ considerably from the actual name of the individual as found in his military file. Few, however, seem to be as far off the mark as this. Records of the unit in which this man served, Company B, Fifty-Third Georgia Infantry regiment, show that his name was actually J A Lummius. He enlisted on May 1, 1862 at Snapping Shoals, Georgia and was present from Feb 1862 until mid-September, 1862. From the 13th of that month until the 30th, he was reported on sick furlough. Returned to his regiment, he served with it continually until wounded and left in Federal hands at Gettysburg. He arrived at David's Island, New York, on July 21, 1863, and died there two days later as a result of his wound. He is buried in grave number 648.

LANCASTER, J. L. - Cemetery records show him to be a member of the Fourteenth South Carolina Cavalry regiment, but there was no unit with this designation.. He was, in fact, a member of the Fourteenth South Carolina Militia. Records of this unit show that he was married (his wife's name was May) and that he was captured at Lynch's Creek, South Carolina, on February 25, 1865. He was received at Hart Island, New York, on April 10, 1865, and he died there of Typhoid Fever on April 15, 1865. He is buried in grave 2543.

LANGSDEN, J. L. - This soldier's name, according to the records of his unit, was J L Lansdon. He enlisted in Florida (no specific location mentioned) on September 5, 1862, in Company F, First Alabama Artillery Battalion and was present with the battalion from enlistment until February 28, 1863. Granted sick leave, he was absent from the unit until the end of April, 1863. He was then present with the unit through April 30, 1864. From December 16th to the 30th, 1863, he was detailed daily with the Quartermaster's Department in Mobile, Alabama. He again served on this duty for at least the month of June, 1864. On August 23, 1864 he was captured when Fort Morgan, Alabama, fell to Federal troops. Sent to New Orleans, he was confined in Steam Levee Press #4. On September 24, 1864, he was hospitalized at St Louis General Hospital, New Orleans, suffering from acute diarrhea. He was released from the hospital six days later. Transferred to Ship Island, Mississippi, he was moved from there to Fort Columbus, New York, arriving on November 10th Less than a month later, on December 2, 1864, he died there on Chronic Diarrhea. He was buried in grave number 1463.

LAWLESS, J. J. - Nothing has been found to show when Lawless became a member of Company "L", First Georgia Infantry, but it is known that he was captured at Cheraw, South Carolina, on March 5, 1865. Moved to New York by way of Newberne, North Carolina, he died at Hart Island, New York, of chronic diarrhea, on June 3, 1865. He was buried in grave 2940.

LAWRENCE, Ira J. - A small number of military records give this soldier's name as J L Lawrence rather then as identified above. He enlisted at Atlanta, Georgia, on September 25, 1861, and was assigned to Company I, Thirty-Fifth Georgia Infantry regiment. Incomplete regimental records show him present with the unit from November, 1861, until December, 1862. Lawrence was wounded and captured at Gettysburg, Pennsylvania. Sent north, he was received at DeCamp General Hospital, Davids Island, New York, where he died on August 23, 1863, a victim of his wound. He was buried in grave number 819.

LEDFORD, William - William B Ledford or W B Ledford, was a twenty-eight year old native of Wilkes County, North Carolina, when he enlisted in Company B, Fifty-Eighth North Carolina Infantry regiment on June 16, 1862. He stood five feet, seven inches tall. After joining the unit at Burnesville, North Carolina, Ledford was reported present with the until April 23, 1863. He deserted at Clinton, Tennessee, on that date. An entry dated June, 1863, reads "Expected to return." And return he appears to have done because the next entry mentioning him, dated September 19, 1863, reports that he had again deserted, this time near Lafayette, Georgia. A final entry in his records, dated January 26, 1864, shows that he had been dropped from the rolls. No additional information has been found on him to indicate when or where he returned to the regiment, when or where he was captured or sent north, yet cemetery records show that he was buried in grave number 2726 on May 26, 1865.

LEONARD, J. D. - One item has been found in the Miscellaneous Unfiled file for this man. This shows that he was a member of Company B, Thirteenth South Carolina Infantry regiment. He was wounded and left at Gettysburg. Arriving at DeCamp General Hospital, Davids Island, New York, he died there on July 20, 1863, as a result of his wound and was buried in grave number 670.

LEONARD, Levi - Military records show that he was carried on some rolls as Levi Leonart. A resident of Davidson County, North Carolina, he was a thirty-nine year old conscript who was enrolled in Company I, Thirty-Fifth North Carolina

Infantry on April 1, 1863, for a three year term of service. Incomplete unit records show that he signed a clothing receipt on March 26, 1864, and that he was admitted to General Hospital Number 11, Charlotte, North Carolina, on May 15, 1864, He signed an additional clothing receipt on September 1, 1864 and was present with the regiment until from November, 1864 through February, 1865. Leonard was captured at Five Forks, Virginia, on April 1, 1865, and sent to Hart Island, New York. He arrived there on April 7, 1865. On May 20, 1865 he died at the Post Hospital of Chronic Diarrhea. He was buried in grave 2837.

LEROACH, William T. - Records of his unit, Company A, First (Butler's) South Carolina Infantry, show that his name was William Laroche (sometimes shown as William LaRoche). No information has been found on him prior to his capture at Cheraw, South Carolina, on March 3, 1865. Transported north, he arrived at Hart Island on April 10, 1865 where he died there of Consumption on June 7, 1865. He is buried in grave number 2903.

LIGHT, Charles - Light enlisted on June 20, 1861 at Hermitage Camp, Virginia, for a one year term of service. He was assigned to Company F, Thirty-Eighth Virginia Infantry. Incomplete regimental records show him present during July and August, 1861, March and April, 1862, and May and June, 1863. He was wounded and left at Gettysburg. Received at DeCamp General Hospital, Davids Island, New York, on July 17, 1863, he died there as a result of his gun shot wound on July 30, 1863. He was buried in grave 710.

LITTEN, George - Litten enlisted on March 27, 1862 at Lebanon, Virginia, for a three year term of service. He was assigned to Company G, Twenty-Ninth Virginia Infantry regiment. He was present from enlistment through February, 1863. During the latter month he was present with the unit, but reported sick. Existing unit records show him present from April 1 - June, 1864. On June 8, 1864 he signed a clothing receipt with his mark. He was again present during the last two months of 1864. Litten was captured at Dinwiddie Court House, Virginia, on April 1, 1865. Sent north, he was received at Hart Island, later that month (the exact date is not given) and he died there, on Typhoid Fever, on May 23, 1865. He was buried in grave number 2860.

LITTLE, James - Although burial records list his name as above, unit records show that his name was actually John B Little. He enlisted on July 26, 1863 in Company B of the Cobb Guards Georgia Infantry Battalion at Calhoun, Georgia. Members of this unit was transferred to Company B of the Twenty-Second Georgia

Artillery Battalion on September 19, 1863. He was present with the battalion during September and October, 1863, and again from April 1864 until October, 1864. The muster of September and October includes the notation "On extra Duty as Company Cook." There is no record of his having been captured but prison records show that he died at Hart Island, New York, on April 11, 1865, no cause being given. Cemetery records give his date of death as April 10, 1865, however. He was buried in grave number 2425.

  LIVINGSTON, John - Livingston was born in Wilkes County, North Carolina. He was seventeen years old, five feet seven inches tall when he enlisted on September 24, 1861, for a one year term of service. He was assigned to Company F, Thirty-Seventh North Carolina Infantry. He re-enlisted for two additional years on June 16, 1862 and was sent to the Confederate General Hospital at Lynchburg, Virginia shortly thereafter. No information has been found showing when or where he was captured but cemetery records show that he was buried in grave number 146 on June 3, 1862.

  LOGAN, J. M. - Rolls of Company B, Twenty-Eighth North Carolina Infantry regiment also show his name as G M Logan. He enlisted on July 30, 1861 at Dallas, Gaston County, North Carolina, for three years. He was eighteen years old at the time. On March 1, 1862, he received a $50.00 bounty for re-enlisting for an additional two years. Logan was wounded and captured at Gettysburg, Pennsylvania. Transported north, he arrived at DeCamp General Hospital, Davids Island, New York, on July 19, 1863. He died there of Pyaemia on August 15, 1863. He was buried in grave number 762.

  LOGAN, T. C. - Thomas C Logan was fifty years old when he enlisted at Vernon, Mississippi on April 18, 1861 in the Beauregard Rifles Mississippi Volunteers. He was mustered into that unit on May, 1861. Born in Liehram, Ireland, Logan stood five feet six inches tall, had fair complexion, blue eyes, and gray hair. His occupation was listed as a laborer. On May 23, 1861 his company became Company I of the Eighteenth Mississippi Infantry regiment at Corinth, Mississippi. Records show him present from enlistment until June, 1862 having re-enlisted on April 26, 1862, at Lee's Mills, Virginia for two years, On August 16, 1862, Logan was discharged "on account of being overage." but records from September and October, 1862, show him present. On November 1, 1862, he was admitted to Howard's Grove Hospital, Richmond, Virginia. He was transferred to General Hospital Number 2, Richmond, on December 23, 1862, suffering from debilitis and rheumatism. He returned to the regiment on February 7, 1863, and was present with it until he was wounded at Gettysburg, Pennsylvania. Logan was among the Confederate wounded left behind there when Confederate forces retreated from that battle. Transported north, he was received at DeCamp General Hospital on July 23, 1863 and died there on September 8, 1863, of an Abcess of his Hip. He was buried in grave number 849.

LONG, Reuben - Long was twenty-three years old when he enlisted in Company H, Twenty-Fourth North Carolina Infantry regiment on July 15, 1861, in Person County, North Carolina. His original term of enlistment was for one year but on April 29, 1862 he re-enlisted for two years or the duration of the war. Long was wounded at the Battle of Malvern Hill, Virginia, July 1, 1862, and was furloughed to Person County. He returned to the regiment in September, 1862. On December 2, 1862, he was admitted to the Confederate General Hospital, Charlottesville, Virginia, suffering from Debilitis. Long returned to service on January 8, 1863. He was promoted to the rank of Sergeant on June 18, 1864. One day later he was wounded and captured. While traveling north on the steamer "Western Metropolis" his left leg was amputated. He arrived at Lovell General Hospital, Portsmouth Grove, Rhode Island, in early July, 1864. Records show that he died there on July 24, 1864 as a result of the amputation but contradictory cemetery records reveal that he was buried at Cypress Hill Cemetery on July 23rd in grave number 3427.

LONG, Richard - Long enlisted at Greensboro, North Carolina, on February 22, 1862 for three years, He was twenty-five years old at the time. Assigned to Company E, Twenty-Second North Carolina Infantry, he was present with the unit until June 20, 1862. On that day he was admitted to the Confederate General Hospital at Danville, Virginia, and returned to duty on August 13, 1862. Medical records in his file show that he was again absent due to sickness in mid-June, 1864, and again from July to October, 1864. His file also contains clothing receipts he signed, dated March 31, June 30, December 5, and December 23, 1864. Long was captured at Petersburg, Virginia, on April 3, 1865. Transported north, he arrived at Hart Island, New York, on April 7, 1865 from City Point, Virginia. He died there of Typhoid Fever on June 2, 1865 and is buried in grave 2931.

LONG, Simon - He enlisted at New Orleans, Louisiana, on May 7, 1861, and was enrolled at Camp Moore, Louisiana, on June 4, 1861, in Company K, Fifth Louisiana Infantry regiment. Irish born, he was single, and listed his occupation as a Steamboatman. His enlistment records state that he was twenty-four years old but his prison records, dated 1863, give his age as thirty. He was five feet nine and a half inches tall, had black hair, blue eyes, and a fair complexion. He was present from enlistment until the end of 1861. Incomplete regimental records show that he was captured at Fair Oaks, Virginia, on June 1, 1862 and sent to Fort Monroe, Virginia, on June 9, 1862. From there he was moved to Fort Delaware, Delaware. Long was exchanged at Aiken's Landing, Virginia, on August 5, 1862. For a month after his capture he shown as "Sick, in Richmond." Regimental records for September, 1862, show him as "Sick in Winchester." On September 20, 1862 he was employed at a cook at the Winchester General Hospital. On December 4, 1862, he was admitted to the Louisiana Hospital, Richmond, Virginia. In early 1863 he was reported at the Farmville General Hospital. Long was then shown as present until May 6, 1863. Again hospitalized (this time at Chimborazo, Hospital Number 5, Richmond) for debility, he returned to his regiment on June 14, 1863, at Winchester, Virginia. He was wounded (Compound Fracture of Left Arm) and captured at Gettysburg, Pennsylvania. He was received at DeCamp General Hospital, Davids Island, New York, on July 17, 1863. Long died there of Pyaemia on September 11, 1863, and was buried in grave number 854.

LUNDY, James - Lundy enlisted on May 25, 1863, at Fort Sumter, South Carolina and was assigned to Company C, First South Carolina Artillery. Not long afterward he was admitted to the City Hospital, Charleston. He deserted from the hospital in June, 1863, but incomplete regimental records show him back with the unit in September, 1863. On November 5, 1863, he was admitted to the First Georgia Hospital, Charleston. Records show him present from January to October, 1864. Long was captured at Bentonville, North Carolina, on March 22, 1865. Sent north to Hart Island, New York, he died there of Chronic Diarrhea on June 15, 1865. He was buried in grave number 3006.

LYLE, Samuel A. - Lyle was a resident of Charlottesville, Virginia. He was five feet nine and a quarter inches tall, had a dark complexion, dark hair, and dark eyes. He was conscripted into Company E, Fourteenth Virginia Infantry regiment on September 1, 1863. He was present with the unit from then until May 15, 1864 when he was wounded. Previously, in March, 1864, his pay had been stopped for loss of twenty cartridges. After being wounded, he returned to the unit in July, 1864 and served with it through the end of 1864. On April 1, 1865, he was captured at Five Forks, Virginia. He was received at Hart Island, New York, on April 7, 1865. Here he took the Oath of Allegiance on June 20, 1865. A day later he died of remittent fever at the Hart Island Post Hospital although cemetery records give the date as one day later, June 22, 1865. He was buried in grave number 3036.

LYNCH, George - Cemetery records show that a man with this name, a Private in Company D, Tenth Virginia Artillery, was buried in grave number 2883 on May 26, 1865. No military records of any kind have been found about him, however.

MACKLENERY, B. C. - His military records show that his name was actually B H McGlamery, a Private in Company B, Twenty-Second North Carolina Infantry regiment. It is not known when he entered the service but he signed clothing receipts on November 23rd, November 26th, and December 2, 1864. He was captured at "Hatch's Run [sic]", Virginia, on April 2, 1865. Sent north, he died at Hart Island, New York, on May 10, 1865, of Chronic Diarrhea. He was buried in grave number 2749.

MARTIN, Brice E. - Martin was a thirty-one year old farmer who enlisted in Company F, Fifty-Seventh Virginia Infantry, on September 20, 1861, at Mount Vernon Church, Henry County, Virginia. On November 23, 1861 he was reported sick in camp. Incomplete regimental records show that he received a thirty day furlough in September, 1862. For some unspecified reason, his pay was stopped for $5.10 in November, 1862. He was present with the regiment until May 11, 1864. On that date he was admitted to Chimborozo Hospital Number 9, suffering from a Contusion of his leg. Martin returned to duty on August 26, 1864 and was promoted Second-Corporal on October 20, 1864. He signed a clothing receipt on November 19, 1864. Captured at Five Forks, Virginia, on April 1, 1865, he was moved to Hart Island, New York, arriving there on April 7th. He died there on April 16, 1865 of "Inflammation of Bowels". He was buried in grave number 2530.[17]

MARTIN, R. M. N. - The only records found regarding this individual shows that he was buried in grave number 213 on July 16, 1862. It is not known what unit he served in or when or where he enlisted or where he had been captured.

---

[17] A recent visit to the cemetery (May 25, 2002) revealed that a new stone had been placed on his grave. It is, however, a Federal marker.

MASSEY, R. R. - The records of his unit, Company B, Forty-Ninth North Carolina Infantry, show that he name was actually R R Massie. A resident of Franklin County, North Carolina, it is not known when or where he enlisted. He was captured at Hatcher's Run, Virginia, April 2, 1865, and was received at Hart Island, New York, on April 7th. He died on Chronic Diarrhea on May 25, 1865. Massey was buried in grave number 2885.

MASSINGALE, R. H. - He enlisted in Company K, Thirty-Eighth North Carolina Infantry regiment, in Johnson County, North Carolina on September 1, 1864. Unit records show that his name as R H Massingill. He signed a clothing receipt on December 22, 1864. On April 2, 1865, he was captured at Petersburg, Virginia. Received at Hart Island, New York, on April 7, 1865, he died there of Typhoid Pneumonia on May 18, 1865 and was buried in grave number 2815.

MATHIS, Thomas - Mathis traveled 112 miles to enlist at Lightwood Hot Springs, South Carolina, on August 17, 1861, in Company G, Fourteenth South Carolina Infantry regiment. He was reported present from enlistment until early 1862. He was then reported hospitalized at Gordonsville, Va., and, later, at Lynchburg, Va. The nature of his illness is not given in the records. He received a furlough to return to his home on October 11, 1863, but on his return was rehospitalized at Jackson Hospital, Richmond, Va. In February, 1864, he finally returned to active service but on June 30, 1864, he was again briefly hospitalized in Richmond. Mathis returned to his regiment in September, 1864, and was captured at Sutherland Station, Virginia, April 2, 1865. Sent to Hart Island, New York, from City Point, Va., he died there of Typhoid Fever on May 16, 1865. He was buried in grave 2803.

MATTHEWS, E. - He enlisted on August 10, 1861 in Company A, First (Provisional Army) South Carolina Infantry regiment at his birthplace, Barnwell, South Carolina. Slightly more than a week later, on August 19, 1861, he was mustered into service at Richmond, Va. He was admitted to Camp Winder Hospital, Virginia, on May 28, 1862, suffering from diarrhea, returning to service on June 5, 1862. He was reported present with the unit until June, 1863, although an entry in his rolls shows that he returned from being absent, sick, at Gordonsville, Va., in November, 1862. Matthews was wounded and left at Gettysburg, Pa. when Confederate forces retreated. He was sent north, arriving at DeCamp General Hospital, Davids Island, New York, on July 17, 1863. He died there as a result of his gunshot wound on July 27, 1863. He is buried in grave number 691.

MATTHEWS, James - Records indicate that this man's correct name was James Mathews but, along with the spelling on his burial records, he was also carried on various rolls as James M Mathis and James M Mathes. He was a twenty-eight year old resident of Alamance County, North Carolina, when he enrolled at Graham, North Carolina, on May 8, 1861. He was mustered in a month later and Garysburg, North Carolina, as a Private Company E, Thirteenth North Carolina Infantry. Matthews was present with his regiment until wounded and captured at Gettysburg, Pennsylvania. Transferred noreth to DeCamp General Hospital, Davids Island, New York, he died there, August 6, 1863, of Typhoid Fever. He was buried in grave number 747.

MATTOX, R. F. - A private in Company E, Eighteenth Virginia Infantry, this man's correct name was Richard T Mattocks. His name also appears on rolls also as K Mattocks, R T Mattocks, and R F Mattoc. On May 8, 1861 he enlisted for a twelve month term of service at Haymarket, Virginia. He subsequently reenlisted for the duration of the War and was present with the unit until June, 1863, except for a brief absence due to illness in October, 1862. A comment on the regiment's rolls for September/October, 1863 reads: "Went into the Battle of Gettysburg and has not been heard of since." Federal reports show that he had been wounded and left at Gettysburg and was sent from Chester Point, Maryland, to the Point Lookout Prison Camp. He was paroled from there on March 20, 1864. Contradictory Confederate reports follow. One states that he received a Furlough in May, 1864 and, in June, 1864, he "Retired on account of wounds received at Gettysburg, July 3, 1863." Another report dated May 18, 1864, however states he was "[a]ssigned to Invalid Corps...to be re-examined November 25, 1864." A final report states "Ordered to return to regiment." This entry is dated December 1, 1864. No additional information regarding his capture or death have been found. Cemetery records show that he died on May 18, 1865, and was buried in grave number 2821.

MAXWELL, Hudson - No information except a burial record, has been found for the individual, buried in grave number 2958. This record shows he was a Private in Company K, Twelfth Virginia Infantry, and that he died on June 5, 1865. Cemetery records give his death date as June 6th, however.

MAY, John D. - May was a resident of Craven County, North Carolina. He was 32 years old when he enlisted on May 12,

1861 as a Sergeant in Company F, Second North Carolina Infantry. He was reported present until June, 1863. For some reason not mentioned in his records, he was reduced to the rank of Private in late 1861. May was wounded and left at Gettysburg in early July, 1863. He was received at DeCamp General Hospital on July 19, 1863, where he died, on July 31, 1863, as a result of his gun shot wound. He was buried in grave 735.

MAY, William H. - Company records show that May was a resident of Pittsylvania County, Virginia. He stood 5 five seven inches tall and had dark complexion, dark hair, and dark eyes. He enlisted and was mustered in at Bachelor's Hall, Va., July 22, 1861, as a Private in Company I, Fifty-Seventh Virginia Infantry. May was present until May, 1862, when he was reported "sick in camp". He returned to duty in July, 1862 and was with his regiment through at least November, 1864. On July 30, 1864 he was assigned to the position of Musician. May was captured at Five Forks, Virginia, April 1, 1865. Transferred to Hart Island, New York, he died there of Chronic Diarrhea on June 11, 1865. He was buried in grave number 2988.

MC CANN, Austin - A forty-five years old resident of Danville, Virginia, McCann enlisted in Company E, Fifty-Ninth Virginia Infantry on September 2, 1862, at Richmond. He was present with the unit until admitted to Chimborazo Hospital, Richmond, on September 14, 1863. The nature of his illness does not appear in unit records and he returned to active duty on October 27, 1863. McCann was captured at Nottaway Bridge, Virginia, May 8, 1864, and sent to Point Lookout prison camp. He was exchanged on October 29, 1864, and sent to Chimborzzo Hospital, suffering from diarrhea. McCann was recaptured on April 2, 1865 at South Side Railroad. Moved to Hart's Island, New York, by way of City Point, Virginia, he died there of "Inflammation of Brain" on May 26, 1865, and was buried in grave number 2983.

MC CARLEY, Green - McCarley was a 22 year old farmer who enrolled at Ripley, Mississippi. Sent to Virginia, he was mustered in at Lynchburg, Va., on May 10, 1861 in Company B, Second Mississippi Infantry regiment and was present from enlistment until June, 1862. He had been detailed as regimental teamster on April 23, 1862. McCarley was admitted to the Soldier's Home Hospital, Richmond, on July 8, 1862 and returned to duty on August 22, 1862. He was reported sick in quarters briefly in the spring of 1863. McCarley was wounded and captured at Gettysburg, Pa. Sent north, he arrived at DeCamp General

Hospital, Davids Island, July 23, 1863. He died there on October 13, 1863, of Pyaemia. He is buried in grave number 899.

MC CARTY, Michael - He enlisted on May 9, 1861, at Covington, Virginia, for a three year term of service. He was assigned to Company C, First Virginia Infantry Battalion and was present with the unit until April 5, 1862. On that date he was admitted to the General Hospital at Orange Court House, Va., suffering from Venereal Disease. He returned to duty in June, 1862 and was present until mid-July, 1863 when he was hospitalized at General Hospital #4, Richmond. McCarty returned to duty in the fall of 1863 but was admitted to General Hospital #9 on June 17, 1864. He appears to have been dismissed the following day. Records show that he was present with the battalion until January 12, 1865. A report dated January 24, 1865 shows that he returned to active service on that date. His name appears on a list of "Refugees and Rebel Deserters sent from City Point, Va., to Philadelphia, Pa." dated April 12, 1865. No details have been found concerning his capture or death but cemetery records show that he was buried in grave number 2810 on May 18, 1865.

MC CLELLAN, _____ - Unfiled Miscellaneous records show this man as a "Prisoner of War" who was admitted to the U S General Hospital, Fort Columbus, New York, June 13, 1862. He died there of Typhoid Fever on June 19, 1862. No grave number is given in any records.

MC CONIELL, R. T. - Records also this man's name as R T McConniel. He enlisted on May 2, 1862 at Tunnel Hill, Georgia in Company G, Eleventh Georgia Infantry regiment. No other records exist for him until he was wounded in the ankle at Gettysburg, Pa. Sent north, he arrived at Hart Island, New York, July 17, 1863. Transferred to DeCamp General Hospital, Davids Island, he died there on July 30, 1863. (A second record gives the date as August 1, 1863 but cemetery records support the July date.) He was buried in grave 709.

MC CURLEY, David - McCurley enlisted at Cedar Bluff, Alabama, on June 8, 1863, for a three year term of service in Company E, Forty-Seventh Alabama Infantry regiment. He was wounded and left at Gettysburg, Pa. when southern forces retreated. Moved to DeCamp General Hospital, Davids Island (no date is given), he died there on September 8, 1863, he was buried in grave 851. The cause of death is given as "Amputation of Leg."

MC CURRY, John D. - After travelling 252 miles to Camp Butler, South Carolina, McCurry enlisted on September 3, 1861, in

Company I, Fourteenth South Carolina Infantry regiment. He was present until August 31, 1862. On that date he was admitted to Huguenot Springs Hospital, Virginia, suffering from Debilitis. He was transferred to Chimborazo Hospital in early 1863. In February, 1863, he was furloughed home. McCurry returned to service in March, 1863. He was wounded at Gettysburg, Pa. and was among the many Confederate wounded left there when southern troops retreated. Moved to DeCamp General Hospital, Davids Island, on July 19, 1863, he died there on September 12, 1863 following the amputation of his right leg. He was buried in grave number 855.

  MC DERMITH, Alex - Alexander H McDermith enlisted on May 24, 1862 at Selma, Alabama, in Company C, Gee's Alabama Artillery Battalion. This battalion was subsequently redesignated the First Alabama Artillery Battalion. He was present from enlistment until April 30, 1864. In February 1863 his pay was stopped for the loss of his haversack and in April, 1863, for the loss of his holster. On February 6, 1864, he was admitted to the Post Hospital, Fort Morgan, Alabama, but returned to active duty three days later. He was captured when Fort Morgan surrendered on August 23, 1864. First sent to New Orleans, McDermith was transferred to New York City on September 18, 1864, arriving there on September 28th. He died at the Fort Columbus Post Hospital on October 8, 1864, of Chronic Diarrhea. He was buried in grave number 1999.

  MC DONALD, Chris. - Christopher McDonald was a 20 year old farmer when he enlisted in Company K, Thirty-Eighth North Carolina Infantry regiment. No enlistment date is given in his records. A resident of Fayetteville, North Carolina, he was unmarried, the son of Ballamb McDonald. Clothing receipts dated December 23rd and 26th, 1864, bear his signature. Captured at Petersburg, Va., on April 2, 1865, he was sent north, arriving at Hart Island on April 7, 1865. On April 29, 1865, he was transferred to DeCamp General Hospital, Davids Island where he died on May 11, 1865 on Chronic Diarrhea. He was buried in grave 2685.

  MC DONNELL, William - McDonnell was 23 years old when he was conscripted into Company C, Sixth North Carolina Infantry regiment. He was a resident of Burke County, North Carolina. McDonnell was present until wounded in the arm at Gettysburg, Pa. Left in the hands of Federal forces, a note in his file reads: "Recovery, Doubtful." Moved to DeCamp General Hospital, he arrived there on July 17, 1863 and died there as a result of his gunshot wound on July 28, 1863. He was buried in grave 696.

MC DOWELL, D. C. -Burial records list his name as above but all of his military records give his name as David E McDaniel, D E McDaniel, or D C McDaniel. He enlisted on May 27, 1861, for "36 months" at Lynchburg, Va. in Company E, Twelfth Virginia Infantry. On March 7, 1863, he was transferred to Company K, Twenty-Fourth Virginia Infantry, in exchange for a Thomas Ratlife. At the battle of Gettysburg, Pa., McDowell was wounded in the right foot and captured. He was cared for at the XII Corps Hospital until July 20, 1863. Sent north, he arrived at DeCamp General Hospital, Davids Island, arriving there on July 28, 1863. He died there, no cause given, on July 31, 1863 and was buried in grave 707.

MC GILL, John - The 19 year old son of Neill McGill, he enlisted on February 15, 1862 in Cumberland County, North Carolina, in Company K, Thirty-Eighth North Carolina Infantry regiment. He was present until August 17, 1862, when he was admitted to Chimborazo Hospital #5, Richmond, for Debility. He received a 40 day furlough from the hospital on October 11, 1862. On his return, he was listed as present with his unit until he was wounded and left at Gettysburg, Pa. He was received at DeCamp General Hospital, Davids Island, on July 19, 1863. Three days later he died there as a result of his wound. McGill was buried in grave 667. On February 3, 1865, his father filed a claim for his pay. The war ended before the claim could be settled, however.

MC HENRY, Alcana -Regimental records also list this soldier's name as Alkana McHenry and A McHenry. He was a 23 year old carpenter when he enlisted on February 16, 1861, at Friar's Point, Mississippi, in the Coahoma Fencibles Mississippi Infantry Company. On May 13, 1861 he enlisted in Company B, Eleventh Mississippi Infantry regiment. Existing records show him present until June 25, 1862, when he was admitted to the C S General Hospital, Petersburg, Va., suffering from "G S Left Breast." It is not known when he returned to active service but was again wounded and captured at Gettysburg, Pa. Sent to DeCamp General Hospital, Davids Island, New York, he arrived there on July 23, 1863. He died there on August 23, 1863, the cause being given as "Amputation Right Thigh." McHenry was buried in grave number 820.

MC KENZIE, H. T. - Although burial records give his name as above, regimental records show his name as T H McKenzie. He enlisted in Company B, Twenty-Second Georgia

Artillery Battalion, at Savannah, Georgia, on August 1, 1864. He was present until the end of 1864. McKenzie was captured at Cheraw, South Carolina, on March 7, 1865 and was received at Hart Island, New York on April 10, 1865. The final entry in his records reads that he died of Typhoid Pneumonia on May 23, 1865, at Darlington South Carolina. Cemetery records, however, show that he was buried in grave number 734 on the same date. There is no explanation of this contradiction in the files.

MC KETHAN, J. A. - Records of his unit, Company L, First (Regular Army) South Carolina Infantry, also show his name as J A Keathan and J A McKeathan. He was 28 years old when he enlisted for the War at Charleston, South Carolina. He was mustered in at Lightwood Hot Springs, near Columbia, South Carolina, on September 3, 1861. Present until the summer of 1863, he was wounded and left in the hands of Federal forces when Confederate troops withdrew. Sent to DeCamp General Hospital, Davids Island, on July 19, 1863, he died there of his gunshot wound on August 3, 1863. He was buried in grave 734.

MC RILEY, Samuel - Cemetery records give his name as above but regimental records show his name as Samuel McNeily. He was a 39 year old resident of Cleveland County, North Carolina when he enlisted in February, 1863. He was wounded and left at Gettysburg, Pa. Received at DeCamp General Hospital, Davids Island, New York, on July 17, 1863, he died there of his gunshot wound on August 3, 1863. He was buried in grave number 730.

MC VICKER, William - McVicker was a Private in Company K, Thirty-Eighth North Carolina Infantry regiment. A resident of Cumberland County, he was five feet, seven inches tall, with dark complexion, dark hair, and dark eyes. He enlisted at Robeson, North Carolina for a three year term of service on September 1, 1864. Captured at Petersburg, Va., on April 2, 1865, he was received at Hart Island, New York, on April 7, 1865. Admitted to the Post Hospital there on June 19, 1865, he took the Oath of Allegiance there on June 30, 1865 but died the same day of Typhoid Fever. He was buried in grave 3057.

MEDLIN, F. M. - He was a 35 year old farmer, a native of Wake County, North Carolina, when he enrolled in Company I, Forty-Seventh North Carolina Infantry on Feb. 24, 1862. Clothing receipts show that he was unable to sign his own name. Medlin was mustered in near Raleigh, North Carolina, and was present with his unit until the fall of 1863. He was admitted to the Wayside Hospital #8, Richmond, on November 10, 1863, but was shown as present from January to October, 1864. Medlin was captured at Petersburg, Va., April 3, 1865, and sent to Hart Island, New York, where he arrived on April 7th. On April 16, 1865, he was admitted to the Post Hospital and died of Typhoid Fever on April 18th. He was buried in grave number 2554.

MEYER, J. H. - Cemetery show that Meyer was a Private in Company F, First South Carolina Artillery, and that he died on May 3, 1865. No military records have been found regarding him or his career, however. Meyer was buried in grave 2682.

MICHAEL, J. W. - Michael was a Private in Company A, Third North Carolina Reserves. Cemetery records incorrectly show his unit as the Third North Carolina Infantry regiment. He was five feet, six and a half inches tall, a resident of Guilford County with dark complexion, light hair, and gray eyes. He enlisted on November 16, 1864 at Camp Holmes, North Carolina. Michael was captured at Bentonville, North Carolina on March 22, 1865. (The date of his capture is also given as February 22, 1865 in his service file.) Sent from Newberne, North Carolina to Hart Island, New York, arriving on April 10, 1865, he died there of Chronic Diarrhea on June 18, 1865. He was buried in grave 3022.

MIDDLETON, H. P. - Nothing is known about when or where Middleton enlisted. A private in Company G, Forty-Fourth Alabama Infantry regiment, he was wounded and left at Gettysburg, Pa. Sent north, he was received at DeCamp General Hospital, Davids Island, New York, on July 19, 1863. He died there on his wounds on July 24, 1863, and was buried in grave 675.

MILBANK, W. J. - The only information found on this individual comes from cemetery records. These show that he was a Private in the Twelfth South Carolina Infantry regiment who died on April 19, 1865. He was buried in grave 2560.

MILLARD, John J. - Millard was a Private in Company K, Sixty-Sixth North Carolina Infantry regiment. Burial records identify his unit as the Sixty-Sixth North Carolina Cavalry. He was 40 years old when he enlisted at Wilmington, North Carolina. Married to Chairy Millard, his home was identified as Mount Olive, Wayne County, North Carolina. He was present from enlistment until July 7, 1864. On that date it was reported that he had deserted. He obviously returned to the unit because on March 15, 1865 he deserted again near Petersburg, Virginia (a second report indicates that he deserted "in the field in North Carolina.) He was captured at Piney Grove, North Carolina, on March 19, 1865. Millard arrived at Hart Island, New York on April 10, 1865, by way of Newberne, North Carolina. Admitted to DeCamp

General Hospital, Davids Island, he died there of Typhoid Fever on April 21, 1865. He was buried in grave number 2852.

MILLS, Gilbert - His name is also carried on some rolls at Gilbert Miles. He enlisted in Company K, Fifty-Sixth North Carolina Infantry regiment on October 29, 1864, at Camp Stokes, North Carolina. He was present until the end of 1864. Mills was captured at Five Forks, Virginia, on April 1, 1865. He was sent north and arrived at Hart Island, New York, on April 7, 1865. On April 24, 1865 he was admitted to the Post Hospital. Mills died there two days later of Typhoid Fever. A note in his records show that his effects were burned after his death. He was buried in grave 2614.

MITCHELL, William L. - His name is also carried on a small number of rolls as William L Mitchael. He was 20 years old when he enlisted on July 3, 1861, at Atlanta, Georgia, in Company D, Eleventh Georgia Infantry regiment. Born in Cherokee County, North Carolina, he was a six foot tall farmer. Mitchell was shown as "Sick, present" in the fall of 1861 but was hospitalized in Richmond on Christmas Eve, 1861, with Intermittent Fever. He returned to the regiment in the spring of 1862. He is mentioned in no other records until July, 1863, when he was reported wounded in the left arm at Gettysburg, Pa. Captured there, he was moved to Hart Island, New York. Transferred to DeCamp General Hospital, on July 19, 1863, he died there on August 7, 1863, after the amputation of his left arm. He was buried in grave number 749.

MIXON, Richard - Mixon enlisted on March 4, 1862 in Randolph County, Georgia for a three year term of service. Assigned to Company H, Fifty-First Georgia Infantry, he received a $50.00 bounty for enlisting. A report in his file dated July 1862 reads "Sick furlough expired - still sick." Mixon returned to duty on October 11, 1862, and was present until the summer of 1863. He was wounded in the stomach and side at Gettysburg, Pa., and was captured when Federal troops occupied the Confederate hospitals. He arrived at DeCamp General Hospital, Davids Island, New York, on July 12, 1863, and died there of his wounds on July 23, 1863. He was buried in grave number 665.

MODLIN, Alpha - Modlin enlisted in the Seventeenth North Carolina Infantry regiment on May 1, 1861 at Hatteras, North Carolina. He was a laborer, and a resident of Matlin County. Information in his service file indicates that he was unable to sign his name. Modlin was captured when Fort Hatteras fell to Federal forces. He died on October 4, 1861. Burial records, however, show that he died on November 24, 1861, and that he was a member of the Seventh North Carolina Infantry[18]. He was buried in grave number 4450.

MONTGOMERY, W. - Only burial records have been found for this man. They provide his death date (July 16, 1862) and the fact that he was buried in grave number 214. No unit is mentioned and none of the Confederate soldiers named Montgomery match the little known of him.

MOORE, G. E. - Records show that his full name was George Moore. He enlisted at Nashville, Tennessee, on May 25, 1861, in Company G, First (Field's) Tennessee Infantry. Incomplete records show that he was present from August through December, 1862, and was detached in early 1863. A note in his file reads: "Deserted, Feb. 20, 1863." but he is shown as present in April, 1863. There are is no additional information in his service file to identify his activities or his capture. Cemetery records show that he died on September 10, 1863, and was buried in grave 852.

MOORE, M. P. - Moore was a Private in Company H, Second North Carolina Infantry regiment. There are no records as to when or where he enlisted or of his service prior to July, 1863. He was wounded and left at Gettysburg. Moore was transferred to DeCamp General Hospital (no date given) and from there to Fort Wood, Bedloe's Island, New York. He died there on November 16, 1863, as a result of his gun shot wound. He was buried in grave number 935.

MORAN, J. A. - In addition to the name shown above, Moran is also carried on the records of his unit, Company G, Twenty-Sixth North Carolina Infantry regiment, as John A Moran and John A T Moran. He enlisted for a twelve month term of service at Matthews, North Carolina, on June 10, 1861, but was not mustered in until August 12th. He was shown as present until the end of 1861 and that his pay was stopped for $6.50 in October, 1861. No reason for this was given, however. Existing regimental records show that he was present in the spring of 1862 and that he was wounded and left at Gettysburg, Pa., in July, 1863. There is no record of when he was sent north only one showing that he died at DeCamp General Hospital on August 22, 1863 and that he was buried in grave number 811.

---

[18] The Seventh North Carolina State Infantry regiment was this unit's original designation. In the autumn of 1861, after the fall of Fort Hatteras, the first ten North Carolina units were redesingated because there was a duplication of State and Volunteer unit numbers. As a result of this redesignation, the Seventh was renamed the Seventeenth North Carolina Infantry regiment.

MORRIS, D. C. - Regimental records give his full name as David C Morris. He enlisted on February 4, 1864 at Carthage, N C, and was assigned to Company C, Thirty-Fifth North Carolina Infantry. On August 27, 1864, he was furloughed from Camp Winder General Hospital, Richmond, "to go to Jonesboro, N. C.". Morris was present from November 1864 through February, 1865. He was captured at Five Forks, Virginia, on April 1, 1865, and was sent to Hart Island, by way of City Point, Va. No date is given as to when he arrived in New York. He died of Typhoid Pneumonia on May 3, 1865, and was buried in grave number 2526.

MORRIS, James - Conscripted at the age of eighteen, Morris was a resident of Montgomery County, North Carolina. He was enrolled at Raleigh on July 24, 1863, and assigned to Company H, Fourteenth North Carolina Infantry regiment. A note is his file dated August 30, 1863 reads "Sent to Hospital." He is shown present from September 1863 though August, 1864. Clothing receipts with his signature, dated November 20, 1864 and December 28, 1864, show that he was at Charlottesville General Hospital late in 1864. On the same date that he signed the December clothing receipt he was ordered to return to his regiment. Morris was captured at Petersburg, Va., on April 3, 1865, and arrived at City Point, Va. four days later. Nothing in his file shows when he was sent north, only that he died at DeCamp General Hospital on May 11, 1865, of Typhoid Fever. Morris was buried in grave 2769.

MORRIS, John S. Burial records show that he was a member of the Fourteenth South Carolina Cavalry. He was, however, a member of the Fourteenth South Carolina Militia according to military records. There is no record of when he began his active service, or where or when he was taken prisoner. Morris arrived at Hart Island on April 10, 1865 and was admitted to the Post Hospital there on April 12th. On the 15th, he was transferred to DeCamp General Hospital, Davids Island, where he died of Chronic Diarrhea on April 20, 1865. He was twenty-one years old. Morris was buried in grave 2588.

MORRISON, Angus - Morrison was a Private in Company A, First (Butler's) South Carolina Infantry who enlisted on May 1, 1862, at Fort Moultrie, South Carolina. He was present with his unit until early September, 1863. On the 6th of that month he was "Captured by Enemy's Barges." On September 26, 1863, he arrived at Fort Columbus, New York. Subsequently exchanged on March 3, 1864, he was reported present until the end of 1864. Morrison was captured a second time at Chesterfield, South Carolina, on

April 1, 1865 and was sent to Hart Island, New York, by way of Newberne, North Carolina, but no date is given in his file. He died there on May 13, 1865 of Chronic Diarrhea. He is buried in grave 2774.

MOSES, Martin F. - Cemetery records list his name as above and his unit as the First North Carolina Infantry, but his military file shows that his name was Martin F Moser and that he served in Company A, Seventh North Carolina Infantry regiment. He was born in Alexander, North Carolina, and was a 19 year old farmer when he enlisted on May 29, 1861 at Charlotte, North Carolina. He stood five feet, nine inches tall. He was present with his unit May 27, 1862, when he was captured at Slash Church (Hanover Court House), Virginia. On June 2, 1862, he was reported at Tripler U S Army Hospital with a fractured thigh. An undated report states that he was moved to White House Landing, Virginia, and that he died at Norfolk, Virginia, on January 19, 1864. A second report, however (which agrees with his burial records) shows that he died on July 14, 1862, at the U S Army General Hospital on Lexington, Avenue, New York City, of "Irritative Fever." He was buried in grave 216.

MULL, J. H. - Regimental records show that his name was Jacob M F Mull although he was sometimes also shown as J M F Marl and J H Mail. No information has been found showing where or when he enlisted in Company F, Eleventh Georgia Infantry regiment. He was wounded in the shoulder at Gettysburg, Pa., and was among the Confederate wounded left there when southern forces withdrew. Sent north, he arrived at DeCamp General Hospital, Davids Island,, on July 23, 1863 and died there of Pyaemia on August 6, 1863. He was buried in grave 718,

MUNN, C. D. - Calvin D Munn enlisted at Raleigh, North Carolina on August 17, 1864, and was assigned to Company K, Thirty-Fourth North Carolina Infantry regiment. An entry in his file reads "Absent since Sept. 17, 1864." There is no additional information in his file. Burial records, however, show that he died on May 27, 1865, and was buried in grave 2896.

MURDOCK, J. G. - Murdock was a private in Company F, Fifty-Eighth North Carolina Infantry regiment. There is nothing in his file to show when or where he enlisted. He was captured at the Edisto River, South Carolina, on February 12, 1865. Sent from Newberne, North Carolina, to Hart Island, New York, he arrived there on April 10, 1865. Murdock died there on May 31, 1865 of Chronic Diarrhea. He was buried in grave number 2926,

MURPHY, E. E. - Enoch E Murphy enlisted on August 30, 1861, at Monticello, South Carolina, for the duration of the War. He was mustered in at Lightwood Hot Springs, near Columbia, in Company E, Fifteenth South Carolina Infantry regiment on September 6, 1861. Records show that he was present until April, 1862. The next entry in his file shows that he was furloughed for twenty days from Winder Division #3 Hospital, Richmond, Va., on October 18, 1862. It is not know why he had been hospitalized. Murphy returned to his regiment and was wounded (flesh wound in the leg) and captured at the Battle of Gettysburg. He was received at DeCamp General Hospital on July 17, 1863, and died of Pyaemia on September 20, 1863. He was buried in grave number 863. His father, John Murphy, applied for a final settlement of his account on July 26, 1864.

MURRAY, John - Murray enlisted on July 22, 1861 in Company C, Tenth Louisiana Infantry for the war at Camp Moore, Louisiana. He was an Irish born laborer, thirty years old, unmarried, and a resident of New Orleans. A list of engagements in which he took part shows that he was on the firing line at Dam #1, April 16, 1862, Williamsburg, May 4, 1862, Savage Station, June 29, 1862, and Malvern Hill, July 1, 1862. From May 22 - June 9, 1862 Murray was reported hospitalized at Winder General Hospital, Richmond, suffering from "Fever." He was then present with the regiment until December 3, 1862 when he was returned to Winder General. Ordered back to duty the following day, he served with the regiment until the spring of 1863. On April 4, 1863, he was transferred from Winder General Hospital to Huguenot Springs, Virginia, suffering from Chronic Rheumatism. He appears on no other regimental record but he signed clothing receipts on August 12, 1863, at Jackson Hospital, Richmond, and on November 20, 1864 (no place indicated). A clothing receipt dated "Fourth Quarter, 1864" shows him assigned to Company G, First Battalion, Confederate Invalid Corps. He was captured on April 3, 1865 at Petersburg, Va. and sent to Hart Island, New York. He was received there on April 7, 1865. He died there of Meningitis on May 7, 1865. He was buried in grave number 2738.

MURRAY, Michael - His name appears on regimental records as spelled above and as Michael Murry. He enlisted in Company H, Fifth Virginia Infantry, for the war, on March 10, 1862, at New Market, Virginia. He was present with the unit until June 2, 1863. On that date he was detached as "Ordnance Guard." A report dated July 18, 1863 shows him at General Hospital #1, Richmond, and reads "Rheumatism is improving." He returned to duty later that month but returned to the hospital in September, 1863. During the following month he was transferred to the General Hospital at Staunton, Virginia. He signed a clothing receipt there on April 20, 1864, and was back with his unit on August 31, 1864. In the fall of 1864 he was reported Absent Without Leave but no date is given. Murray was captured at Petersburg, Virginia, on April 2, 1865. Sent to Hart Island by way of City Point, Virginiaa., he arrived at the prison camp on April 7, 1865. He died there of Typhoid fever on June 11, 1865, and was buried in grave 2985.

NAKEEP, Daniel - Cemetery records list his name as above but military records give his name was Daniel A Kanup (also carried on rolls as D A Kanup). He enlisted on July 7, 1862, in Rowan County, North Carolina, in Company K, Fifty-Seventh North Carolina Infantry regiment. He was reported present with the regiment until the spring of 1863. On April 15, 1863, he was sent to an unnamed General Hospital in Richmond, Va.., and on the 28th was admitted to Chimborazo Hospital #3 suffering from Typhoid Pneumonia. He was subsequently transferred to the General Hospital in Danville, Virginia. It is not known when he returned to his regiment but he was wounded severely in the hip and he was among those left at Gettysburg, Pa. Received at Hart Island, New York, he died there on August 21, 1863, of Chronic Diarrhea. He was buried in grave 812.

NIX, Jacob - Only cemetery records exist for this individual. These show that a man with this name was buried in grave 3050 on June 24, 1865. His unit is not identified.

NORWOOD, Jos. J. - Joseph J Norwood was a Sergeant in Company E, Forty-Seventh North Carolina Infantry regiment. He was born in Wake County and was twenty-five years old when he enlisted at New Hope, North Carolina on January 20, 1862. He was five feet, eight inches tall. Incomplete regimental records show him present in the summer of 1862 and early in 1863. On June 21, 1863, he was admitted to Chimborazo Hospital #3, Richmond. Norwood returned to duty on July 13, 1863. Additional records show him present in the spring of 1864 and the fall of 1864. Clothing receipts with his signature dated November 17th, 25th, and December 1st, 1864, are found in his file. Norwood was captured at Petersburg, Va., on April 2, 1865, and was received at Hart Island on April 7th. He died there on May 26, 1865 of Double Pneumonia. He is buried in grave 2892.

NOWELL, J. Henry - Nowell was 39 years old (a second report gives his age as 40) when he enlisted at Franklin, North

Carolina on March 1, 1862. Born in Franklin, he was a farmer, standing five feet, eleven inches tall. He was present with his unit until January, 1863. He was then recorded as Absent, "Hospital Attendant." In the spring of 1863 he returned to his regiment but is next mentioned as having been admitted to the General Hospital, Wilmington, North Carolina, in August, 1863. He was hospitalized for the remainder of the year, suffering from Dysentery. He appears in no other reports until September, 1864, when he was shown as again being absent, serving as a Nurse, at General Hospital #4, Goldsborough, North Carolina. He signed clothing receipts dated December 1st, 17th, and 27th, 1864. Nowell was captured on April 2, 1865, at Petersburg, Virginia. and was moved to Hart Island, New York, by way of City Point, Virginia. He died there on May 21, 1865 of Double Pneumonia. He was buried in grave number 2843.

O'CONNOR, Patrick - Regimental records show his name as above and also as Patrick O'Connell and Patrick Connell. Born in Ireland, he was a 42 year old private in Company C, First South Carolina Artillery. He enrolled at Nashville, Tennessee, on October 8, 1861 and was mustered in on October 14th at Fort Sumter, South Carolina, for three years or the war. Records show that he was present with the regiment until the end of 1864. He was captured at Fayetteville, North Carolina, on March 12, 1865. Sent from Newberne, North Carolina, to Hart Island, New York, he arrived there on April 10, 1865. O'Connor died there of Typhoid Fever on April 27, 1865 and was buried in grave number 2613.

OLIVIA, P. D. - Although buried under this name and listed as a member of Company E, Fourth Louisiana Cavalry, this individual's name, according to unit records, was P Olive. He was a member of Company A of that regiment. It is not known where or when he enlisted but he was captured at Lavinia, Louisiana on October 13th, 1864 (a second report gives the date as October 18th). He was moved to New Orleans and then, on October 27, 1864, to Ship Island, Mississippi. On November 5, 1864 he was transferred to New York, arriving at Fort Columbus on November 16, 1864. He died there on December 12, 1864 of Chronic Diarrhea and was buried in grave 2164.

OTTS, Martin - Records show that a man with this name enlisted in the Third South Carolina Reserves on November 25, 1862, for a 90 day term of service. His rank is shown as Fifth Corporal. The only other record with his name shows that he died at Hart's Island on June 9, 1865, of Chronic Diarrhea. He is buried in grave 2978. There is nothing in the file to show when or where he was captured or any details regarding what must have been at least a second term of service.

OVERFELT, R. - Overfelt enlisted on April 17, 1862 at Fort Dillard, North Carolina, for a three year term of service and was assigned to Company F, Fifty-Seventh Virginia Infantry regiment. He is reported to have deserted on August 8, 1862 but was reported back with his command at Winchester, Virginia, on October 17, 1862. He next appears as present with the regiment until December 11, 1862 when he was reported as hospitalized at Richmond, Virginia, suffering from pneumonia. Rolls show him present from May 1863 until August 7, 1863, when he deserted a second time. On September 27, 1863 he returned to his unit and a subsequent court martial sentenced him to forfeit his pay for four months. He was next present until October, 1864. Clothing receipts with his name, dated November 12th and December 31st, 1864, are found in his file. On March 27, 1865 he was admitted to the General Hospital at Petersburg, Virginia, suffering from Acute Bronchitis. He returned to service on March 31, 1865 and was captured at Five Forks, Virginia, the following day. Overfelt was received at Hart Island, New York (no date given) and died there on May 17, 1865 of Chronic Diarrhea. He was buried in grave number 3016.

OWENS, A. P. - Albert P Owens enlisted on August 12, 1861 in the Marion District, South Carolina. He was assigned to Company E, First (Butler's) South Carolina Infantry regiment and was present with the regiment through October, 1862. Owens was wounded at the Battle of Sharpsburg, Maryland, and "sent to hospital." On September 24, 1862, he was promoted to the rank of Corporal while at Receiving and Wayside Hospital (General Hospital Number 6), Richmond, Virginia. Owens is next reportd as present from January, 1863, until July, 1863. He was wounded at Gettysburg, Pennsylvania, and was among those left in Confederate field hospitals when the Army of Northern Virginia retreated. He was sent to DeCamp General Hospital, New York, arriving there on July 24, 1863. Owens died there as a result of his wound on August 6, 1863, and was buried in grave 717.

OWENS, W. H. - William H Owens was mustered into service in Company E, Fiftieth North Carolina Infantry, at Goldsboro, North Carolina, on February 27, 1864, for a three year term. He was a resident of Goldsboro (a second report gives his home at Whiteville), North Carolina. Not long after being mustered into service he was admitted to General Hospital #4, Wilmington, North Carolina, with Syphilis. Owens returned to his unit on March 21, 1864. He signed clothing receipts on March 25th and July 5th, 1864, and was admitted to General Hospital #3, Goldsboro, North Carolina, on August 27, 1864. He was captured at Hamburg, South Carolina, on February 7, 1865. Owens was sent to Hart Island, New York, by way of Newberne, North Carolina (no date given). He died there of Pneumonia on May 12, 1865, and was buried in grave 2771.

PARKER, James - Parker enlisted on March 1, 1863, and was assigned to Company F, Third South Carolina Artillery. Existing records show him present from enlistment until October, 1864. He was captured at Cheraw, South Carolinas, on March 6, 1865, and was sent to Hart Island, New York. He died there on April 10, 1865 of Typhoid Fever. He was buried in grave 2797

PARRISH, James M. - He enlisted at Warrenton, Alabama, on April 7, 1862, for a three year term of service and was assigned to Company C, Forty-Eighth Alabama Infantry regiment with the rank of Sergeant. A incorrect report in his file states that he was killed at Cedar Run, Virginia, on August 9, 1862. Rather, he was wounded in the side and lung at Gettysburg and captured. Sent to DeCamp General Hospital, Davids Island, New York, he died there on July 28, 1863, of his gun shot wound. He was buried in grave 684. His father, John Parrish, applied for settlement of his account in the fall of 1862 but it was cancelled on December 27, 1862. He reapplied on October 31, 1864 but nothing in the file indicates whether or not the claim was ever resolved.

PATTERSON, Neal - According to the rolls of his unit, McDougald's North Carolina Infantry, his first name was actually Neill. He enlisted at Wilmington, North Carolina, on August 13, 1863 and was present with the unit until the summer of 1864. In July, 1864, he was reported as a Guard at Hilton Ferry, North Carolina. Patterson was reported as Absent Without Leave in September, 1864. He had not returned by the end of December, 1864 but was captured at Bentonville, North Carolina, on March 20, 1865. Moved to Hart Island, New York, by way of Newberne, North Carolina, (no date given), he died there on May 18, 1865 of Chronic Diarrhea. He was buried in grave 2818.

PEASE, John - His unit is not given on the burial records and no one with this name was found in various records. The Miscellaneous unfiled Confederate records contain an entry for him that states he was wounded and captured at Gettysburg and was received at DeCamp General Hospital on July 17, 1863. He died there on July 24th (burial records give the date as July 25th), "Hemorrhage of Bladder" and was buried in grave 689.

PEGRAM, Joseph E. - Pegram was 22 years old when he enlisted on October 1, 1862 in Company K, Fifty-Second North Carolina Infantry. Incomplete records show him present from February 1863 until he was captured at Gettysburg, Pa. Sent to Davids Island, New York (no date given), he died there on August 1, 1863 of Diarrhea. He was buried in grave 727.

PERRY, H. H. -He enlisted on July 24, 1861 at Clarksville, Georgia, and was assigned to Company E, Sixteenth Georgia Infantry. In November, 1861, he was reported as Absent, on "Extra or Daily Duty." On May 13, 1862 he was admitted to Chimborazo Hospital #4, Richmond. It is now known when he returned to duty but he was wounded severely in the knee and captured at Gettysburg, Pa. Perry was moved north to DeCamp General Hospital, Davids Island, New York (no date given) and was transferred to Fort Wood, Bedloe's Island, New York, on October 24, 1863. He died there on November 23, 1863. No cause of death is given. He was buried in grave 944.

PERRY, Robt. - Perry was either 34 or 38 (records with both these ages are found in his file) when he enlisted in Wake County, North Carolina, on May 9, 1862, for a three year term of service. He was married, a resident of Rossville, Wayne County, and was unable to sign his name. He was assigned to Company B, Forty-Seventh North Carolina Infantry regiment. Perry next appears as being detached at the Confederate General Hospital, Petersburg, Va., on December 24, 1862. It is not known when he returned to service but he was present from July 1863 through February, 1864 when he was granted a "furlough of indulgence." He returned to duty in late March, 1864 and was present through October, 1864. Clothing receipts with his mark are found dated November 6th and December 11th, 1864. Perry was captured on April 2, 1865, probably at Petersburg, Virginia, but no exact place is mentioned in the records. He was received at Hart Island, New York, on April 7, 1865 and died there of Chronic Diarrhea on May 8, 1865. He was buried in grave 2462.

PERSIL, L. - Persil was a 22 year old farmer, native of Duplin County, North Carolina, who enlisted on October 1, 1861 in Company A, Thirty-Eighth North Carolina Infantry regiment.(A second report gives his age at enlistment at eighteen.) He was mustered in there on December 31, 1861. Persil was present from then until August, 1862. He is next shown as present from November 1862 through mid-February, 1863. A note on the roll of February, 1863 reads: "Home on Furlough for 20 days from Feb. 20, 1863." He returned to duty in mid-March, 1863 and was promoted Third-Sergeant on March 15, 1863. Persil was wounded and left at Gettysburg, Pa. He was received at DeCamp General Hospital, Davids Island, but no date is given. He died there on January 13, 1864 (burial records, however, give the date as January 19th) and is buried in grave 985

PETTY, William E. - Petty enlisted in Company B, First Tennessee Artillery on October 28, 1861 for a 12 month term of service. He was present from enlistment until captured at Fort Morgan, Alabama, on August 23, 1864, having re-enlisted for the duration of the war in the fall of 1862. He arrived in New York on September 18, 1864, from New Orleans, Louisiana. Admitted to the U S General Hospital at Fort Columbus, New York, on December 4, 1864, he died there on December 28th of Variola. No grave number is given but cemetery records show that his remains were subsequently removed and sent to Paducah, Kentucky.

PHELPS, David - On December 19, 1863, Phelps enlisted in Company A, First Alabama Artillery Battalion, at Starlington, Butler County, Alabama. He was present from that time until captured at Fort Morgan, Alabama, on August 23, 1864. Sent to New York by way of New Orleans on September 18, 1864, he arrived at Fort Columbus, New York on the 28th. He died there on October 22, 1864 of Chronic Diarrhea and Variola. He was buried in grave number 2074.

PHILLIPS, E. W. - Unit records show that his name was E W Phillippi. He was a Private in Company B, Thirty-Ninth Virginia Infantry. Nothing is known about where or when he enlisted or where or when he was captured. He died at the U S Post Hospital, Hart Island, New York, June 26, 1865. No cause of death is given. He was buried at "8 a.m., June 27, 1865" in grave 3065.

PHILLIPS, Richmond - A 20 year old farmer, born in Franklin County, North Carolina, Phillips enlisted on February 27, 1862 in Company B, Forty-Seventh North Carolina Infantry and was mustered in with the rank of Sergeant. Phillips stood six feet, one inch tall. He next appears on unit records with the rank of Private on September 24, 1862, when he was admitted to the General Hospital at Petersburg, Va. No explanation is found explaining his reduction of rank. He returned to service on November 24, 1862 and was present with the unit until wounded and captured at Gettysburg, Pa. A note in his file shows that he was released from the hands of the Medical Department and turned out to the Provost Marshall as a Prisoner of War, at Fort McHenry, Baltimore, Maryland, in August, 1863. From there he was transferred to the prison camp at Point Lookout, Maryland, on August 21, 1863. Phillips was exchanged on March 17, 1864. He signed clothing receipts dated March 22nd, May 3rd, July __, 1864, and December 11, 1864. He was captured at the South Side R. R. on April 3, 1865 and sent north, arriving at Hart Island, New York, on April 7, 1865. On June 17, 1865, he took the Oath of Allegiance at the Post Hospital. Phillips died there on Chronic Diarrhea on June 28, 1865, and was buried in grave number 3069.

PHIPPS, Jno. - Buried under the name of John Phipps, regimental records show that his first name was actually Joseph. He enlisted in Company F, Twenty-Second North Carolina Infantry for a 12 month term of service on July 27, 1861, at Raleigh, North Carolina. He was 21 years, a native of Alleghany County, five feet eleven and a half inches tall, with dark complexion, dark hair, and gray eyes. He was present during the summer of 1861 but appears on no other regimental record until he was captured at the Appomattox River, Va., on April 3, 1865. He was received at Hart Island, New York on April 11, 1865. He died there on June 18, 1865, of Chronic Diarrhea, the day before he was scheduled to take the Oath of Allegiance. Phipps was buried in grave 3019.

PLEMMONS, W. C. - On February 25, 1862, Plemmons enlisted in Company F, Eleventh Georgia Infantry, at Gilmer, Georgia. On July 1, 1862 he was reported on extra duty at the Richmond Fortifications. Plemmons was admitted to Chimborazo Hospital, Richmond, on August 12, 1862, suffering from Chronic Diarrhea. He was transferred from there to the General Hospital at Farmville, Va. A report dated October 27, 1862, shows that he had returned to his regiment but that he was suffering from "Camp fever." In February, 1863, it was reported that he had been furloughed from the General Hospital, Farmville, and that he had not returned at the expiration of the furlough. On June 12, 1863, he was again admitted to the General Hospital at Farmville and returned to his regiment on June 23, 1863. Plemmons was wounded and left at Gettysburg, Pa. Sent north, he arrived at DeCamp General Hospital on July 17, 1863, where he died on August 6, 1863. He was buried in grave 746. An item dated November, 1914, is found in his files that dates that he "deserted on March 13, 1864, dropped from rolls." In light of the other regimental and burial records, this last item is in error.

POLLARD, J. W. - Cemetery records show that an individual with this name, a Private in the First Virginia Artillery, died on June 24, 1865, and was buried in grave number 3056. The only J W Pollard found among the files of Confederate troops in Virginia organizations that he enlisted on May 4, 1861 in the James City Virginia Artillery Company for a twelve month term of service. He was reported to have been discharged but no date is given. On September 27, 1862, he re-enlisted in this unit at Petersburg, Virginia, for the duration of the war and was present through the fall of 1863. After a brief stay at the General Hospital in Petersburg, he returned to duty in either late November or early December, 1863. On December 4, 1863 he was "Detailed as carpenter." Special Order, No. 107, Department of North Virginia, dated April 18, 1864, reassigned him to "Company I Cavalry" but no regimental designation is given. Ten days later he was admitted to Chimborazo Hospital suffering from Phthisis. A report dated September 3, 1864 shows him as absent, sick, from the artillery company, and present at Chimborozo Hospital. On October 4, 1864, he is reported to have died there of Dysentery. It is impossible to reconcile these conflicting reports.

POOR, J. W. - According to records of his unit, Company G, First South Carolina Artillery, his name was actually James M Poor. He was 32 years old, a resident of Anderson District, South Carolina, with light complexion, light hair, and blue eyes. He was six feet, two inches tall. Poor enlisted on June 18, 1862 in the Lawrence District, South Carolina and was mustered in at Columbia, South Carolina, on July 10, 1862, as a Private in Company A, Sixth South Carolina Cavalry. On October 31, 1862 he was reported absent, on detached service in search of deserters from his company in Anderson, Spartanburg, and Pickens Districts. Subsequent records show him present with his regiment from March 1863 through the end of that year. In January, 1864, he was reported present, but sick. On February 29, 1864, he was transferred to Company G, First South Carolina Artillery, by Special Order #65, Department of South Carolina, Georgia, and Florida. He was present with the unit thereafter until October 4, 1864, when he was shown as Absent Without Leave. Returned to his unit in November, 1864, his pay was stopped $2.00 because of the loss of his haversack, canteen, and strap. On March 22, 1865, Poor was captured at the Bentonville, North Carolina. Moved to Newberne, North Carolina, he was sent north not long afterwards. Poor was received at Hart Island on April 10, 1865. Chronic Diarrhea claimed his life there on June 18, 1865. He was buried in grave number 3024.

PORTER, John E. - Nothing has been found in Porter's file to indicate when or where he was enlisted or captured. Cemetery records show that he was a Private in the Second Texas Cavalry who died at Fort Columbus, New York, on November 24, 1864, of Chronic Diarrhea. He was buried in grave 2173.

POWELL, H. A. - Unit records show that his name was Andrew J Powell but other rolls list him as Andrew Jackson Powell and Jackson Powell. He enrolled at Cleveland, North Carolina, on September 17, 1861 and was mustered in on October 25, 1861, at Camp Fisher, North Carolina. He was assigned to Company F, Thirty-Fourth North Carolina Infantry regiment. Powell was a 22 year old farmer, five feet nine inches tall. In early 1862 he was reported "Absent-Sick-Hospital, Goldsboro, N. C." He was present with his unit from March 1862 until he was wounded and captured at Gettysburg, Pa. He arrived at DeCamp General Hospital, Davids Island, New York, on July 23, 1863 and died there of Pyaemia on August 2, 1863. His father, J W Powell, filed a claim for the settlement of his account in April, 1864.

POWELL, Thomas - Buried in grave number 2808 on May 17, 1865, records of the Second Georgia Infantry regiment show that his name was actually James M Powell. He was also carried on the rolls as J W Powell and S W Powell. He enlisted at Buena Vista, Georgia, on April 15, 1861, and was present through the summer of 1861. On July 31, 1862 he was reported on "Extra Duty, Medical College of Virginia" and he remained as such until August 7, 1862. He was admitted to the Institute Hospital Richmond, Va., December 14, 1862, as a result of a gun shot wound. A day later he was transferred to Winder Division Number 1 Hospital, Richmond. Powell returned to his regiment on December 30, 1862, only to be wounded and captured at Gettysburg, Pa. On July 7, 1863 he was transferred from Harrisburg to Philadelphia, Pa. On July 12th he was moved to Fort Delaware, Delaware. He is reported to have died at Point Lookout, Maryland, on February 25, 1864. In this face of these conflicting reports, it is not possible to determine if the individual buried in Cypress Hills Cemetery is the same individual mentioned in the regimental reports.

POWER, T. B. - Power was a resident of Pickens District, South Carolina. He had blue eyes, brown hair, and a light complexion. He was five feet, seven inches tall. On July 20, 1861, he enlisted in Company A, Orr's South Carolina Rifles, for three years or the war. Regimental records show that he was unable to sign his name. He was present through April, 1862. There is a gap in unit records and he next appears as Present in November, 1862. Power was wounded at Gettysburg, Pa. on July 3, 1863, and was captured at Falling Waters, Maryland, on July 14, 1863. Moved to Washington, D C, he was held at the Old Capitol Prison until August 9. 1863. He was next transferred to Point Lookout, Maryland, and was exchanged on March 3, 1864. On May 8, 1864, he was wounded by a Minie ball in the head, and did not return to active service until September, 1864. Power was captured at Petersburg, Virginia, on April 3, 1865 and received at Hart Island, New York, on April 7, 1865. He died there of Chronic Diarrhea on May 17, 1865, but no grave number is listed in either cemetery or unit records. Two additional reports are found in his file. One shows that he was released at City Point, Virginia, on June 6, 1865, and the other that he was released there on June 15th. These last two reports appear to be in error.

PRATT, Thomas - A thirty year old conscript, Pratt was mustered into service on September 1, 1862, in Company K, Forty-Fifth North Carolina Infantry regiment, He was a resident of Rockingham County. Pratt was present with the unit until May 22, 1863, when he was admitted to Chimborazo Hospital #3, Richmond, suffering from Debilitis. His stay in the hospital was for only two days, however. He was wounded in the chin at Gettysburg, Pa., and left there when Confederate forces withdrew. Pratt arrived at DeCamp General Hospital on July 23, 1863 and he died there on July 26th, as a result of his wound. He was buried in grave 682.

PRESTWOOD, E. - Records of Company F, Twenty-Sixth North Carolina Infantry regiment show that this man's name was Ervand Preswood. He is also carried on the rolls as E Presswood. He enlisted on October 8, 1864, in Lenoir County, North Carolina and was present until captured on April 2, 1865, at Hatcher's Run, Virginia. Sent north, he arrived at Hart Island on April 11th where he died there on June 11, 1865. He is buried in grave 2994.

PRIDGEN, John O. - Pridgen was 35 years old when he enlisted in McDugald's North Carolina Infantry Company at Wilmington, North Carolina, on July 20, 1863. He was present with the unit for the next six months and was then briefly detached as a guard along the Wilmington Railroad. Returned to his company, he served with it until November, 1864, and was then detached as "Telegraph Guard." He was captured on March 20, 1865 at Bentonville, North Carolina. Sent north, he arrived at Hart Island, New York (no date given) and was hospitalized on April 20, 1865, suffering from Chronic Bronchitis. He died on June 4, 1865 of "Nostalgia." He was buried in grave 2943.

PROCTOR, Thomas D. - On March 11, 1862, Proctor, a Tobacco Roller, enlisted in Company A, Forty-Fifth North Carolina Infantry regiment. Born in Rockingham County, he was 20 years old, and stood five feet ten inches tall. He entered service as Spring Garden or Grogansville, North Carolina and he was present with the unit until wounded and left at Gettysburg. Proctor arrived at DeCamp General Hospital on July 17, 1863, and died there of Pyaemia on August 16, 1863. He was buried in grave 792.

PUGH, Eli - Pugh was a Private in Company D, Fiftieth Virginia Infantry regiment. Nothing in his file indicates where or when he enlisted or anything regarding his service until he was wounded and captured in a "Hospital around Gettysburg." Sent north, he arrived at Hart Island on July 23, 1863. On August 8, 1863, he died there as a result of his gun shot wound. He was buried in grave 758.

QUACKENBUSCH, J. G. - He enlisted at Greensboro, North Carolina on February 22, 1862, and was assigned to Company E, Twenty-Second North Carolina Infantry regiment. He was 29 years old at the time and was present with his unit until August 28, 1862. On that date he was "Sent to Richmond". Quackenbusch was admitted to the General Hospital at Danville, Virginia on October 9, 1862, and he served as Surgeon's Orderly for an unknown period of time. In early October, 1863, he was admitted to Receiving & Wayside Hospital (General Hospital #9), Richmond, and on the 9th of that month was transferred to Winder Hospital #5, Richmond. Clothing receipts of Oct 22, 1863, June 30, 1864, October 21, 1864, November 15, 1864, and December 1, 1864 bear his signature. He was captured at "Hatch's [sic] Run, Va., April 1, 1865. He was moved to City Point, Va., and then to Hart Island, New York, but no date is given. Quackenbusch died at Hart's Island on May 14, 1865, of Typhoid Fever, and was buried in grave 2780.

RAINEY, James - He enlisted as a Private in Company D, Fourteenth Georgia Infantry regiment on July 9, 1861, in Cherokee County, Georgia. Incomplete unit records show him present through the fall of 1861 and that he was admitted to the General Hospital at Danville, Virginia. on September 9, 1862. He was returned to duty on September 15th. Rainey was wounded at the battle of Fredericksburg, Va., in December, 1862, and appears on no further records until May, 1864. At that time, bearing the rank of First-Sergeant, he is listed as present and remains so until February, 1865. Rainey was captured at Petersburg, Va. on April

3, 1865 and sent to City Point, Va. He arrived at Hart's Island, New York, on April 7th. He died there of Double Pneumonia on May 29, 1865 and was buried in grave 2917.

RANDLEMAN, A. T. - August T Randleman, 26 years old, enlisted at East Bend, North Carolina, on June 18, 1861, for a twelve month term of service. A resident of Forsyth County, North Carolina, he was assigned to Company F, Twenty-Eighth North Carolina Infantry with the rank of Sergeant. He was present from enlistment until the end of 1861. Randleman was reported on Sick Leave during May and June, 1862 but was present with the unit from July, 1862 until November 29, 1862, when he was admitted to the Confederate General Hospital at Charlottesville, Virginia, suffering from "Erysepelas" and he was transferred to the General Hospital at Lynchburg later the same day. It is not know when he returned to duty but on February 13, 1863 he was admitted to General Hospital #4, Wilmington, North Carolina with "Febrious Typhosis." He returned to duty on February 22, 1862. Randleman was among the wounded who were left at Gettysburg, Pa.. He was received at DeCamp General Hospital on July 22, 1863 and died there the next day, the cause being given as "Hemorrhage of lungs." He was buried in grave 677.

RANSOM, John H. - A resident of Whitesville, Harris County, Georgia, Ransom enlisted there on July 27, 1861, and was attached to Company E, Twentieth Georgia Infantry regiment. He was present from enlistment until the end of 1861. In early 1862 he was reported "Sick" but was present again in March, 1862. On June 30, 1862 he was admitted to General Hospital #13. Richmond. It is now know why he was hospitalized or when he returned to service but he was readmitted to that hospital on December 4, 1862. Shortly afterwards, he was transferred to General Hospital #4, Richmond, suffering from Phthisis. On February 13, 1863 he was again hospitalized, this time at General Hospital #11. A week later he was transferred to Winder Hospital #1, Richmond. He was hospitalized one more time, on April 5, 1863, at Winder Hospital #2, Richmond, pneumonia as the diagnosis. Ransom was wounded severely in the thigh at Gettysburg and was captured there. Sent north to DeCamp General Hospital, no date given, he died there on August 23, 1863, no cause being given. He was buried in grave 822.

RAPE, S. M. - A 19 year old farmer, married to Sarah A Rape, of Union County, North Carolina, he was mustered into service on November 20, 1861 in Company D, Thirty-Seventh North Carolina Infantry regiment for a one year term of service.

He stood 5 feet eight and a half inches tall, had light hair, blue eyes, and a florid complexion. He was present until captured at Hanover Court House, Va., on May 28, 1862. Rape had, in the meantime, reenlisted for the duration of the war. Sent north (no date mentioned in his file), he died on Fibrus Typhus on July 4, 1862 at the Post Hospital, Governor's Island, New York. (Cemetery records state that he died on July 6, 1862.) On September 1, 1863, his widow was paid the balance of his pay.

RAST, William R. - Rast was a private in Company C, Fourteenth South Carolina Militia. Nothing is known about when or where he began his active service. He was captured at Lynch's Creek, South Carolina, on February 25, 1865. Received at Hart Island, New York by way of Newberne, North Carolina (no date given), he died on May 5, 1865, and was buried in grave #2781.

RAY, A. J. - Buried under this name, unit records show, however, that his name was Joseph A Ray. A conscript from Moore County, North Carolina, he was 26 years old when he enrolled at Troy, North Carolina on March 5, 1863. He was mustered in on April 4, 1863 at Camp Gregg, Va. Ray was wounded and captured at Gettysburg, Pa. and was moved north to DeCamp General Hospital, Davids Island, arriving there on July 19, 1863. He died there on July 31, 1863, the cause being given as "Amputation of leg." He was buried in grave number 711.

REDDIX, James - No information has been found on the man buried in grave 2962 in regimental records. Burial records show that he was a private in Company A, Fifty-Eighth North Carolina Infantry who died on June 8, 1865.

REDMAN, T. O. - Born in Northumberland County, Va., Redman was commissioned Second-Lieutenant, Company C, Fortieth Virginia Infantry at Heathville, Va. on May 26, 1861. He was present with the unit until wounded and captured at Gettysburg, Pa. On April 23, 1862, he was, in the meantime, appointed First-Lieutenant to fill the vacancy caused by a death. From January to April, 1863, he was listed as "Commanding Company." Redman was wounded in the thigh at Gettysburg and left there when Confederate troops retreated. Received at Hart Island, New York, on July 17, 1863, he died there on August 2, 1863, of Pyaemia. No grave number is found in his file. An undated item in the file states that his body was "In receiving Tomb, Brady's, Second Ave., New York City," It is probable that he was never actually buried at Cypress Hills and that his body was sent south at the request of his family. On November 9, 1863, a claim was partially paid to the Administrator of his estate, Warren Eubank. Of the $279.00 claimed, $126.00 was paid.

REESE, Samuel - Burial records state that he was a Private in Company "B", Third Virginia Infantry who died on June 9, 1865 and was buried in grave 2968. Nothing is found on him in the records of that unit, however.

REEVES, Sanders - Reeves enlisted in Company K, Second North Carolina Infantry regiment on May 14, 1864, at Raleigh, North Carolina. Rolls show him present with the unit until the end of 1864, and that he signed a clothing receipt for the fourth quarter of 1864. Captured at Petersburg, Va., on April 3, 1865, he was sent north and received at Hart Island, New York but no date is listed. He died there on May 8, 1865, of Typhoid Fever and was buried in grave 2745.

RESNER, Henry - A resident of Richmond, Resner enlisted on May 2, 1862, at Halifax, Virginia, in Wright's Virginia Heavy Artillery Company. He was five feet, eight inches tall, had dark complexion, dark hair, and gray eyes. He was listed as present with the unit until August 9, 1862. At that time he was hospitalized near Yorktown, Virginia. On October 25, 1862, a remark in his file reads "Deserted". Resner does not appear in additional reports until late 1863 when he was marked present. Clothing receipts with his signature are included in his file. They are dated September 12, 1864, October 31, 1864, and November 10, 1864. He was captured at Petersburg, Va., on April 2, 1865. He arrived at Hart Island, New York on April 7, 1865, where he died on Chronic Diarrhea on June 10, 1865. He was buried in grave 2993.

RICHARDSON, Robert N. - On May 5, 1862, he enlisted into Company K, Fifty-Third Georgia Infantry regiment at either Forysth or Griffin, Georgia (Both places are mentioned in his file). He was present with his unit until the summer of 1862 when a note in his file reads "Left sick at McLaws Sick Camp, near Richmond, Va." Richardson was admitted to Howard's Grove General Hospital on September 9, 1862 suffering from Rubiola. On October 4, 1862, he was reported as having been assigned to Extra Duty at that hospital. Not long afterwards he was furloughed for sixty days. Richardson returned to his regiment on February 28, 1863, and was present with it until wounded at Gettysburg, Pa. Captured along with other Confederate wounded when southern forces withdrew from Gettysburg, Richardson was sent north and arrived at DeCamp General Hospital, Davids Island, New York, on

July 19, 1863. He died of Peritonitis on August 8, 1863, and was buried in grave 753.

RIGGS, Augustus L. - One record states that he was 32 while a second gives his age as 34 when he was mustered into service on March 6, 1861, at Iuka, Mississippi as a member of the Mississippi Rifles Company. Born in Monroe County, Alabama, Riggs, a carpenter, stood five feet, ten inches tall, with dark complexion, blue eyes, and black hair. He was mustered out of the infantry company an April 30, 1861, and enrolled in Company K, Second Mississippi Infantry at Tishomingo on May 1, 1861, but he was not officially mustered into the unit until May 10, 1861 at Lynchburg, Va.. Riggs was reported "Sick, in camp" during July and August, 1861, and present from September 1861 through May, 1862. At that time he was again reported sick in camp at Danville, Va., suffering from Dysentery. On June 17, 1862 he was transferred to Chimborazo Hospital #2, Richmond, not returning to his regiment until November, 1862. In the following month his pay was stopped for $2.75 for the loss for his blanket. Riggs was wounded and left at Gettysburg. He was received at DeCamp General Hospital on July 19, 1863 and was transferred to Fort Wood, Bedloe's Island, New York, on October 24, 1863. He died there of Phthisis on December 5, 1863, and was buried in grave number 952.

RIGGS, George W. - Born in Tennessee, Riggs was a resident of Hernando, Mississippi, a farmer, when he enlisted in Company C, Forty-Second Mississippi Infantry on May 14, 1862 at Grenada, Mississippi. His term of enlistment was for three years or the duration of the war. Riggs was present from the time he joined the unit until July, 1863. In January, 1863, his pay had been stopped $1.00 for one "cock screw lost." He was wounded and left in the hands of Federal troops at Gettysburg. Sent to DeCamp General Hospital, Davids Island, New York, he arrived there on July 19, 1863, where he died as a result of his gunshot wound on October 5, 1863. He was buried in grave number 886.

ROBERSON, McG. - Roberson was mustered into Company F, Seventeenth North Carolina Infantry regiment, at Hatteras, North Carolina, on July 26, 1861. The regiment was subsequently redesignated the Seventh North Carolina Infantry. A native of Martin County, his occupation was listed as laborer. He was captured at Fort Hatteras, North Carolina, and sent north. Nothing has been found to show when he arrived in New York or where he was held. He died on October 10, 1861, and was buried in grave 4446. Cemetery records give his date of death as October 11th.

ROBERT, Jno. W. - Records of his unit show that his name was John A W Roberts. He enlisted in Company G, Eleventh Georgia Infantry at Atlanta, Georgia, on July 3, 1861. He was present with the unit until hospitalized at the General Hospital, Orange Court House, Virginia, on October 5, 1861. He returned to his unit on December 4, 1861 and was present until May, 1863. On May 8th he was admitted to Receiving & Wayside Hospital (General Hospital #9), Richmond, but was subsequently transferred to Winder Hospital. It is not known when he returned to the regiment but he received a head wound at Gettysburg, Pa., and was left there when Confederate troops withdrew. He was admitted to DeCamp General Hospital, Davids Island (no date given) and died there on September 14, 1863 of a Cerebral Abcess. He was buried in grave 857.

ROBERTS, John M. - Roberts enlisted at Macon, Georgia, on March 4, 1862, in Company A, Forty-Fifth Georgia Infantry regiment. Incomplete regimental records show that he received a $50.00 bonus on March 4, 1863 for r-enlisting and that his name appears on a clothing receipt dated May 5, 1863 at Camp Winder General Hospital, Richmond. He was present with the unit from May 1864 through February 1865 and was promoted to the rank of Fifth Sergeant on November 12, 1864. Roberts was captured at Petersburg, Va., on April 3, 1865 and sent north, arriving at Hart Island on April 7, 1965. Suffering from Double Pneumonia, he died on June 1, 1865, and was buried in grave 2841.

ROBERTS, William D. - Roberts was 22 years, unmarried, a native of Giles County, Tennessee, when he enlisted at Nashville, Tennessee on January 1, 1862. He was assigned to Company D, Fifty-Third Tennessee Infantry regiment. When Fort Donelson, Tennessee, fell to Federal forces on Feb. 15, 1862, Roberts was sick in the post hospital. Captured there. he was sent north and held at Camp Morton, Indianapolis, Indiana. On August 28, 1862, he was exchanged at Vicksburg, Mississippi, and hospitalized at the General Hospital in Richmond, Louisiana. Returned to his regiment, Roberts was again captured when Port Hudson, Louisiana, fell to Federal forces in July of 1863. Once again he was exchanged at Vicksburg, on October 8, 1863. Continuing a career of captivity, he was again taken by Federal forces, this time and Connersville, Tennessee, shortly after being exchanged. He was sent to Nashville, Tennessee, on October 17, 1863, and on the 21st to Louisville, Kentucky. From there he was moved to Fort Delaware, arriving there on March 22, 1864. On the last day of September, 1864, Roberts was paroled at Fort Delaware "pending exchange." It is not known when the returned to his regiment but at the Battle of Bentonville, North Carolina, he was wounded by a shell in the left knee and hospitalized at Thomasville, North Carolina, where he was again captured. On November 2, 1865, he was reported as a Convalescent at the U S Post Hospital, Morehead City, North Carolina. Soon afterwards he was moved to DeCamp General Hospital, Davids Island, New York. He died there of Phthisis on December 13, 1865 and was buried in grave 3254. Roberts was the last Confederate Prisoner of War to die in New York. Having been captured four times, few men of either side could equal the number of different times that he was captured and released.

ROBERTSON, T. C. - Thomas C Robertson, a Private in Company I, Eighteenth Mississippi Infantry regiment, was born in South Carolina. He was a resident of Brownsville, Mississippi, when he enrolled at Corinth, Mississippi, on May 23, 1861. He was mustered in there for twelve months on June 7, 1861. Most records give his age as 27 when he enlisted but one shows it as 30. He was present with the regiment until mid-January, 1862. On the 12th of that month Robertson was admitted to the hospital at Leesburg, Virginia, suffering with Parocitis. He returned to this regiment on January 20, 1862. On April 26, 1862 he re-enlisted for two additional years of service and he received a thirty day furlough in July, 1862. Robertson was listed as Present from September through December, 1862, but he was detailed as a nurse at the hospital in Winchester, Virginia, and, later, at Receiving and Wayside Hospital, Richmond. He returned to active service with the regiment in January, 1863 and was wounded in the leg at the Battle of Gettysburg. He was among the large numbers of Confederate wounded who were captured when southern troops withdrew from there. Transferred north, he arrived at DeCamp General Hospital, Davids Island on July 21, 1863. He died there as a result of his wound on September 21, 1863, and was buried in grave 865.

ROBINETT, L. G. - Lawson G Robinett enlisted in Company G, Thirty-Seventh North Carolina Infantry, at Camp Fisher, Transylvania County, North Carolina, in December, 1861 (no exact date given). He was five feet eleven and a half inches tall, eighteen years of age, a resident of Alexander County. He was present with the unit through February, 1863. His original term of service having been for twelve months, he re-enlisted for two more years in April, 1862. Records show that he was promoted Fifth-Sergeant in December, 1862, and was "Absent, On Detached service" in early 1863. The nature of this service is not reported in the files. Bearing the rank of First-Sergeant, he was wounded and left at Gettysburg. Sent to DeCamp General Hospital, Davids Island, New York, arriving on July 23. 1863. He died of Typhoid Fever on August 9, 1863, and buried in grave 766. On March 5, 1864 a claim for his back pay was filed by an attorney acting in behalf of his parents. They are not named in his records, however.

ROBINSON, James - Records reveal that the individual buried under this name was actually James L Robertson (also carried on some regimental rolls as J L Robberson). He enlisted for three years in Company D, Sixteenth North Carolina Infantry on October 14, 1863 at Rutherford, North Carolina and was present from enlistment until October, 1864. Clothing receipts dated November 5th and November 14th, 1864, are found in his file. Captured on April 3, 1865, at Petersburg, Virginia, he was sent to Hart Island, New York, by way of City Point, Virginia. He arrived in New York on April 11, 1865, where he died of Chronic Diarrhea on June 1, 1865. He was buried in grave 2925.

ROGERS, J. B. - Cemetery records identify his unit as the Thirteenth North Carolina Infantry regiment. He was, however, a Private in Company D of the Thirteenth North Carolina Light Artillery Battalion. Unit records also give his name as John B Rodgers and J B Rodgers. He was captured on April 3, 1865 at Petersburg, Va. Sent to Hart Island, New York, by way of City Point, Virginia, he arrived there on April 13, 1865, and two days later was admitted to DeCamp General Hospital, Davids Island. He died there of Chronic Diarrhea on April 28, 1865. He was buried in grave 2657.

ROGERSON, David L. - Rogerson was a 46 year old private in Company F, Seventeenth North Carolina Infantry regiment.Cemetery records, however, identify his unit as the Seventh North Carolina Infantry regiment. He was a five feet, ten inch tall farmer, a resident of Martin County, North Carolina, who was unable to sign his name. On March 21, 1862, he was "Hired as a substitute for Joseph G A Parker" and was present with the regiment until November, 1862. He was then detailed as "Hospital Nurse". In February, 1863, he was still detailed but his duties were identified as "Hospital Nurse & Washer." From May 1863 through February, 1864, he was shown in the same capacity at the hospital at Hamilton, North Carolina. In March, 1864, he was detailed as nurse at the regimental hospital by order of General

Kirkland. No other information has been found on him and it is not known where or when he was captured. Burial records indicate that he died on October 8, 1864, and that he was buried in grave 4445. No cause of death has been found.

ROLADES, J. G. - On May 3, 1862, Rolades enlisted in Company K, Forty-Eighth Alabama Infantry, at Mount Polk, Alabama, for the war. An injury to his testicles caused him to be admitted to Chimborazo Hospital #4, Richmond, Va. This entry in his records is undated. He does not reappear on unit records until May, 1863, when it was shown as Present. Rolades was wounded "Ball in shoulder" at Gettysburg and left there when Confederate forces retreated. Sent to DeCamp General Hospital, Davids Island, New York (no date given), he died there as a result of his wound on July 28, 1863. He was buried in grave 695.

ROLAND, Charles - Roland enlisted in Company K, Thirty-Eighth North Carolina Infantry regiment on July 25, 1864, at Yadkin, North Carolina. Existing regimental records show him present from enlistment through the end of October, 1864. He signed clothing receipts dated November 5th, November 17th, November 26th, and December 1st. On April 3, 1865, he was captured at Petersburg, Virginia. Sent north, he arrived at Hart Island, New York, on April 7, 1865, and he died there on May 30, 1865. His cause of death was given as Remittent Fever. He was buried in grave 2915.

ROLLINS, Thomas - On February 14, 1864, he enlisted in the First (Regular) South Carolina Infantry at Muttonville, South Carolina. From March 15th through the 28th, he was reported "Sick in Rest Hospital, Mt. Pleasant, SC." Rollins was present from May through October, 1864 and Absent without Leave from December 18th to 26th, 1864. Nothing has been found to show when or where he was captured. Rollins was admitted to the Transit Hospital, New York City, on June 2, 1865. He died there two days later, on the 25th. and was buried in grave 3048.

RONNINGER, J. - A man with this name, a private in Company G, Second North Carolina Infantry, died on August 3, 1863, and was buried in grave 741 according to cemetery records. Nothing has been found about this man in any unit records, however.

ROYAL, William H. - Nineteen years old when he enlisted at Camp Mangum, North Carolina, on October 16, 1861, Royal's records show that he was also carried on regimental rolls as William B Royal and William H Royall. Born in Sampson, North Carolina, he stood five feet, eleven and a half inches tall and had a dark complexion, brown hair, and hazel eyes. He was a farmer. Royal was mustered in as Second-Sergeant, Company B, Thirty-Eighth North Carolina Infantry regiment. Incomplete records show him present from January, 1862, to November 16, 1862. Suffering from Debility, he was admitted to the Confederate General Hospital, Charlottesville, Virginia, on that date. On June 10, 1863, he was reported "Absent, sick." in Richmond, Virginia. An item dated April 7, 1864 reported him at Jackson Hospital, Richmond, Virginia. Royal is next reported, early in July, 1864, as having been wounded and that he was absent, at his home. He failed to return as scheduled and on August 10, 1864, he was reported Absent without Leave. Finally returning to his regiment, he was reduced to the rank of Sergeant on September 12, 1864. He signed clothing receipts on December 25, 1863, November 6, 1864, and November 14, 1864. Royal was captured on April 1, 1865 at Hatcher's Run, Va. He was sent to Point Lookout Prison, Maryland and was scheduled to be released on June 19, 1865. He is reported to have died on June 3, 1865, however, and was buried in grave number 2939. It is not known if the information regarding his being sent to Point Lookout is incorrect or, if not, when he was sent to New York.

RUSSELL, A. - Abednego Russel, Private Company K, Fifty-Third North Carolina Infantry regiment, enlisted in Wilkes County, North Carolina for three years on March 26, 1863. He was wounded in the knee at Gettysburg and left in the hands of the enemy. Russell arrived at DeCamp General Hospital, Davids Island, New York, on July 17, 1863. He died there of Pyaemia on September 30, 1863. He was buried in grave 862.

RYLE, A. J. - Adam J Ryle was 40 years old when he enlisted at Gordon, Georgia. He was appointed Corporal and assigned to Company B, Fourteenth Georgia Infantry regiment. Ryle, born in Wilkinson, Georgia, had blue eyes, dark hair, and a light complexion. He was five feet, six inches tall. Ryle was Absent, Sick, at Rockbridge Alum Springs, Virginia, in September, 1861. Incomplete regimental rolls next show Ryle as being admitted to Chimborazo Hospital #1, Richmond, on August 9, 1862, suffering from rheumatism. It is not known when he returned to active service but he was wounded and captured at Gettysburg, Pa. Sent to DeCamp General Hospital, Davids Island, he arrived there on July 23, 1863. On August 9, 1863, he died there of Pyaemia. He was buried in grave number 767.

SALE, Wm. - William Augustus Sale was a Private in Company G, First (Provisional Army) South Carolina Infantry regiment who had enrolled on August 16, 1861 at Hamburg, Edgefield District, South Carolina, for the war, He was mustered into service at Richmond, Va., three days later. Records show him present from November, 1861, until he was wounded and left in the hands of the enemy at Gettysburg, Pa. Sent north, he was received at DeCamp General Hospital, Davids Island, New York, arriving there on July 17, 1863. He died on Pyaemia on October 23, 1863, and was buried in grave 902.

SAPP, F. M. - He enlisted on May 20, 1861, at Greenville, Alabama, for the duration of the war and was assigned to Company F, Eighth Alabama Infantry regiment. Incomplete unit reports show him present from May 21, 1861 to August, 1861. He was wounded on July 2, 1863, at Gettysburg and was captured when Federal troops occupied the Confederate field hospitals there. Sent north, he was received at DeCamp General Hospital but no date was given. He died there of Peritonitis on August 28, 1863. He was buried in grave 828.

SAVAGE, Braxton - Savage enlisted on May 1, 1863 for the duration of the war and was mustered into Company B, Fifty-Third Georgia Infantry regiment. He was 39 years old, stood five feet, ten inches tall, had blue eyes, dark hair, and a dark complexion. Born in Newton County, he was a farmer. Savage was present from enlistment until September 9, 1862. On that date he was granted a forty day sick furlough. Reported back with his unit in early 1863, Savage was wounded and left at a Confederate field hospital at Gettysburg. He was captured there on July 4, 1863. On July 12, 1863 he was sent to DeCamp General Hospital, where he arrived on July 17, 1863. He died there of Typhoid Fever on July 22, 1863 and was buried in grave 671. His wife, Louisa Savage, was awarded a settlement of $121.68 on December 10, 1863.

SAWYER, Robinson A. - A resident of Hyde County, North Carolina, Sawyer enlisted at Swan Quarter, North Carolina, on November 8, 1861. He was assigned to Company H, Thirty-Third North Carolina Infantry regiment. He was present with his unit until the spring of 1862 and was reported Missing on March 14, 1862. There are no details of his capture but he was admitted to the U S Post Hospital, Fort Columbus, New York (no date given) suffering from Febris Typhoides. He died there on June 29, 1862 and was buried in grave 145.

SAWYER, William B. - Sawyer enlisted in Company B, Thirty-Second North Carolina Infantry regiment at Elizabeth City (reported as "E. City" in his service file) for 12 months on August 23, 1861. He was captured at Cape Hatteras, North Carolina, on

August 29th. He was sent to Fort Warren, Boston, Massachusetts, but released from there on February 3, 1862. There are no further details of any kind in his service file. Cemetery records, however, show that he was buried on July 21, 1862, and was buried in grave 243.

SCHRADER, Samuel - He enlisted on May 18, 1861 at Franklin, Virginia, for a one year term of service and was mustered in as a Private, Company K, Twenty-Fifth Virginia Infantry regiment. Incomplete regimental records next show him present in early 1863. On March 1, 1863 he was promoted to the rank of Corporal. Schrader was wounded in the foot at Gettysburg, Pa. and captured when Federal troops occupied the Confederate field hospitals there. He was received at DeCamp General Hospital, Davids Island, New York, on July 17, 1863. He died there of Pyaemia on August 9, 1863 and was buried in grave number 759.

SCOTT, Henry - Scott enlisted at Camp Mangum, North Carolina, on May 30, 1862, and was assigned to Company A, Fifty-Fifth North Carolina Infantry regiment. He was a farmer, five feet, eight inches tall, born in Wilson, North Carolina. He was twenty-two years old when he enlisted. Scott was present until wounded at Gettysburg and captured there. He was sent to Davids Island, New York (no date given) and died there on July 31, 1863, as a result of his wound. He was buried in grave 723.

SEARS, Robert - His service file shows that he was carried on most regimental rolls as Barb Sears. He enlisted on Feb. 1, 1862 at Camp Branch, Newberne, North Carolina, for the war and was assigned to Company B, Thirty-Fifth North Carolina Infantry regiment. A native of Wake County, North Carolina, Sears was unable to sign his name. He was seventeen years old when he enlisted, had fair complexion, light hair, gray eyes, and stood five feet, six and a half inches tall. He was present from enlistment until at least 1862. When he re-enlisted for two years on June 17, 1862, he received a $50.00 bounty. Most of the unit's records for the next year and a half do not exist. There are clothing receipts with his mark dated March 25, 1864, and was reported present from November, 1864 through February, 1865. Sears was captured at Five Forks, Va. on April 1, 1865. He was transferred from City Point, Va. to Hart's Island, New York, but no date is given. He died there on June 24, 1865 of Febris Typhoides and was buried in grave number 3053.

SHARP, John W. - Cemetery records give his name as above but regimental rolls list him as James W Sharp. He enlisted on September 1, 1863 at Camp Vance, North Carolina, for the duration of the War and was assigned to Company A, Thirty-Fourth North Carolina Infantry regiment. Present from enlistment until June, 1864, Sharp was admitted to the General Hospital at Petersburg, Virginia. on June 23rd of that year. One day later he was transferred to an unidentified General Hospital in Richmond, suffering from "Sclopeticum". He deserted on August 29, 1864 and a note in his file dated late October, 1864 reads "Drop from roll for Desertion." Despite this, he appears to have rejoined the unit at some time and he was captured at Petersburg, Va. on April 3, 1865. He was received at Hart Island, New York (no date given) by way of City Point, Va. On June 20, 1865 he died on Typhoid Pneumonia. He was buried in grave 3034.

SHAVER, William - Shaver enlisted on May 7, 1862, at David Mills, South Carolina, and was assigned to the Fifteenth South Carolina Infantry regiment. Incomplete records show him as "Absent, sick" from November, 1862 through February, 1863. An entry in his file dated August, 1863 reads "Missing since we recrossed the Potomac." There are no other records of his activities yet burial records, however, show that he died on May 15, 1865, and was buried in grave 2782.

SHAW, Hugh - It is not known when or where Shaw entered the service only that he was a Private in the Forty-Seventh North Carolina Infantry regiment. A clothing receipt dated December 29, 1864 shows his mark. He was captured at "Hatch Run" [sic], Va., April 2, 1865. On April 7, 1865 he was received at Hart Island, New York, where he died on June 10, 1865 of Chronic Diarrhea. He was buried in grave number 2991.

SHORE, William L. - A Private in Company D, Twenty-First North Carolina Infantry regiment, Shore enrolled on October 22, 1864, at Winston, North Carolina, for the duration of the War. He was captured on April 3, 1865, at Petersburg, Va. and arrived at Hart Island, New York, on April 7, 1865 by way of City Point, Va. He died at Hart Island of Chronic Diarrhea on June 18, 1865. Shore was buried in grave 2955.

SHORT, Robert - Buried under the name shown above, military records give his name as Benjamin F Shortt, however. He enlisted on May 11, 1861 at Petersburg, Va. and joined Pegram's Virginia Artillery Company. He was unable to sign his name. Short was present from enlistment until October, 1863. His pay was stopped in October, 1862, for $28.75 but no reason was given. Incomplete reports show him present from May to October, 1864. A clothing receipt dated November 30, 1864 bears his mark. Short was captured at Petersburg, Va., on April 3, 1865. He was sent north and arrived at Hart Island, New York, on April 7, 1865. He died there, of pneumonia, on June 8, 1865. He was buried in grave 2963.

SHULER, Daniel M. - Nothing is known about where or when Shuler enlisted. A private in Company C, Fourteenth South Carolina Militia, he was captured at Camden, South Carolina, on March 1, 1865. Sent north, he was received at Hart Island, New York, on April 10, 1865. Shuler died there on May 5, 1865, of Chronic Diarrhea, and was buried in grave 2707.

SHUTTLESWORTH, Samuel - On March 28, 1863, Shuttlesworth enlisted at Grant's Island, Alabama, and was placed in Company C, First Alabama Artillery Battalion. He was present from enlistment until April 20, 1864. A note in his file with that date reads "Absent on Recruiting furlough for 40 days since April 20, 1864." He was captured on August 23, 1864 when Fort Morgan, Alabama, fell to United States forces, and was transported to New Orleans. From there he moved to New York, on September 11, 1864. He arrived at Fort Columbus on September 28, 1864. He died on November 17, 1864 (no cause given) and was buried in grave 2030.

SIEGEL, N. M. - Burial records give his name as above but military records show that his name as Noah W Seagle. A small number of entries in his file also give his name as N W Seagel. He enlisted at Lincolntown, Lincoln County, North County, on May 23, 1861, for a one year term of service. He was twenty-six years old. Existing records show him present from February through March 17, 1862. He re-enlisted for the duration of the war on that date and received a $50.00 bounty and a fifteen day furlough. Suffering from Mumps, he was admitted to Chimborazo Hospital #1 in early May, 1862. He returned to his unit on May 20, 1862. He was wounded and captured at Seven Pines, Virginia on May 31, 1862. Moved to Portsmouth Grove Hospital, Rhode Island, he died there on July 12, 1862 of "gunshot wound of right knee followed by gangrene." There are no records of his remains being sent to New York but he was buried in grave 3321. An undated item in his file shows that his father, George Seagle, received $108.40 as settlement.

SIMON, W. - A private in Company K, Fifty-Seventh Virginia Infantry, burial records show that he died on August 24, 1863, and was buried in grave 823. No other details have been found regarding where or when he enlisted, his career, or when and where he was captured.

SIMPSON, _____ - Miscellaneous Confederate files show him as a Prisoner of War who was admitted to the U S General Hospital, Davids Island, New York on September 26, 1861 suffering from Typhoid Fever. He died there of Variola on November 19, 1861, and was buried in grave 4449.

SIMPSON, Richard - Simpson enlisted on March 30, 1864, at Camp Holmes, North Carolina, for the duration of the war. He was assigned to Company C, Thirty-Eighth North Carolina Infantry regiment and was present with his regiment until August, 1864. On September 11, 1864 a report shows him "At his home on Sick Furlough." He returned to his regiment in October, 1864. Simpson was captured at the South Side Railroad on April 2, 1865. He was moved to City Point, Virginia, and then to Hart Island, New York. No date is given for his arrival there. On July 1, 1865, he was admitted to DeCamp General Hospital, Davids Island, and he died there, on July 6, 1865, of Chronic Diarrhea. Simpson was buried in grave 3093.

SKELTON, Alex - He enlisted on June 6, 1861 at Fort Powhatan (a second record says Richmond), Virginia, and was assigned to Company A, Montague's Virginia Infantry Battalion. On December 1, 1862, this company was redesignated Company A, Fifty-Third Virginia Infantry regiment. Skelton was present from his enlistment until February, 1862. He next appears on regimental records in September, 1862, when he was reported "Sick in Hospital." In November, 1862, he was reported "Absent, with leave." He returned to the unit in late January, 1863 and "showed cause to explain his absence." Skelton was present until he received a wound at Gettysburg, on July, 1863, and was left in the hands of Federal troops. He was received at DeCamp General Hospital, Davids Island, New York (no date reported) suffering from a gunshot wound to the left hip. In October, 1863, he was transferred to Fort Wood, Bedloe's Island, New York. He died there on December 4, 1863 as a result of his wound compounded by Chronic Diarrhea. He was buried in grave 953.

SLAUGHTER, Selim - On July 10, 1861, Slaughter enlisted for twelve months at West Point, Virginia. He was attached to Company B, Tomlin's Virginia Infantry Battalion. This company became Company D, Fifty-Third Virginia Infantry on December 1, 1861. He was reported sick on December 28, 1861. Returning to his regiment soon afterwards, he was present with the unit thereafter until June, 1863. He had, in the meantime, reenlisted for the war in May, 1862 and received a bounty. In June, 1862, he was sentenced to forfeit 20 days pay by order of a

General Court Martial. No record has been found to show why he was court-martialed, however. Wounded at Gettysburg, Pa., Slaughter was absent from the unit until September, 1863. Incomplete regimental records show him present until December, 1863, and during July and August, 1864. He signed a clothing receipt on June 30, 1864, and on November 30 and December 31. On April 1, 1865, he was captured at Five Forks, Virginia and sent to Hart Island, New York. Slaughter arrived there on April 7, 1865. he was admitted to the Post Hospital on April 18, 1865, and died there, on April 20, 1865, of Pneumonia. He was buried in grave number 2572.

SMITH, A. M. - Alonzo M Smith enlisted on March 6, 1862, for one year at Fort Pillow, Tennessee. He was assigned to Company B, First Tennessee Heavy Artillery. His name also appears on regimental rolls as A H Smith, A Smith, A W Smith, and Alonzo H Smith. Smith was absent, hospitalized in May and June, 1862, but was present through October 4, 1862. On that date he hospitalized at Mississippi Springs, Mississippi. Returning to duty in late November, 1862, he was reported present through early 1863. Smith was captured at Vicksburg, Mississippi, on July 4, 1863 and moved to the Parole Camp at Demopolis, Alabama, where he received his parole on December 20, 1863. Smith reported to his unit at Fort Morgan, Alabama. He was present through May 11, 1864, when he was admitted to the Post Hospital suffering from Intermittent Fever. On May 14th he returned to duty. He was captured on August 23, 1864, when Fort Morgan fell to Federal troops and was transported to New Orleans, Louisiana, soon thereafter and, on September 18, 1864, to New York City. He arrived at Fort Columbus, New York, on September 28, 1864 and was hospitalized there on December 5, 1864, suffering from diarrhea. He was scheduled to be moved to the prison camp at Elmira, New York, on January 11, 1865, but he was still hospitalized, suffering from Variola. He was next scheduled to be moved to City Point, Va., in February 1865, but was remained in the hosptail, too ill to be relocated. On March 28, 1865, he died at the General Hospital, Fort Columbus, of Mumps and Chronic Diarrhea. Smith was buried in grave 2427.

SMITH, George A. - A forty year old resident of Cabarrus County, North Carolina, Smith enlisted at Concord, North Carolina on March 22, 1862, and was assigned to Company H, Twentieth North Carolina Infantry regiment. A note in his file states that he was "Present at Cold Harbor, Malvern Hill, South Mountain, Fredericksburg, Chancellorsville". Twice wounded, once on June 27, 1862 and again on September 16, 1862, Smith was admitted to General Hospital #2, Richmond, Virginia, on September 30, 1862, receiving a thirty day furlough in October, 1862. Smith was wounded a third time on April 27, 1863, and was briefly hospitalized at Chimborozo Hospital #3, Richmond. He rejoined his regiment at Danville, Virginia, in late May, 1863. At Gettysburg, Pa., Smith was wounded a fourth time, receiving a gun shot wound in his foot. Left in a Confederate field hospital at Gettysburg, he was captured by U S forces and sent to DeCamp General Hospital, Davids Island, New York, arriving there on July 19, 1863. Smith died on Pyaemia on August 12, 1863 and was buried in grave 776,

SMITH, Henry - On March 4, 1862, Smith enlisted at Perry, Houston County, Georgia, for three years or the war. He was assigned to Company H, Forty-Fifth Georgia Infantry regiment. He was thirty-one years old and married when he enlisted. On April 24, 1862, he was reported sick "left at Magnolia, Georgia." It is not known when he returned to his regiment but he was paid ($53.90) on August 3, 1862 and was captured on September 14, 1862, at Boonsboro, Maryland. Sent to Fort McHenry, Maryland, Smith was exchanged at Aiken's Landing, Virginia, on October 3, 1862. Prior to being exchanged, however, he had been reported sick at Fortress Monroe, Virginia. He was reported Absent, with Leave, in late 1862. Smith's name appears on a list of sick and wounded captured at Gettysburg. He arrived at DeCamp General Hospital, Davids Island, on July 19, 1863. He died there on Pyaemia on February 19, 1864 and was buried in grave 1042. His effects were listed as one flannel shirt, one pair of drawers, one pair of pants, a uniform coat, a pair of shoes, one handkerchief, a knife, a tin cup, haversack, and pipe. These effects were sold on April 4, 1866 for $1.00 and the proceeds turned over to Brigadier-General Alvord, Paymaster.

SMITH, J. A. - Cemetery records show a man with this name as a private in Company D, Fifty-Seventh Georgia Infantry regiment. He died on August 20, 1863 and was buried in grave 777. The service file for this individual, however, shows that he was captured at Vicksburg, Mississippi, and was subsequently paroled. No additional information is found in his file. Another J A Smith served in Company D of the Fifty-Fourth Georgia Infantry. Information in his file shows that he was wounded and captured at Gettysburg and was sent to DeCamp General Hospital, Davids Island, New York, arriving there on July 19, 1863. No additional information is found in his file concerning where or when he enlisted or if and when he died in captivity. It seems almost certain that the J A Smith buried in grave 777 is the latter individual.

SMITH, J. H. - On August 31, 1861, Smith enlisted at Yorkville, York District, South Carolina, for the war. He was assigned to Company D, Twelfth South Carolina Infantry regiment. Smith was eighteen when he enlisted. Incomplete unit records show him present in early 1862 and that the was wounded in the right thigh on June 30, 1862. He was admitted to Chimborazo Hospital #1 and returned to duty on August 16, 1862. Soon afterwards, on August 29, 1862, he was wounded and captured at Manassas, Virginia. Held as a prisoner of war at Old Capital Prison, Washington, D C, he was exchanged on Nov. 10, 1862. A note in his file dated November 10, 1862, states "Captured by Genl. Sickles." Smith was marked present with his regiment until early 1863 and was shown "Absent, sick" until the spring of 1863. Smith was among the wounded left at Gettysburg, Pa. Sent north, he was received at DeCamp General Hospital, Davids Island on July 19, 1863. He died there on August 2, 1863, of Pyaemia. He was buried in grave 733.

SMITH, Major - Burial records show that a man with this name was buried in grave 234. His date of death is given as July 18, 1862. His unit is not identified and no record of a soldier with this name has been found. Because of the large number of men sharing this surname it has been impossible to check them all. There is also a possibility that this man's rank was Major and his first name is not recorded.

SMITH, William A. - A twenty-eight year old resident of Burke County, North Carolina, Smith enlisted on February 1, 1862 in Burke County for three years or the war. He was assigned to Company B, Eleventh North Carolina Infantry. Records show he was present with his unit from enlistment until August 21, 1862. On that date he was admitted to Confederate General Hospital #4, Wilmington, North Carolina, but he returned to his regiment on August 27th. He was present thereafter until April 30, 1863. From April 30 to May 21, 1863, he was on detached service in Burke County "[i]n search of deserters." He received $15.75 commutation for rations during this period. Smith returned to the unit and was wounded and left in the hands of Federal troops at Gettysburg. Moved north, he was received at DeCamp General Hospital, Davids Island, New York, on July 17, 1863. Smith died there as a result of his gun shot wound on October 1, 1863. He was buried in grave 875.

SMITH, William B. - Smith enlisted in Company A, First Alabama Artillery Battalion on September 29, 1863 at Starlington, Butler County, Alabama. He was present from enlistment until May 3, 1864. He was then reported in the Post Hospital, Fort Morgan, Alabama, suffering from Remittent Fever. He was again hospitalized from June 26 to July 13, 1864, this time with a diagnosis of diarrhea. Two weeks later, on July 27th, he was hospitalized a third time, suffering from diarrhea. Returned to active duty on August 6, 1864, Smith was hospitalized one more time on August 9 suffering from "Volocus". On August 21st he returned to active service and two days later, on the 23rd, was captured when Fort Morgan surrendered to Federal forces. Moved to New Orleans, he was transported from there on September 18th to New York. He arrived at Fort Columbus, New York, on September 28th. Smith died there on October 25, 1864 of Variola and Chronic Diarrhea. He was buried in grave number 2092.

SMITH, Zemerick N. - A private in the Sixteenth North Carolina Cavalry Battalion (burial records identify his unit as the Sixteenth North Carolina Cavalry regiment but there was no such regiment), Smith was a seventeen year old resident of Clinton Creek, North Carolina. It is not known where or when he enlisted. Captured at Hatcher's Run, Virginia on April 1, 1865, he was sent north and admitted to the Hart Island Post Hospital on April 29, 1865. On May 5, 1865, Smith died there of Typhoid Fever and Measles. He was buried in grave 2701.

SNOW, Jesse L. - Snow was a private in Company L, First (Provisional Army) South Carolina Infantry regiment. He enlisted on March 16, 1864, at Marion, South Carolina, receiving a $50.00 bounty. He was present until July 31, 1864. On that date he was admitted to Receiving and Wayside Hospital, Richmond, but was transferred to Jackson Hospital, Richmond, the following day, suffering from Remittent Fever. Snow returned to service on September 13, 1864 and was present for the remainder of 1864. He was captured at the South Side Railroad on April 2, 1865, and arrived at Hart Island, New York, on April 7, 1865. He died there on May 10, 1865 of Double Pneumonia. He was buried in grave 2770.

SOLLER, R. E. A. - An individual with this name, identified as a Private in Company K, Eighteenth North Carolina Infantry regiment, is buried in grave 864. He had died on September 21, 1863. No military records of any kind have been found for an individual with this name in this or any other Confederate unit.

SOUTHARD, William R. - Southard enlisted on August 15, 1861, at Bachelor's Hall, Virginia, for twelve months. He was assigned to Company I, Fifty-Seventh Virginia Infantry regiment. Records show that he was unable to sign his name. He was reported present, sick in camp, in late 1861, and on January 10, 1862, he was granted a thirty-four day furlough. Returned to his regiment, he was present with it until December 22, 1862. On that date he was reported hospitalized in Richmond. He returned to the unit soon afterwards but on January 17, 1863, was again hospitalized, suffering from Diarrhea. Southard returned to duty on April 2, 1863, but, on May 8, 1863, he was again hospitalized. Admitted to Episcopal Hospital, Richmond (no reason given), he remained there until June 13, 1863. He was then present with his regiment until February 13, 1864. A note in his file reads "Absent - deserted from company while on march from Kinston, North Carolina to Richmond, Virginia." He is next mentioned in unit records in September, 1864, with the following note: "Absent. Undergoing sentence of court martial [and] confined at hard labor for the period of three months with ball and chain attached to left leg and to forfeit his pay for twelve months in consideration of his unauthorized absence." On October 11, 1864, Southard was admitted to Chimborazo Hospital with Intermittent Fever only to be returned to confinement the following day. Nothing in his file shows when he returned to active service but he was captured at Five Forks, Virginia, on April 1, 1865, and sent north to Hart Island, New York (no date given). He died there of Chronic Diarrhea on May 17, 1865, and was buried in grave 864.

SPROULES, F. J. - Although it appears that this soldier's name was F J Sproule, he was also carried on various rolls as above as well as F J Sprawls and J Sprawls. He was a member of Company A of the First (McCreary's) South Carolina Infantry regiment. He enlisted on August 10, 1861 in Barnwell District, South Carolina, and traveled five hundred miles to be mustered in on August 19, 1861. On December 14, 1861, he was promoted to the rank of Corporal and assigned as Color Corporal in March, 1862. On May 15, 1862, he was detailed with the Ordnance Sergeant and remained so until October, 1862. He was admitted to the General Hospital at Charlottesville, Virginia, on December 15, 1862, suffering from "Velu. Sclopt." Three days later he was transferred to the General Hospital at Lynchburg, Virginia. Sometime later he was released from the hospital and furloughed. He returned from the furlough on March 15, 1863, and was paid $267.65 in back pay, clothing allowance, bonus, etc. He was also promoted to the rank of sergeant, apparently during his absence, dating from February 28, 1863. Sprules was wounded and left at Gettysburg, Pa. in early July, 1863. He was received at DeCamp General Hospital on July 17, 1863 and died there on July 25th, as a result of his wound. He was buried in grave 685.

STATON, Malachi - A twenty-eight year old farmer, Staton enlisted in November 20, 1861, at Camp Fisher, North Carolina. He was assigned to Company D, Thirty-Seventh North Carolina Infantry with the rank of Sergeant. Records show that he was five feet ten and a half inches tall. He was present with his unit until October, 1862. His original enlistment having been only for twelve months, he re-enlisted in March, 1862, for an additional two years. In late 1862 he was hospitalized at Lynchburg, Virginia. Conflicting reports show that he was present from January to March 1863 and that he was Absent at his home on sick furlough during the same period. Staton was wounded on May 1, 1863, at the Battle of Chancellorsville. He was wounded a second time, in the left shoulder, at Gettysburg, Pa. and was captured there when Federal troops occupied the Confederate field hospitals. He was sent to DeCamp General Hospital, Davids Island, New York (no date given) where he died, as a result of his wound, on August 15, 1863. He was buried in grave 791.

STEELEY, S. - Burial records list his name as above but military rolls show that his name was Thomas Staley. At the age of nineteen he was conscripted into Company K, Seventh North Carolina Infantry on May 1, 1863. He was a native of Guilford County. He joined his regiment in mid-May. Steeley was wounded and captured at Gettysburg, Pa. Received at DeCamp General Hospital, Davids Island, New York, on July 17, 1863, he died there on July 22nd. He was buried in grave 674.

STELLING, Hassan - No military records have been found for a man with this name. Burial records identify him as a Private in Company F, Twenty-Sixth North Carolina Infantry regiment who died on August 26, 1863, and that he was buried in grave 827

STEPHENS, C. A. T. - Stephens enlisted in Company K, Ninth Georgia Infantry, on June 11, 1861. Incomplete records show him present through the spring of 1862. He was wounded at Gettysburg on July 3, 1863, and was among those captured when southern forces retreated. Sent north (no date given), he died at DeCamp General Hospital, Davids Island, and was buried in grave number 726..

STEVENSON, James M. - Stevenson was thirty-seven years old when he was commissioned a Captain in the Thirty-Sixth

North Carolina Infantry regiment on June 15, 1861. He was shown as present until early 1862, when his record reads "Absent in Wilmington attending Court Martial as witness." No other details concerning the court martial are found in his file. He returned to the unit and, on June 14, 1862, was reported sick in Sampson County. Incomplete unit records show him as present for the remainder of the summer of 1862 but he does not appear again until January, 1864, when he was Absent on Court Martial duty in Wilmington. Stevenson was promoted to the rank of Major on July 23, 1864, and was captured at Fort Fisher, North Carolina, on January 15, 1865. He was sent north and died at the General Hospital at Fort Columbus, New York, of Pneumonia on February 18, 1865. Although originally buried at Cypress Hills, records indicate that his remains were removed and returned to North Carolina.[19]

  STILL, Isaac - A private in Company A, Fourteenth South Carolina Militia, Still was captured at Lynch's Creek, South Carolina, on February 25, 1865. Nothing has been found showing when or where he began his active service. He was received at Hart Island, New York on April 10, 1865, and died at the Post Hospital there on Chronic Diarrhea on May 16, 1865. He was buried in grave 2805.[20]

  STILL, Thomas - Thomas Still was captured at Lynch's Creek, South Carolina on February 25, 1865, while serving as a Private in Company B, Fourteenth South Carolina Militia. It is not known when or where he began his active career. Received at Hart Island, New York, on April 10, 1865, he died there on Chronic Diarrhea on April 28, 1865. He was buried in grave 2637. [21]

  STOKES, B. B. - Stokes, twenty-two, was captured at Fort Morgan, Alabama, on August 23, 1864. It is not known when or where he entered the service and "Conjugal Condition, Not Known" is noted in his file. Originally moved to New Orleans, La., he was transferred from there to New York on September 18, 1864. He arrived at Fort Columbus, New York, on Sept. 28, 1864, and was admitted to the General Hospital there suffering from diarrhea and edema of the left leg on November 11, 1864. Scheduled to be transferred to Elmira, New York, on December 4,

---

[19] A brief biography and summary of Stevenson's military carre appears on pages 265-66 of the June, 1898, "Confederate Veteran" magazine. This states that his remains are now in Wilmington, North Carolina.
[20] It is possible that he was related to Thomas Still, below.
[21] It is possible that he was related to Isaac Still, above.

1864, he was considered too ill to be moved. Stokes died at Fort Columbus of Variola on December 19, 1864. He was buried in grave 1630.

STONE, Green P. - Stone was twenty-six years old when he enlisted on March 8, 1862, at Chulahoma, Marshall County, Mississippi for the war. He was assigned to Company I, Nineteenth Mississippi Infantry regiment. Slightly more than a month later (on April 21, 1862), he was admitted to the Episcopal Church Hospital, Williamsburg, Virginia. On April 24th he was transferred to Chimborazo Hospital #2, Richmond, suffering from Debility and Diarrhea. He returned to his regiment on May 3, 1862 but was rehospitalized in July, 1862. Incomplete records show him hospitalized through May, 1863 for sickness (although the roll of September/October 1862, probably in error, indicates that he had been wounded.) Once he returned to the regiment in May, 1863, records show him as present until December, 1864. Stone was captured at Petersburg, Virginia, on April 3, 1865 and that he was sent to Hart Island, New York, where he arrived on April 7, 1865. He died there of Remittent Fever on June 3, 1865, and was buried in grave 2934.

STOWE, J. N. - A resident of Gaston County, North Carolina, Stowe was eighteen when he enlisted for a one year term of service on June 12, 1861. His file does not show where he enlisted only that he was assigned to Company H, Twenty-Third North Carolina Infantry regiment. Stowe was present with the unit through the spring of 1862. Records of his unit for the next few months are missing, and he is next shown as having been captured at South Mountain, Maryland, on September 14, 1862. Exchanged at Aiken's Landing, Virginia, on October 4, 1862, he was promoted to the rank of Sergeant on May 6, 1863. Stowe was wounded in the thigh and neck at Gettysburg and was among those left behind when Confederate troops withdrew. He was received at DeCamp General Hospital, Davids Island, on July 17, 1863, and died there, as a result of his wounds, on August 3, 1863. He was buried in grave 735

STREET, P. S. - Military records show that the soldier buried under this name was named Pinckney S Struit, a private in Company I, Eleventh North Carolina Infantry regiment. He was nineteen, a resident of Lincoln County, when he enlisted for three years or the war at Lincolntown on March 15, 1862. He was present from his enlistment until wounded and captured at Gettysburg, Pa. Moved north, he arrived at DeCamp General Hospital on July 19, 1863. He died there, of Pyaemia, on August

18, 1863 and was buried in grave 797. His mother, Rhoda Struit, filed a claim for his back pay on December 21, 1863, but there is no record of whether or not the claim was ever settled.

STRICKLAND, Henry - Strickland was twenty-seven years old when he enlisted on February 26, 1862 at Marlboro, South Carolina. He was assigned to Company D, Twenty-Sixth South Carolina Infantry regiment. Incomplete unit records show him present from September 1862 through August 1863. He was then carried as "Absent Without Leave." The roll for January/February, 1864 reads "Present, In Arrest Awaiting sentence of court martial." Nothing has been found showing what this sentence might have been. There is no further mention of him until October 1, 1864, when he was admitted to the General Hospital in Petersburg, Virginia. Indicating that he might have still been under sentence, he was turned over to the Provost Marshall when he was released in October 18, 1864. On December 6, 1864, he was again hospitalized in Petersburg, and, on the 16th of that month, again returned to the hands of the Provost Marshall. He signed clothing receipts in 1864 dated April 14, May 26, July 30, and September 20. Strickland was captured on April 2, 1865, at Petersburg, Virginia. He was received at Hart Island, New York, on April 7, 1865. On April 10th he was admitted to the Post Hospital, where he died of Chronic Dysentery on June 14, 1865. He was buried in grave 3005. His effects - one dress coat, one shirt, one set of drawers, and one pair of shoes - were sold not long afterward for thirty cents.

STROMAN, A. - A Private in Company E, Fourteenth South Carolina Militia, he was captured at Lynch's Creek, South Carolina, on March 1, 1865. It is not known when or where he began his active career. Stroman was received at Hart Island, New York, by way of Newberne, North Carolina, on April 10, 1865. Admitted to the Post Hospital there on April 28, 1865, he died the following day. Cemetery records show that he was buried in grave 2665 on May 1, 1865, "at 8 a.m."

STRUM, G. B. - Records of the Fourteenth South Carolina Infantry regiment show that this soldier's name was George B Strom. He was a private in Company D of that regiment who had enlisted at Columbia, South Carolina on June 27, 1864 for the war. He was present from enlistment until September 14, 1864. On that day he was admitted to Jackson Hospital, Richmond, Virginia (no reason given) and did not return to duty with his regiment until October 24, 1864. Captured at Petersburg, Virginia. on April 3, 1865, he was received at Hart Island, New York, on April 7, 1865.

He died there on May 17, 1865 of Chronic Diarrhea and was buried in grave 2809.

SULLIVAN, J. V. - James V Sullivan enlisted at Huntsville, Alabama, on November 15, 1863, in the Tenth Alabama Infantry regiment. From January 24 through February 1, 1864, he was on "Extra duty at Third Corps Headquarters as a laborer". Clothing receipts in his file with his signature are dated January 1864, February, 1864, Second Quarter 1864, August 30, 1864, and Fourth Quarter, 1864. On April 3, 1865, he was captured at Chester Court House, Bermuda Hundred, Virginia. Transported north, he arrived at Hart Island., New York, on April 11, 1865. He died there on June 6, 1865 of Chronic Diarrhea and was buried in grave number 2953.

SUTHARD, William R. - A soldier with this name, a Private in Company I, Fifty-Seventh Virginia Infantry, was buried in grave 2811 according to cemetery records. He died on May 17, 1865. There are no military records of a man with this name, however, in this or any other unit.

SWALT, Simeon O. - Military records show that this man's name was Simson Oswalt. Other records show his name as Simon Oswalt. He enlisted on February 12, 1863, in Company C, Fifteenth South Carolina Infantry regiment, at Lexington, South Carolina. He was present until wounded and captured at Gettysburg, Pennsylvania. Swalt was received at DeCamp General Hospital on July 17, 1863. He died there on July 31, 1863, of Typhoid fever, and was buried in grave 706.

SWEETSER, Theodore - Cemetery records show that a man with this name, a member of the First South Carolina Infantry, died on November 23, 1863, and was buried in grave 937. No military records have been found, however, for a man with this name in this or any other unit.

TEMPLETON, H. B. - A private in Company B, Fourteenth South Carolina Militia, Templeton was captured at Lynch's Creek, South Carolina, on February 25, 1865. There are no records which show when or where he began his active service. He was received at Hart Island, New York, on April 10, 1865, and died there on Chronic Diarrhea on June 1, 1865. He was buried in grave 2929.

TEYSON, ____ - Miscellaneous Confederate records show this man as a "prisoner of war" who was admitted to the U S Post Hospital, Fort Columbus, New York, on October 12, 1861. He died there of Typhoid fever on October 16, 1861. No grave number is reported in this file nor in cemetery records. It is not known when or where he enlisted, his unit, or where or when he was captured.

THOMAS, J. M. - Thomas was a Sergeant in Company A, Eighteenth North Carolina Infantry regiment. Nothing is known about where or when he enlisted or his service prior to his being captured in April, 1865 nor are his place of capture and the exact date reported. He was received at Hart Island, New York, on April 10, 1865, from Newberne, North Carolina. He died at Hart Island on May 21, 1865 of Chronic Diarrhea and was buried in grave 2842.

THOMAS, William - Thomas was a Private in Company I, Twenty-Seventh Alabama Infantry regiment. He enlisted at Florence, Alabama, on January 10, 1862. He was captured at Champion's Hill, Mississippi, on May 17, 1863. A second report states that he was captured at Raymond, Mississippi on May 12, 1863. On August 23, 1863, he was reported as present at Fort Delaware as a prisoner of war. His regimental records, however, for the same date, reads "Deserted". There are no additional records concerning him or his career. He is next mentioned on cemetery records. These show that he died on May 10, 1865, and was buried in grave 2767.

THOMPSON, H. F. - Records of his unit, Company B, Forty-Eighth Virginia Infantry, show that his name was H F Thomson. Nothing is known about where or when he enlisted. He was wounded and left at Gettysburg, Pennsylvania, and was received at DeCamp General Hospital, Davids Island, New York, on July 23, 1863. He died there of Typhoid Pneumonia on August 19, 1863, and was buried in grave 798.

THOMPSON, S. M. - Samuel M Thompson was a Private in Company A, Twelfth Texas Cavalry. He was seventeen years old when captured at Bullitt's Bayou, Concordia Parish, Louisiana, on August 25, 1864. It is not known where or when he had enlisted. On September 15, 1864, he was moved to New Orleans, Louisiana, and held at Steam Levee Press #4. He was admitted to the U S Army General Hospital in New Orleans on September 29, 1864, suffeering from Rubeola. He returned to custody on October 18, 1864, and two days later, on October 20th, was moved to Ship Island, Mississippi. He was transported to New York on November 5, 1864, and arrived at Fort Columbus on November 16th. Thompson died of Chronic Diarrhea at the Post Hospital, Fort Columbus, on December 18, 1864, and was buried in grave number 1817, The letter, reprinted below, written two days after his death, is found in his file.

Metamoras, Mexico, Dec. 20, 1864
General E R S Canby,
    My son <u>Samuel M Thompson</u>[22] was captureed by a portion of your forces last September in the state of Louisiana. He belonged to Co. A <u>12th Texas Cavalry</u>, Parsons Brigade. I wish to ascertain where he is imprisoned in order that I might write to him to induce him to abandon the Confederates as I have done. I assure you that I will be under many obligations to you if you will send the information I desire. My son is a mere boy and was compelled to go into the rebel service against his wishes. Please write to C H Thompson care of the U S Consul, Metamoras, Mexico.
    I remain with great respect,
    Charles W Thompson

    TIDWELL, Clark - This soldier was a member of the Gist Guard South Carolina Heavy Artillery Company. In addition to his name being shown on the cemetery records as above, he was also carried on military rolls as J S Tidwell and J S A Tidwell. He enlisted at Lancaster, South Carolina for the war on December 28, 1861. Very incomplete unit records next show him as present from June 1864 through February 1865. Tidwell was captured at the Battle of Bentonville, North Carolina, on March 22, 1865. He was received at Hart Island, New York,, by way of Newberne, North Carolina, on April 10, 1865. He died there on May 11, 1865, the cause of death being given as Inflammation of the Brain. He was buried in grave 2748.

    TILLY, William - Buried under the name shown here, this soldier, according to military records was named William Tilley. He was married to Martha Tilley, and was a 55 year old private in the Fourteenth South Carolina Militia. Nothing is known about where or when he began his active career. He was captured at Lynch's Creek, South Carolina, on February 28, 1865, and was received at Hart Island, New York, on April 10, 1865. He died there of Chronic Diarrhea on April 23, 1865, and was buried in grave 2593.

    TIMBERLAKE, G. W. - George W Timberlake was a 22 year old resident of Lenoir County, North Carolina, when he

---

[22] underlined in original

enlisted on July 8, 1861, at Goldsboro, North Carolina for the war. His name also appears on a small number of records as J W Timberlake. He was assigned to Company A, Third North Carolina Infantry regiment. He was present through December, 1861. In March and April 1862 he was reported as Absent, on Furlough. Returned to his regiment, he was present until July, 1863. On October 1, 1862, he received a promotion to the rank of Corporal, and, on February 20, 1863, to the rank of Sergeant. Timberlake was wounded, his leg fractured, at Gettysburg, and he was left there when Confederate troops withdrew. He arrived at DeCamp General Hospital, Davids Island, New York, on July 19, 1863, and he died there, as a result of his wound, on August 8, 1863, He was buried in grave 754.

TINDALL, H. F. - On February 16, 1863, Tindall enlisted for the war at Pocataligo, South Carolina, and was assigned to Company I, Fifth South Carolina Cavalry. One day after enlisting, he was placed on recruiting service for fifteen days. He was present with the unit thereafter until December 21, 1863, when he received a ten day furlough. Early in 1864 he was reported on "Picket Duty" and was present with the regiment until August 31, 1864. A note on the muster of August, 1864, reads, "In dismounted battalion - Horse and Recruiting Camp." Shown as sick in quarters in September, 1864, Tindall was admitted to Jackson Hospital, Richmond, Virginia, on October 3, 1864, suffering from "Ints. Febris." He signed a clothing receipt dated December 1, 1864. Tindall was captured in the Barnwell District, South Carolina, on February 15, 1865. Moved from Newberne, North Carolina to Hart Island, New York, he arrived in the north of April 10, 1865. He died there of Chronic Diarrhea on May 2, 1865, and was buried in grave 2679.

TISON, William L. - Tison enlisted on June 6, 1861 at Quitman, Georgia, for the duration of the war. He was assigned to Company A, Ninth Georgia Infantry, with the rank of Sergeant and was present from enlistment until October, 1861. Incomplete regimental records next show him present in early, 1863. He was wounded (described as a "Flesh Wound to the Knee") at the Battle of Gettysburg, and captured there. Moved to DeCamp General Hospital, Davids Island, New York, on July 17, 1863, he died there, of Pyaemia, on August 8, 1863. Tison was buried in grave 764.

TITTERTON, Samuel D. - Burial records show that a man with this name, a private in Company F, Seventh North Carolina Infantry, died on October 19, 1861, and was buried in grave 4448.

No military records have been found for a man with this name in the Seventh North Carolina Infantry or any other unit.

TOLAN, S. D. - Burial records show that he was a Private in Company E, Fifty-Ninth Virginia Infantry regiment. His unit, however, was the Fifty-Seventh Virginia Infantry regiment. Burial records also disagree with military records concerning his name. Most records show his name as Samuel D Toler but he was also carried at Samuel D Towler, Samuel D Tolen, and Samuel D Tolar. He enlisted on August 2, 1861, in Pittsylvania County, Virginia and was present through the February 4, 1862. On that date he was reported "on War furlough in Pittsylvania County for thirty days", obviously having received the furlough for re-enlisting. In the early summer of 1862 he was absent, sick, at Drewry's Bluff, Virginia, and, in October, 1862, sick as White Sulphur Springs, Virginia. He was reported back with the unit in November, 1862. On February 21, 1863, he "Deserted on March from Richmond, Va. to Drewry's Bluff." He was apprehended near Manchester, Virginia, on March 6, 1863 and court-martialed. A verdict of guilty was rendered against him. As a result his pay was forfeited for three months and his pay stopped $55.00 for the loss of his rifle and accouterments. On May 8, 1863, Tolan was admitted to the Episcopal Hospital, Williamsburg, Virginia, and transferred to the General Hospital, Farmville, the following day. He returned to duty on July 1, 1863. Subsequent records show him hospitalized (place not identified) from November, 1863, through April, 1864. He was shown as present from May through October, 1864. He signed clothing receipts of November 30 and December 31, 1864, and January 9, 1865. Tolan was captured at Petersburg, Virginia, on April 2, 1865. He was received at Hart Island (no date given) and admitted to the Post Hospital. He died there of Chronic Diarrhea on May 5, 1865. No grave number is given in the cemetery records.

TORRINGTON, J. - John Torrington enlisted on June 1, 1864 as a Private in the Fourth Maryland Artillery Company, at Hanover Court House, Virginia. Incomplete unit records show that he was present for the remainder of the year. A note in his file dated February 20, 1865, states that, by Special Orders #48, Paragraph 6, Department and Army of Northern Virginia he was transferred to Beverly's Company, Gilmore's Battalion[23], but he appears not to have reported to it. He was captured at Petersburg,

---

[23] First Maryland Cavalry Battalion

Virginia, on April 3, 1865 and was received at Hart Island, New York, on April 7th. He died there on June 10, 1865 of Chronic Diarrhea. He was buried in grave 2971.

TOWLER, J. E. - According to burial records, a soldier with this name died on May 5, 1865, and was buried in grave 2703. He was a Private in Company I, Forty-First Alabama Infantry regiment. No records of such an individual have been found in any military files, however.

TOWNSEND, George - Cemetery records show that a man with this name, a private in Company E, Thirty-Seventh North Carolina Infantry, died on June 3, 1862, and was buried in grave 4113. Contradictory information exists in his file however. One report states that he was twenty-three years old when he enlisted; a second gives his age as thirty. He was five feet, ten inches tall, with sandy hair, blue eyes, and a sallow complexion. Townsend enlisted at Kinston, North Carolina on April 5, 1862. On the same day he re-enlisted for two additional years. He was captured at Hanover Court House, Virginia, on May 27, 1862, and moved to Fort Columbus, New York. Admitted to the Post Hospital there, Townsend died of Typhoid fever on June 3, 1862. His file, however, also contains information showing that he was exchanged at Aiken's Landing, Virginia, on July 12, 1863. Still another item shows that he died at an unidentified location in New York City on March 28, 1863. The cause of this contradictory data in his file is not known nor does it seem possible to reconcile the differences.

TRAITOR, William - This soldier is also carried on various rolls at William Traytor, W Traitor, W F Trautor, and W W T Traitor. He enlisted on May 23, 1861, at Columbus, Georgia, for the war. He was twenty years old and was assigned to Company I, Twentieth Georgia Infantry regiment. Records show him present for only a month and he was then reported Absent, Sick, at Culpeper, Virginia. He returned to duty in September, 1861, and was present until mid-August, 1862. At that time he was admitted to the General Hospital at Farmville, Virginia, suffering form Rheumatism. Traitor returned to his regiment on September 1, 1862. Three weeks later, on September 22, 1862, suffering from Rheumatism once more, he was admitted to Marland Hospital (Gwathney Hospital), Richmond. On September 26th he was transferred to the Fourth Division General Hospital, Richmond. He finally returned to his regiment on September 29th. Not long afterwards, on October 15, 1862, he was admitted to Winder Hospital Number 2, Richmond, Virginia, returning to service on November 27, 1862. On February 27, 1863, Traitor was again hospitalized, admitted to General Hospital Number 1, Richmond and it is not known when he returned to service. He was, however, admitted to Winder Hospital Number 7, Richmond, on April 14, 1863. The reasons why he was hospitalized the last few times is not mentioned in his files. Returning to his regiment, he received multiple wounds in the breast, shoulder, thigh, lungs, and eye at Gettysburg, Pennsylvania. Traitor was among the Confederate wounded captured in the southern field hospitals at Gettysburg when Federal troops occupied them. He was received at DeCamp General Hospital, Davids Island, New York, on July 2,1 1863. On October 24, 1863 he was transferred to Fort Wood, Bedloe's Island, New York. He died there of Phthisis on November 21, 1863 and was buried in grave number 963.

TREXLOR, J. J. -Trexlor was a Private in the Eighteenth South Carolina Militia. It is not known when or where he entered active service. He was captured at Lynch's Creek, South Carolina, on March 3, 1865. He was received at Hart Island, New York (no date given) and died there on May 2, 1865, of Chronic Diarrhea.

TROUT, John O. - Nothing is found in his file that shows where or when Trout enlisted as a member of Company C, Fifth Virginia Infantry. He was wounded and captured at Gettysburg, Pennsylvania. Trout arrived at DeCamp General Hospital on July 19, 1863. He died there as a result of his gunshot wound on August 1, 1863. It is not known what grave he was buried in but cemetery records show that his remains were subsequently removed but do not show where.

TURNER, John - Turner enlisted in Company A, Gee's Alabama Artillery Battalion on March 1, 1861, at Mobile, Alabama, for a three year term of service. This unit subsequently became Company A, First Alabama Artillery Battalion. He was twenty-three years old when he enlisted. Turner was present with the unit until mid-December, 1863. On October 27, 1862, he was promoted Corporal and on May 26, 1863, Sergeant. On December 11, 1863, he was reported "Absent on 30 day furlough." He re-enlisted for the duration of the war in early 1864. On January 22, 1864, Turner was reported at the Post Hospital, Fort Morgan, Alabama but returned to duty on January 26th. He was captured at Fort Morgan on August 23, 1864 and transported from New Orleans, Louisiana, to New York, New York, arriving there on September 17, 1864. He was received at Fort Columbus on September 28, 1864, and he died there of Pneumonia on November 22, 1864. He was buried in grave 2172.

TURNHAM, Thomas J. - A private in Company C, Fifty-Ninth Alabama Infantry, Turnham enlisted on September 23, 1863 for three years. He was a native born Alabaman, thirty-five years old, and married to Frances Turnham. Incomplete unit records show him present in January and February, 1864. On June 19, 1864, he was admitted to the U S General Hospital at City Point, Virginia, as a wounded prisoner of war, with a head wound, fractured malar, and a ruptured ear. He was sent to the U S General Hospital, Willett's Point, New York (no date given) and he died there on September 2, 1864 (no cause given). He was buried in grave number 1786.

TUTT, John - Nothing has been found to show when or where Tutt enlisted. He was a Private in Company A, Jeff Davis Mississippi Cavalry Legion. Captured on March 28, 1865, at Goldsborough, North Carolina, he was sent to Newberne, North Carolina, and then to Hart Island, New York. It is not known when he arrived but he died there on May 30, 1865 of Typhoid Pneumonia. Cemetery records do not give his grave number.

TYRE, W. B. - William B Tyre enlisted on March 31, 1862 at Camp Pryor, Virginia, for a three year term of service. He was assigned to Company G, Thirteenth Virginia Cavalry. He next appears in unit records dated in October, 1862. There he was reported "Absent, sick", since September 29, 1862. On October 20, 1862, he was Present at General Hospital Number 11, Richmond, Virginia. He was listed as present from November, 1862, until Aug. 1864, although the roll of July and August, 1863, shows Tyre as "Present, Sick". The roll of November and December, 1864, reads, "Absent without leave since Dec. 21, 1864." On April 6, 1865, his name appears on a list of "Rebel prisoners forwarded to Bermuda Hundred." He was sent from Fort Powhatan, Virginia, to New York, on April 8, 1865, arriving at Hart Island, New York, on April 11th. He died of Chronic Diarrhea there on June 11, 1865, and was buried in grave number 298

TYSON, W. T. - William T Tyson, twenty-one years old, born in Richmond, North Carolina, enlisted on December 31, 1861, at Camp Mangum, North Carolina. He was six feet tall, a planter. When mustered in, he was given the rank of Sergeant and he was present with the unit from enlistment until August, 1862. He had, in the meantime, been reduced to the rank of Corporal on April 18, 1862 but no reason for his demotion is mentioned. Sometime in late August, 1862, he was admitted to Chimborazo Hospital Number 2, Richmond, suffering from diarrhea, but he returned to his unit, Company E, Thirty-Eighth North Carolina Infantry on

September 5, 1862. In late 1862 he was shown as "Present, sick, General Debility" and on Sick Furlough on January 18, 1863. On February 20, 1863, Tyson's furlough was extended for another twenty days. Wounded in the "Left Chest" at Gettysburg, Pa., he was among the wounded captured there when Federal troops occupied the Confederate field hospitals. He was received at DeCamp General Hospital on July 7, 1863, and died there of Pyaemia on July 26, 1863. He was buried in grave number 687.

UNKNOWN - Five individuals buried in Cypress Hills National cemetery are listed as Unknown. For those buried in graves 66 and 68 nothing is known, not even a date of death. The soldier buried in grave 666 died on July 23, 1863. The listed death date for the man in grave 672 is July 24, 1863. Finally, the individual buried in grave 4432 died on July 25, 1863.[24]

VANDERGRIFF, Joseph - He was a twenty-eight old married painter, an Irish-born resident of New Orleans, who enlisted at Camp Moore, Louisiana on July 22, 1861. He had brown hair, blue eyes, and a fair complexion. He stood five feet seven and a half inches tall. Assigned to Company C, Tenth Louisiana Infantry, he was present with his unit until November 30, 1861. On December 1, 1862, Vandergriff was admitted to Chimborazo Hospital Number 4, Richmond, Virginia, suffering from Acute Diarrhea. He returned to duty on February 17, 1863. Included in his file is a list of engagements in which he took part. Those named are Chancellorsville, May 1 - 5, 1863, Winchester, June 15, 1863, and Gettysburg, July 1 - 3, 1863. He was wounded at this last engagement and was among those captured when U S troops occupied the Confederate field hospitals. He was received at DeCamp General Hospital, Davids Island, New York, on July 17, 1863, and he died there as a result of his gun shot wound on July 31, 1863. He was buried in grave 721.

VARN, Hangford D. - Varn was a private in Company K, Fourteenth South Carolina Militia. It is not known where or when he was placed on active service. He was captured at Lynch's Creek, South Carolina, on February 25, 1865 and arrived at Hart Island, New York, on April 10, 1865. He died there on May 11, 1865 of Chronic Diarrhea. He was buried in grave 2753.

VAUGHN, A. G. - This soldier's burial records show his name as above but his military records list his name as G A Vaughn. There is no record of his enlistment or service prior to

---

[24] on the basis of the death dates of the last three, it would appear that they, at least, had been captured during the Gettysburg Campaign.

being captured. A Private in Company B, Tenth Georgia Cavalry, Vaughn was captured at Lynch's Creek, South Carolina on February 26, 1865. He was received at Hart Island, New York, on April 10, 1865, and he died there of Chronic Dysentery on April 18, 1865, He was buried in grave number 2638.

VAUGHN, William L. - A private in Company F, Thirty-Fourth North Carolina regiment, Vaughn enlisted at Camp Holmes, North Carolina, on April 20, 1864. He was present with his regiment until October, 1864. On April 2, 1865 he was captured at the South Side Railroad. Transported north, he was received at Hart Island, New York (no date given). He died of Typhoid Fever on June 17, 1865, and was buried in grave 3023.

VENDRICK, J. A. - Vendrick enlisted at Greenville, North Carolina, on April 20, 1861, for one year. His name also appears as Vendricke on a number of files. He was single, the son of Mrs. Nice Vendrick of Johnson's Mills, Pitt County, North Carolina. He was assigned to Company H, Twenty-Seventh North Carolina Infantry regiment. Vendrick was present from enlistment until December, 1862, having re-enlisted for three years in early May, 1862. On May 18, 1862, he was court-martialed for insubordination and forfeited his pay for six months. Vendrick was given a thirty day furlough after being wounded at Sharpsburg, Maryland, in September, 1862. On July 7, 1863 (having been promoted to the rank of Corporal) he was admitted to Receiving and Wayside hospital (General Hospital Number 9), Richmond, Virginia., with "Cronic [sic] Diarrhea." Vendrick signed clothing receipts on March 2, 1864, June 17, 1864, and September 13, 1864. He was captured at Sutherland Station, Virginia, on April 7, 1865. He arrived at the Post Hospital, Hart Island, New York, on April 16th and died there on April 28th of Typhoid Fever. Hospital records show he was twenty-three when he died. He was buried in grave number 2652.

VENSON, W. J. - William J Venson was single and twenty-three when he enlisted in Company E, First Alabama Artillery, on March 7, 1861 at Autauga, Alabama. His term of enlistment was for three years. On May 24, 1861 he was reported at the Post Hospital, Fort Morgan, Alabama. He returned to duty on June 30, 1861, and was present thereafter until February 12, 1862 when he was admitted to the General Hospital, Mobile, Alabama. It is not known when he returned to his unit but he was present from April 1862 through October 21, 1862. On that date Venson received a ten day furlough, returning to duty on November 3, 1862. He was present until the last day of the year when he was reported "Sick in quarters", not returning to active service until February 28, 1863. Venson was listed as present until May 18, 1863 when he was hospitalized briefly. He returned to duty two days later and was present from May 20 to December 16, 1863, when he re-enlisted for the duration of the war. On that date he was given a thirty day furlough but appears to have returned to his unit on December 31, 1863. Venson was then present with the unit until mid-February, 1864. On the 15th of that month he was admitted to the Post Hospital, Fort Morgan, once again, suffering from diarrhea. He returned to service on February 23, 1864, remaining on active duty until April 19, 1864. On that date he was given a fifteen day furlough, perhaps the continuation of his previous furlough. Venson was captured when Fort Morgan was taken by Federal forces on August 23, 1864 and sent to New Orleans. From there he was moved to New York, arriving at Fort Columbus on September 27, 1864. He died at the Post Hospital there on December 13, 1864 of Variola and was buried in grave 2187.

WADSWORTH, E. E. - Eli Wadsworth was a Private in Company I, Thirty-Fifth North Carolina Infantry regiment. He was conscripted in Davidson County, North Carolina, on April 1, 1863. Conflicting reports give his age at enlistment as twenty and twenty-two. A clothing receipt (which he signed with his mark), dated March 26, 1864, is found in his file. Unit records show him present from November 1864 through February, 1865. He was captured at Five Forks, Virginia, on April 1, 1865. He was transferred to City Point, Virginia, and, from there, to Hart Island, New York, where he arrived on April 7, 1865. Wadsworth was admitted to the Post hospital on April 11, 1865. He died there on Diarrhea and Typhoid fever of April 27, 1865, and was buried in grave number 2621.

WALKER, J. C. L. - This soldier, a twenty-one year old resident of Lagrange, Georgia, enlisted in Company G, Twenty-Seventh Georgia Artillery Battalion, at Columbus, Georgia, on September 14, 1863. He was present with his unit until August, 1864. Records of Quincy Hospital, Savannah, Georgia, show him a patient there from August 4, 1864, until November 16, 1864. He was then with the battalion until the end of the year. Walker was captured at a hospital in Cheraw, South Carolina, on March 7, 1865. Moved to the U S General Hospital at Newberne, North Carolina, on April 10, 1865. He was subsequently moved to Hart Island, New York, and from there, to DeCamp General Hospital, Davids Island. No date is given for either move. On May 2, 1865 he died of Pleuritis and Diarrhea and was buried in grave 2676.

WALKER, Lee - Cemetery records show that a man with this name died on July 6, 1862, and was buried in grave 167. No other information of any kind has been found on him in any military records.

WALLACE, William - Wallace was a Private in Company A, Forty-Sixth North Carolina Infantry. Born in Wayne County, North Carolina, he was twenty-seven years old when he enrolled on February 8, 1862 at Lumberton, North Carolina. Wallace was a laborer, standing five feet, nine inches tall. Records show that he was Absent Without Leave between April 16, 1862 and July 31, 1862. There are no details as to when he returned or what punishment, if any, he received. His name appears on no further rolls but his mark (he was unable to sign his own name) appears on Clothing receipts of November 29, 1864 and December 6, 1864. Nothing in his file indicates where or when he was captured. He died at DeCamp General Hospital, Davids Island, New York, on June 16, 1865. He was buried in grave 3011.

WARD, W. H. - This soldier was a private in Company H, Forty-seventh North Carolina Infantry regiment. Nothing is known about when or where he enlisted or his service prior to his capture. He had light complexion, blue eyes, light hair, and was five feet, six inches tall. Ward was captured at Hatcher's Run, Virginia, on April 2, 1865, and was transported to Hart Island, New York, by way of City Point, Virginia. He arrived at Hart Island on April 7, 1865 and he died there on June 9, 1865, no cause being given. Cemetery records, however, indicate that he died and was buried on June 1, 1865. It is not know which is correct. He was buried in grave 2970

WARRICK, W. P. - At the age of twenty, Warrick enlisted on August 20, 1861, at Ridgeway, South Carolina, for the duration of the war. He was assigned to Company C, Twelfth South Carolina Infantry regiment. Incomplete unit records show him present in early 1862 and from November 1862 through June, 1863. Warrick was wounded and left at Gettysburg, Pennsylvania. He was received at DeCamp General Hospital on July 19, 1863, and died there on July 26, 1863 of Pyaemia. He was buried in grave 678.

WATKINS, William H. - Watkins enlisted at Camp Mangum, North Carolina, on April 11, 1862, for three years. He was a resident of Kittrell Springs, North Carolina, twenty-two years old, single, the son of Charlotte Watkins. Upon enlisting he was assigned to Company G, Forty-Seventh North Carolina Infantry regiment with the rank of Private. Incomplete records show him present in early 1863. In July, 1863, he was reported hospitalized at the General Hospital, Lynchburg, Virginia, but no reason is given. Watkins was present again from March through July, 1864, with his rank shown as Corporal. At that time he was reported in General Hospital Number 9 (Receiving and Wayside Hospital), Richmond. He signed clothing receipts on July 13, 1864, August 18, 1864, December 1, 1864, and December 9, 1864. Watkins was captured at Sutherland Station, Virginia, on April 2, 1865. Sent north by way of City Point, Virginia, he was received at DeCamp General Hospital, on April 29, 1865 and died there, a victim of Chronic Diarrhea, on July 15, 1865. He was buried in grave 3105. His effects were listed as one uniform coat, one pair of boots, one cap, and one pair of stockings.

WATSON, T. J. - Watson enlisted at the age of eighteen at Covington, Alabama, on December 5, 1863. Assigned to Company C, First Alabama Artillery Battalion, he is also carried on a number of the battalion's rolls as J J Watson. He was present from enlistment until June 7, 1864. On that day he was admitted to the Post Hospital, Fort Morgan, Alabama, with "Febris Ret." He was captured when Fort Morgan fell on August 23, 1864, and was sent to New Orleans, Louisiana, and then to New York, where he arrived on September 28, 1864. He died at Fort Columbus on October 22, 1864 of Chronic Diarrhea and was buried in grave number 1607.

WAYNE, Francis A. - A member of Company L, First (Provisional Army) South Carolina Infantry regiment, Wayne enlisted on August 12, 1861 in the Marion District of South Carolina. He was mustered in with the rank of Corporal at Richmond, Virginia, on August 19th and was present with the regiment through the early 1864. In the meantime he had been assigned as Color Corporal in March, 1862, and been promoted to Sergeant on September 24, 1862. For some reason not explained in his file he was demoted to the rank of Private on November 14, 1863. Wayne received a "Furlough of Indulgence" from February 29 to March 15, 1864, and, on his return, was present with the regiment until December, 1864. He was captured on April 2, 1865 at the South Side Railroad, Virginia. and sent to City Point, Virginia. Transferred to Hart Island, New York, he was received there on April 7, 1865. Wayne died of Double Pneumonia on May 11, 1865 and was buried in grave 2747.

WEATHERBY, J. M. - Burial records spell his name as above. Military records, however, give his name Weathersbee. One report states that he enlisted into Company A, First (McCreary's) South Carolina Infantry regiment at Barnwell, South Carolina, on August 22, 1861. A second report, however, shows him being mustered in at Richmond, Virginia, on August 19, 1861. Incomplete records show him present from November 1861 through February, 1862 and from April through October, 1862. On October 31, 1862 a note in his file reads "Sent to Hospital from Leesburg and is now in Richmond sick." The entire entry, however, has been crossed out and further records show him present through June, 1863. He was wounded and left at Gettysburg and subsequently transferred north. He arrived at DeCamp General Hospital, Davids Island, New York, on July 17, 1863 and died there of Pyaemia on August 1, 1863. He was buried in grave 774.

WEBB, John H. - Although buried under this name, this soldier was identified in military records as John N Webb. There is nothing in his file to show when and where he enlisted only that he was a Private in the Tenth Georgia Cavalry who was captured at Columbia, South Carolina, on February 18, 1865. Sent north, he was received at Hart Island on April 10, 1865, where he died on Chronic Diarrhea on May 20, 1865. He was buried in grave number 2916.

WEBB, Levi - Cemetery records identify the soldier buried in grave 2992 as above. He was a Corporal in the Eighth Florida Infantry regiment who died on June 11, 1865. No military records have been located for him in this or any other unit.

WHEEY, J. A. - Another of the many Confederate soldiers buried in Cypress Hills National Cemetery whose name is different than military records, this individual's correct name was J A Wherry. He was eighteen when he enlisted on August 13, 1861, at Rock Hill, South Carolina. Wheey was present from enlistment through mid-November, 1861, and again in January and February, 1862. A note in his file reads "Discharged July 23, 1862". Despite this, records for May and June, 1863, show his as present. He was wounded and left at Gettysburg. Received at DeCamp General Hospital, Davids Island, New York, on July 19, 1863, he died there on July 22, 1863 from a gun shot wound. He was buried in grave 669

WHITE, E. - White enlisted at Spartanburg, South Carolina, on August 27, 1861, and was assigned to Company E, Thirteenth South Carolina Infantry. Incomplete records show him present through November, 1861. In November, 1862, he was promoted to the rank of Corporal, and he was present until he was wounded at Gettysburg, Pennsylvania. He had, in the meantime, been promoted to the rank of Sergeant in March, 1863, and First-Sergeant in May, 1863. Transported north, he arrived at DeCamp General Hospital on July 19, 1863. He died there the following day as a result of his gunshot wound and was buried in grave number 654.

   WHITE, Franklin - Nothing is known about where or when Franklin White enlisted. He was a Private in the Sixty-seventh North Carolina Infantry regiment who was captured at Moseley Hall, North Carolina, on March 31, 1865. He was sent to Hart Island, New York, from Newberne, North Carolina, arriving on April 10th. White died of Typhoid Fever on May 24, 1865 and was buried in grave 2875.

   WHITEHURST, _____ - Material in the Unfiled and Miscellaneous Confederate records file shows that his name was L Whitehurst. In this file he is identified only as a Prisoner of War and it is not known what unit he served in, when he enlisted, or where he was captured. He was admitted to the U S Post Hospital, Fort Columbus, New York, on October 12, 1861, and died there the next day of Febris Typhoides. No grave number is recorded.

   WHITING, William H. C. - William Henry Chase Whiting was born on March 22, 1864, at Biloxi, Mississippi. He graduated from the U S Military Academy in 1845, having attained the highest overall grades ever made to that time. He served with the Engineers in California and various locations in the south thereafter. At the start of the War he was named Chief Engineer of the Army of the Shenandoah and was promoted Brigadier-General on the field of First Manassas personally by President Jefferson Davis on July 21, 1861. During the Valley Campaign and the Seven Days Battles, he commanded a division under Stonewall Jackson. Shortly after the battle of Malvern Hill, he was sent to North Carolina where he was instrumental in the construction of Fort Fisher which guarded the approaches to Wilmington, North Carolina. On April 22, 1863, Whiting was promoted to Major-General on April 22, 1863. In the summer of 1864 he served briefly in the Petersburg, Virginia, area. At Port Walthall Junction, Virginia, he was unable to get his command into action and rumors of his being under the influence of alcohol or narcotics surfaced. Returned to the North Carolina coast, he was severely wounded when Fort Fisher fell on January 15, 1865. Against the advise of both Federal and Confederate surgeons, he was transferred north. He died of his wounds at Fort Columbus,

New York, on March 10, 1865. His remains were later exhumed and transferred south and now lie in Oakdale Cemetery, Wilmington, North Carolina.25

WILKINSON, George - Nothing has been found to show where or when Wilkinson enlisted. He was a Sergeant in Company D, Fourteenth Virginia Infantry when he was captured at Five Forks, Virginia, on April 1, 1865. He was sent north to Hart Island, New York (no date given). He died at the Post Hospital there on April 20, 1865 of Dysentery and was buried in grave 2570.

WILLIAMS, _____ - An item in the Miscellaneous Unfiled Confederate file reads: "Indian, Prisoner of War." According to this entry he was admitted to the U S General Hospital at Fort Columbus, New York, on September 3, 1863. He died there on September 4, 1863, of Phthisis Pulmonitis. He was buried in grave 839. No additional information on his enlistment, career, or capture has been found.

WILLIAMS, C. D. - Military records show that this individual's name was actually D C Williams. He enlisted at Rexboro, North Carolina, on March 10, 1863, for a three year term of service and was assigned to Company E, Thirty-Fifth North Carolina Infantry regiment. He was thirty-five at the time of his enlistment. He appears on none of the unit's existing rolls. Williams was wounded in the left leg on June 19, 1864, near Petersburg, Virginia, and captured. Placed on the steamer "Western Metropolis" for transfer to New York, Williams died en route to Hart Island. He was buried in grave 3389 at Cypress Hills.

WILLIAMS, R. F. - Although buried under this name, military records show that his name was Killis F Williams. A Private in Company K, Thirty-Fifth North Carolina Infantry, he was eighteen when he enlisted at Kinston, North Carolina, on April 17, 1862. Williams was a farmer, five feet five inches tall, a resident of Alleghany County who had been born in Ashe County. Regimental rolls show that he was present until August 27, 1862. On that date he was admitted to the General Hospital at Charlottesville, Virginia, suffering from debility. He returned to his regiment on the next day. He was admitted to the Danville General Hospital on September 11, 1862 with "Jeterus" and returned to duty on November 3, 1862. On the same date he was

---

25 It is almost certain that Whiting's remains were not buried at Cypress Hills but rather on Governor's Island.

reported "Under Arrest at Lynchburg." This entry may be in error however, since he was shown as present from November through February, 1863. Williams was wounded and left at Gettysburg, Pennsylvania. Sent north, he arrived at DeCamp General Hospital, Davids Island, New York, on July 17, 1863,. He died there on August 19, 1863, as a result of his gun shot wound. He was buried in grave 801.

WILLIS, Billy - Willis enlisted on January 4, 1862 in Company C, Deneale's Regiment Choctaw Warriors and was present through July 14, 1862. The 1860 Federal census for the State of Arkansas erroneously included a small part of the Choctaw Nation and enumerated Billy Willis, a farmer, who had been born at Towne Pees. He was living with a Charles Lyons, thirty-six, an Occultist. A second record shows that Willis enlisted on June 30, 1862, at Camp Granite, Indian Territory and was assigned to Company K, First Choctaw and Chickasaw Mounted Rifles for two years. No information has been found as to when or where he was captured. Burial records show that he died on May 12, 1863 (no cause given) and that he was buried in grave number 2758.

WILLIS, James - Cemetery records show that a man with this name, identified as a member of Company A, Eighth Tennessee Infantry, died on May 12, 1865, and was buried in grave 2758. No records of an individual with this name has been found in any available records.

WILSON, David - At the age of twenty-seven, David Wilson enlisted in Company G, Eleventh Georgia Infantry regiment. Incomplete records show that he was admitted to Chimborazo Hospital Number 1, Richmond, Virginia, on September 2, 1862, with Typhoid Fever. The day before he had received $44.00 back pay plus a $25.00 clothing allowance from which $9.50 was deducted (but no reason was given), Wilson was wounded "Ball [in] Breast" at Gettysburg and was among those left there when Confederate forces retreated. He was received at DeCamp General Hospital, Davids Island, New York, on July 23, 1863 where he died there on August 21, 1863. Wilson was buried in grave 831. No cause is given.

WILSON, G. S. - George S Wilson was a Private in Company K, Twenty-Second North Carolina Infantry regiment. He enlisted at Petersburg, Virginia, on September 11, 1864 and was present through the end of October. He signed a clothing receipt dated November 5, 1864. Wilson was captured at the South Side R R on April 2, 1865, and was received at Hart Island, New York, on

April 7, 1865, He died there on May 18, 1865 of Double Pneumonia. He was buried in grave number 2813.[26]

WILSON, J. E. - James E Wilson enlisted in Company K, Twenty-Second North Carolina Infantry regiment on September 11, 1864, and was present through October, 1864. He signed a clothing receipt dated November 17, 1864. On April 2, 1865, he was captured at the South Side Railroad, Virginia. He was received at Hart Island, New York, on April 7, 1865, and died there on May 16, 1865. The cause named was Typhoid Pneumonia. He was buried in grave 2804.[27]

WILSON, John W. - Wilson enrolled in Company E, Fifty-Fifth North Carolina Infantry regiment at Greenville, North Carolina, on April 28, 1862. He was mustered in at Camp Mangum, North Carolina, for the war. Born in Pitt County, North Carolina, he was a twenty-five year old farmer when he enlisted. He stood six feet, four inches tall, considerably taller than the average Confederate soldier. Incomplete reports show him present through June 1862 and from May through June, 1863. Wilson was captured at Gettysburg, Pennsylvania and sent to Fort McHenry, Maryland and from there to Fort Delaware, Delaware. On February 18, 1864, he was exchanged at Aiken's Landing, Virginia. He signed a clothing receipt in December, 1864, at which time his rank was shown as Corporal. He was captured at the South Side Railroad on April 2, 1865, and was transported to Hart Island, New York, where he arrived on April 7, 1865. He died there on Pneumonia on May 16, 1865. No grave number is given in his file.

WILSON, Nathaniel - Burial records show a man with this name, a member of the Eighth Tennessee Infantry, buried in grave 2789. He died on May 15, 1865. No additional information of any kind has been found about him or his career.

WINN, William D. - His name also appears as William D Wynn on some military records. He was a Private in Norwood's Florida Home Guard Company. (Burial records identify his unit as Chisholm's Florida Company.) He was captured on September 27, 1864 at Marianna, Florida. Winn was sent to New Orleans on October 8, 1864, and, from there, to Ship Island, Mississippi, on October 27, 1864. Transferred to New York on November 5, 1864, he was received at Fort Columbus, New York, on November 16,

---

[26] It is not known if he was related to J E Wilson, below.

[27] It is not known if he was related to G S Wilson, above.

1864. He died there (no cause given) on December 21, 1864. He was buried in grave 2194.

WINSTON, Henry M. - Buried under this name, military records show that he name was Henry M Winsor. He was sixteen years old when he enlisted in Company F, Forty-Fifth North Carolina Infantry regiment, on March 11, 1862, at Elm Grove, North Carolina. Despite his youth, he was mustered in with the rank of Sergeant. A resident of Rockingham County, North Carolina, he was a farmer, five feet nine inches tall. He was present from May 1862 through June 1863. Winston was wounded and left at Gettysburg. Sent north, he arrived at DeCamp General Hospital on July 17, 1863, and died there, as a result of his gun shot wound, on August 14, 1863, He was buried in grave 675.

WOLF, Henry F. - A private in Company B, Thirteenth North Carolina Infantry regiment, his name also appears on military records as Henry Wolfe. A resident of Mecklenburg County, Wolf was a twenty-three year old farmer, when he was mustered in at Fort Deslanes, Virginia, July 17, 1861. He was present through mid-August, 1862 but a report with his name states that he was admitted to Cliffburne General Hospital, Washington, District of Columbia and sent to Old Capital Prison June 11, 1862. There is no explanation for this contradictory data in his file. On August 12, 1862, he was admitted to Moore Hospital, General Hospital Number 24, Richmond, Virginia and was furloughed on the same day. He was next shown as present from November 1862 through February, 1863. Wolf was wounded and captured at Gettysburg, Pennsylvania. Received at DeCamp General Hospital on July 9, 1863, he died there on July 19, 1863, a victim of his wounds. He was buried in grave 658.

WOOD, D. C. C. - Wood enlisted at Newport, Tennessee, on August 27, 1863, and was assigned to Company C, Twenty-Sixth Tennessee Infantry regiment. Many rolls give his name as D C Wood. He was present through October, 1863 and again in early 1864. He signed a clothing receipt on March 30, 1864, and was again listed as present from May through August, 1864. Wood was captured at Orangeburg, South Carolina, on February 12, 1865 and sent to Newberne, North Carolina. From there he was moved to Hart Island, New York, where he arrived on April 10, 1865. On May 3, 1865 he was admitted to the Post Hospital on Hart's Island and he died on May 13, 1865 of Typhoid Pneumonia. He was buried in grave 2786.

WOOD, William - An eighteen year old resident of Burke County, Wood enlisted at Morgantown, North Carolina, on March

1, 1862. He was assigned to Company D, Eleventh North Carolina Infantry, Records show him present through June, 1863. He was wounded and captured at Gettysburg, Pennsylvania. Sent north, he was received at DeCamp General Hospital, Davids Island, New York, on July 23, 1863. He died there from his gun shot wound on September 5, 1863, and was buried in grave 838.

WOOD, William H. - Wood, a private in Company B, Forty-Seventh North Carolina Infantry, enlisted on February 27, 1862 and was mustered in at Camp Mangum on April 11, 1862. A resident of French Lick, North Carolina, he was eighteen years old, five feet, ten inches tall, and had a dark complexion. Incomplete records show that in July and August, 1863, he was "At home on furlough for 30 days," He was present in early 1864 and again in May and June of that year. Unable to sign his name, his mark appears on Clothing Receipts of the Third Quarter of 1863, the Second and Third Quarters of 1864, July 25 and October 20, 1864. He was captured at Petersburg, Virginia, on April 3, 1865 and was sent to Hart Island, New York, where he arrived on April 11, 1865. On May 10, 1865 he died of Typhoid Fever and was buried in grave 2768.

WOODALL, A. G. - He enlisted at Crabtree, North Carolina on August 18, 1861, for twelve months. He was present from enlistment (with the rank of Sergeant) until December, 1862, and again in March and April, 1862. The roll of April 1862 shows his rank as Third Lieutenant. Woodall was wounded in the left knee and was captured at Gettysburg, Pennsylvania, when Federal troops occupied the Confederate field hospitals. He was received at DeCamp General Hospital on July 20, 1863, and died there as a result of his gunshot wound on September 8, 1863. He was buried in grave 848.

WOODS, John B. - This soldier enlisted at Hevener's Store, Virginia, on June 11, 1861, for a twelve month term of service. He was assigned to Company F, Twenty-Fifth Virginia Infantry. He was present from enlistment through October 2, 1861 and was then reported as Absent, sick. In November and December, 1861 he was shown as Absent Without Leave. Incomplete records next show him as present from April through December, 1862. In June, 1862, he reenlisted for three more years or the war. In January and February, 1863, he was reported on detached service but the specific duty is not mentioned. Woods was wounded in the patella and left at Gettysburg. He arrived at DeCamp General Hospital on July 7, 1863, and he died there as a result of his gunshot wound on August 9, 1863. He was buried in grave 765.

WRIGHT, H. C. - Henry Clay Wright enlisted in Company A, First Texas Infantry, at New Orleans, Louisiana, on May 16, 1861, for a twelve month term of service. Existing regimental records show him present through July, 1863. In May, 1862, he had reenlisted for an additional three years. He received a flesh wound in the arm at the battle of Gettysburg and was captured there. Wright was transferred to DeCamp General Hospital, Davids Island, New York, arriving there on July 19, 1863. He died there of Pyaemia on August 18, 1863. He was buried in grave 800.

YEDDER, Stephen - According to burial records a man with this name died on May 10, 1865, and was buried in grave 2760. He was reported to have been a Private in Company G, Third South Carolina Infantry regiment. No military information has been found regarding his service, however.

YORK, C. P. - York was a Private in Company E, Twenty-Fourth Georgia Infantry regiment. There are no records as to when or where he enlisted. He was reported at Chimborazo Hospital Number 3, Richmond, Virginia, on June 21, 1862, suffering from Pneumonia. On June 26th he was transferred to the General Hospital at Lynchburg. No other records are found with his name until he was captured, wounded in the right leg at Gettysburg. He was transported north and arrived at DeCamp General Hospital on July 21, 1863. He died there as a result of his wound on August 17, 1863. He was buried in grave 793.

YOUNG, Beverly D. - Unit rolls show that he was also identified to as Bev Young and B D Young. He was thirty-one years old when he enlisted on April 27, 1861, and was attached to Company I, Eleventh Mississippi Infantry regiment. He was mustered in for twelve months at Lynchburg, Virginia, on May 13, 1861 and was present with his unit until February 9, 1862. Having re-enlisted for the war two days earlier, he was granted a furlough. Young was reported back with the unit from March through June, 1862. In December, 1862, he was on detached service with the Brigade Commissary Department. At the Battle of Gettysburg, Young was wounded and captured. He was received at DeCamp General Hospital, Davids Island, on July 19, 1863. He died there as a result of his wound. Three dates are reported in his file for his death: August 15th, August 25th, and August 28th. He was buried on August 29th. His body was subsequently removed and returned to Mississippi.

YOUNG, John - His name is found in the Unfiled and Miscellaneous Confederate file showing that he was a Conscript from South Carolina, a resident of Charleston, unassigned to any unit. Young was captured at Columbia, South Carolina, on February 19, 1865. He was sent north and arrived at Hart Island, New York, on April 10, 1865. He was admitted to DeCamp General Hospital, Davids Island, New York, on June 22, 1865, and died there the next day. No cause of death is given. He was buried in grave 3034.

YOUNGINGER, J. - Burial records show his unit as the Fifteenth South Carolina Infantry regiment. He was, however, a Private in Company H, Fourteenth South Carolina Militia. There are no details of where or when he was captured but he was received at Hart Island, New York on April 15, 1865. On the same date he was transferred to DeCamp General Hospital. He died there on April 29, 1865. The cause of death was listed as "Confederate Typhoid Fever." He was buried in grave 2645.

YOW, John W. - Yow was nineteen when he enlisted at Camp Mangum, North Carolina on April 3, 1862. He was a farmer, residing in Randolph County, who stood five feet, ten inches tall. He was assigned to Company H, Forty-Fourth North Carolina Infantry regiment and was marked present from enlistment until August, 1863, and again from January to February, 1864. Incomplete unit reports next show him present in January, 1864, with the rank of Sergeant. He continued to be shown present until April, 1864. On August 20, 1864, he was furloughed from the General Hospital, Camp Winder, Richmond, Virginia, returning to his unit in November, 1864. Yow signed clothing receipts dated October 5, 1863, December 19, 1863, December 20, 1863, Second Quarter of 1864, August 4, 1864, August 16, 1864, and November 26, 1864. He was captured at the South Side Railroad on April 2, 1865. Sent north, he was received at Hart Island, New York,. on April 7, 1865. He died there of Pneumonia on June 14, 1865. Yow was buried in grave 3004.

ZWEIGLER, George - Regimental rolls show his name as above as well as J Zweigler. He was a German born laborer, twenty-nine years old, single, a resident of St Landry Parish Louisiana, when he enrolled at Camp Moore, Louisiana on July 22, 1861. He was assigned to Company E, Tenth Louisiana Infantry. He was present from enlistment through the end of February, 1862 although on January 1, 1862 he was on temporary detached service at Lebanon Church, Virginia. A list of engagements in which he took part reads: Dam #1, Virginia, April 6, 1862;

Williamsburg, Virginia. May 4, 1862; Savage Station, Va., June 29, 1862; Malvern Hill, Virginia, July 1, 1862; Cedar Run, Virginia, August 15, 1862, Manassas, Virginia, August 30, 1862; Chantilly, Virginia, September 1, 1862, Harper's Ferry, West Virginia, September 15, 1862; Sharpsburg, Maryland, September 17, 1862; Fredericksburg, Virginia, Dec 12 - 15, 1862; Chancellorsville, Virginia, May 2 - 3, 1863; Winchester, Virginia, June 14, 1863, and Gettysburg Pennsylvania, July 1 - 3, 1863, At the last named battle he was wounded "Flesh Wound in Knee" and captured. He was transferred north of July 15, 1863, but no date is given as to when he arrived at DeCamp General Hospital. He died there on August 12, 1863 of "Hemmorrage". He was buried in grave 755.

Appendix I

As mentioned above, there are numerous cases of errors in the cemetery listing of Confederates buried at Cypress Hills National Cemetery. The list below shows the soldier's names, units, and grave numbers as found in the published report. In cases where research in service files has produced different information than that which is on the list, the correct information is printed below the entry.

1) ABERNATHY, WM. R. D - Co. H. Thirty-Seventh North Carolina Infantry - no grave number listed.
2) ADAMS, A. B. - Co. K, Fourteenth South Carolina Infantry - 748.
3) ALLEN, R. F. - Co. C, Thirty-Eighth North Carolina Infantry - 861. Military records show his name as RUFUS F ALLEN.
4) ALLEN, ROBT. H. - Co. I, Forty-Third North Carolina Infantry - 2516.
5) AMOS, DAVID - Co. B, First Tennessee Heavy Artillery - 1937. Military records show that he originally enlisted in the Confederate Ordnance Department and later served in unit named on the cemetery list.
6) ANDERSON, JAMES - no unit listed - no grave number listed.
7) ANDERSON, JOSEPH R. - Co. C, Eighth Virginia Infantry - 2763. Military records show his name as JOSEPH K ANDERSON.
8) ANDERSON LEROY - Co. F, First Maryland Infantry - no grave number - "Taken to Md. by his father". Military Records show that correct unit as the First Maryland Infantry Battalion.
9) ARCHIBALD, E. N. - Co. B, Seventh Alabama Cavalry - 1269. Military records show his name as E M ARCHIBALD but also carried on rolls as E A Archibald.
10) ATTLEBERRY, CHARLES - Co. C, Second Texas Cavalry - 2181. Military records show that he was also carried on rolls as Charles Atteberry, Charles Atleberry, and Charles Atleburg.
11) BAILEY, W. - Co. __, First Georgia Infantry - 148. Military records show his name as WILLIAM R BAILEY and his unit as Co. K, First (Lawton's/Mercer's/Olmstead's) Georgia Infantry.
12) BAKER, G. D. - C. S. A. - 158.
13) BARBURY, J. E. - Co. D, Twenty-Eighth North Carolina Infantry - 4443. Military records show that his name was JAMES E. BARBEE.

14) BARKER, KILLIS C. - Co. K, Thirteenth Mississippi Infantry - 788.
15) BARNES, JAMES - Co. A, First Alabama Artillery - 1840.
16) BARTLEY, SMITH - no unit given - 4452. Military record s show his name as BARTLEY SMITH (the reverse of that carried on the cemetery list) and unit as Co. __, Montgomery Guards.
17) BASS, JETHRO - Co. C, Second North Carolina Infantry - 2932. Military records show his name as JETHROE BASS.
18) BEALL, JOHN YATES - C.S.A. - no grave number given. Military records show that he originally served in Co. G, Second Virginia Infantry and subsequently in the Confederate States Navy.
19) BEARD, JAS. O. - Co. A, First South Carolina Rifles - 2861.
20) BECKMAN, W. H. - Co. K, Thirty-Third North Carolina Infantry - 2820.
21) BELLSHAW, JOHN - Co. E, __ Virginia Militia - 3085.
22) BENNETT, A. W. - Co. ?, 10 Alabama Infantry - 3592.
23) BENSON, JESSE W. - Co. B, Forty-Fifth North Carolina Infantry - 688.
24) BIRD, JOSIAH - Co., A, Third North Carolina Artillery - 2855. Military records show that his name was JOSIAH BYRD and that he served in the Third North Carolina Heavy Artillery.
25) BIRD, W. L. - Co. G, Second South Carolina Infantry - 830.
26) BLAKE, A. P. - Carpenter's Virginia Battery - 789. Military records show that he was also carried on rolls as E. Blake and E. C. Blake. He served in Cutshaw's Virginia Artillery Company and later Crenshaw's Virginia Artillery Company.
27) BLANKENSHIP, J. T. - Co. E, Thirty-Seventh North Carolina Infantry - 432. Military records show that his name was THOMAS BLANKENSHIP. (A James Blankenship also served in the same unit but his records do not match those of the man buried).
28) BLOCK, C. - Co. K, Thirty-Eighth North Carolina Infantry - 659. Military records show that his name was DUNCAN BLOCK.
29) BLOOD, L. W. - Co. G, Thirteenth North Carolina Infantry - 783. Military records show that his name was LEVI WILLIAM BLOUNT.
30) BLOUNT, HOSEA - Co. F, Seventh North Carolina Infantry - 4444. Military records show that he served in the Seventeenth North Carolina Infantry.
31) BLUNT, T. H. - Co. D, Second Georgia Infantry - 755. Military records show that he was also carried on the rolls as T C C Blunt.

32) BOGGS, JOHN D. - Co. C, Fifty-Fifth North Carolina Infantry - no number given.

33) BOUGHMAN, H. L. - Co. C, First South Carolina Infantry - 2844. Military records show that his name was HENRY L BAUGHMAN and that he served in the First (Provisional Army) South Carolina Infantry.

34) BOULDIN, N. H. - Co. F, Fifty-Seventh Virginia Infantry - 2677. Military records show that his name was NATHANIEL H BOULDIN.

35) BOWINE, JAMES - Co. A, Thirteenth Florida Infantry - 651. There was no unit with this designation.

36) BOYLE, STEPHEN - Co. A, Fifty-Fifth North Carolina Infantry - 3049. Military records show that his name was STEPHEN BOYETT.

37) BOZEMAN, M. - Co. E, Twenty-Second Georgia Heavy Artillery Battalion - 2641. Military records show that he served in the Confederate States Navy prior to joining the Heavy Artillery unit.

38) BRADBURY, WILEY - Co. A, Forty-First Georgia Infantry - 3080.

39) BRADLEY, _____ - C. S. A. - 199

40) BRADSHAW, J. P. - Co. E, Thirteenth North Carolina Infantry - 772. Military records show that his name was JAMES P. BRADSHAW.

41) BRANHAM, W. - Co. I, Forty-Sixth Virginia Infantry - 2854. Military record show that his name was WILLIAM BRANHAM.

42) BROWN, _____ - C. S. A. - no number given.

43) BROWN, ELISHA - Co. D, Fifteenth North Carolina Infantry - 3122. Military records show that he appears on some rolls as E. B. Brown.

44) BROWN, H. E. - Co. B, Thirteenth South Carolina Infantry - 898. Military records show that his name was HARRINGTON E. BROWN.

45) BROWN, HENRY - Burdall's Louisiana Artillery - 2615. Military records show that his unit was Burdsall's Louisiana Battery.

46) BROWN, J. J. - Co. I, Sixth South Carolina Cavalry - 2686

47) BROWN, JOHN - Co. H, Thirty-Fourth North Carolina Infantry - 2938.

48) BRYAN, JOHN J - Co. F, Forty-Eighth Mississippi Infantry - 3163. Military records show that his name appears as J. J. Bryant on a number of rolls.

49) BULLIS, DAVID W. - Co. F, Fifty-Second North Carolina Infantry - 742.
50) BULLIS, SIMEON - Co. C, Twenty-Sixth North Carolina Infantry - 847.
51) BURDICK, E. W. C. - Co. G, Fourteenth South Carolina Infantry - 2591. Military records show that his name was EDWARD C BARWICK.
52) BURMINGHAM, JOHN - Co. D, Eleventh Mississippi Infantry - 686.
53) BURNES, PATRICK - Co. __, Fifteenth Texas Volunteers - 1353. Military records show that he served in Co. B, Fifteenth Texas Infantry.
54) BURNETT, WILLIAM T. - Co. E, Thirteenth South Carolina Infantry - 2750.
55) BUSHING, _____ - C. S. A. - 132.
56) CAMDEN, J. S. - Co. H, Twenty-Seventh Virginia Infantry - 832. Military records show his name as JOSEPH CAMDEN and also carried on some rolls at Joseph Camdon.
57) CAMHILL, CHARLES - C. S. A. - 3062. Miscellaneous Confederate records show that he served in the First South Carolina Infantry but they do not specify which of the three units with this designation.
58) CAMP, JAMES - Co. A, Sixth South Carolina Cavalry - 2708.
59) CAMPBELL, E. - Co. A, Sixteenth South Carolina Infantry - 2729. Military records show that he served in Co. A, Fifteenth South Carolina Infantry regiment.
60) CAMPBELL, R. J. - Co. C, Fourth South Carolina Artillery - 2571. Military records show that he served in the Pee Dee South Carolina Artillery Company (Zimmerman's South Carolina Battery). There was no unit designated the Fourth South Carolina Artillery.
61) CAMPBELL, ROBERT - Co. H, First South Carolina Infantry - 2814. Military records show that he served in the First (Provisional Army) South Carolina Infantry.
62) CANNON, JOHN - Co. F, Ninth Florida Infantry - 2302. Military records that he served in Mooty's Florida Infantry Company and the Sixth Florida Infantry battalion prior to serving in the Ninth Florida Infantry.
63) CARLTON, JAMES C. - Co. B, Ninth Florida Infantry - 2334. Military records show that he served in the Sixth Florida Infantry Battalion prior to the Ninth Florida Infantry.
64) CARROLL, JOHN - Co. E, Fourteenth North Carolina infantry - 2715.

65) CARROLL, ROBERT A. - Co. F, Third Alabama Infantry - 1027.
66) CARTER, TIMOTHY - Co. H, First South Carolina - 2819. Military records show that he served in the First (Regular Army) South Carolina Infantry.
67) CARTLAND, FRANCIS - Co. C, Tenth North Carolina - 2900. The Tenth North Carolina regiment was officially the First North Carolina Heavy Artillery.
68) CARVER, LEWIS C. - Co. A, Sixteenth Virginia Artillery Battalion - 2742. Military records show that he served in Sturdivant's Virginia Artillery Company which was Co. B, Twelfth Virginia Artillery Battalion. There was no unit designated as the Sixteenth Virginia Artillery Battalion.
69) CASEY, A. M. - Marion South Carolina Artillery - 2605.
70) CASH, PETER - Co. E, Forty-Eighth Alabama Infantry - 83
71) CHAMBERS, G. W. - C. S. A. - 215. Military records show that his name was GEORGE W CHAMBERS and that he served in Co. F, Thirty-Third North Carolina Infantry.
72) CHAMBERS, HARVEY - Co. G, Forty-Eighth Alabama Infantry - 729.
73) CHAMPION, WILLIAM - Co. F, Second North Carolina Infantry - 3020.
74) CLARK, JOSEPH W - Co., K, Fifty-Third Virginia Infantry - 2948. Military records show that he was identified on a number of rolls as Joseph W Clarke and James W Clarke. He served in the Fifth Virginia Infantry Battalion originally.
75) CLARK, W F - Coit's Virginia Battery - 2740. Military records show that his name was William T Clark and that he served in Pegram's Virginia Battery.
76) CLIFTON, GEORGE - Co. B, Forty-Seventh North Carolina Infantry - 2663.
77) COFFEY, J G - Co. F, Twenty-Sixth North Carolina Infantry - 824.
78) COLEMAN, HAZEL - Co. D, Thirty-Third North Carolina Infantry - 2812. Military records show that he was carried on a number of rolls as Hazel Colman and Azel Coleman.
79) COLLINS, JAMES - C. S. A. - 345.
80) CONDREY, JEFFERSON - Co. D, Fourteenth Virginia Infantry - 3096. Military records show his name as James Condrey and other rolls give his name as J L Condrey.
81) CONETRAIN, J. - C. S. A. - 211.

82) COOK, SAMUEL F - Co. E, Twenty-Eighth Georgia Siege Artillery - 2710. Military records show that he served in the Twenty-Eighth Georgia Heavy Artillery Battalion.
83) COSART, LEWIS - Co. C, Thirty-Fifth North Carolina Infantry - 1266. Military records show that his name was LEWIS CUSSART.
84) COSTELLE, PATRICK - Lee's Virginia Artillery Company - no number given - "Taken by his brother to Hudson City, N. J."
85) COUSINS, JAMES - Co. C, Forty-First Virginia Infantry - 2969. Military records show that he was also identified on some rolls as James Cozzens.
86) COVINGTON, ELIJAH - Co. D, First South Carolina Infantry - 2874. Military records show that he served in the First South Carolina Heavy Artillery.
87) COWARD, N. M. - Co. B, Fourteenth South Carolina Militia - no number given.
88) COX, LEANDER - Co. A, Thirty-Seventh North Carolina - 3331.
89) CRAWFORD, E. P. - Co. G, Fourth North Carolina Infantry - 3003. Military records show that his name was A. D. CRAWFORD.
90) CROUDER, WILLIAM - Lucas Virginia Battalion - 2764. Military records show that his name was WILLIAM CROWDER and that he served in Co. C, Fifteenth South Carolina Artillery Battalion.
91) CUBBAGE, J - Co. D, Fifty-Third Virginia Infantry - 2954.
92) DARROLD, J L - Co. K, Eleventh North Carolina Infantry - 679. Military records show that his name was JAMES C DARNOLD and a small number of records refer to him as J S Darrold.
93) DAVENPORT, M. C. - Co. B, Thirty-Third North Carolina Infantry - 261. Military records show that he also appears on some records as Mac C Davenport, McCarey Devenport, and McKaney Davenport.
94) DAVIDSON, LEWIS - Co. F, Eleventh North Carolina Infantry - 693.
95) DAVIDSON, WILLIAM T. - Co. G, Ninth Alabama Cavalry - 2681.
96) DAVIS, A. - Co. E, First North Carolina Artillery - 2949. Military records show that his name was ALLEN DAVIS and that he served in the First North Carolina Artillery Battalion.
97) DAVIS, J. R. - Co. K, Seventh South Carolina Cavalry - 2759.

98) DAVIS, SAMPSON - Co. E, First Alabama Artillery Battalion - 2294.
99) DE BAR, L. W. - Co. E, Fourteenth South Carolina Infantry - 2568. Military records show that he was carried on military records as Lewis W Debards, L. W. Dabava, L. W. Debarr, L. W. DeBard, L. W. Debard, and L. D. Dubard.
100) DE BRADY, DE YOUNG - C. S. A. - 2713.
101) DEE, PATRICK - Co. L, Twenty-Second North Carolina Infantry - 2856.
102) DIXON, J. J. - Norwood's Florida Home Guards - 1465. Military records show that his name was JOHN J DIXON.
103) DRUMMON, JAMES - Co. B, Fourteenth South Carolina Infantry - 2471. Military records show that his names was JAMES DRUMMOND.
104) DUDLEY, J. - C. S. A. - 725.
105) DUFF, B. R. - Sturdivant's Virginia Artillery Co. - 2639.
106) DUFF, JAMES A. - Co. D. Fourth Virginia Artillery - 2783.
107) DUGGANS, J. R. - Co. M, Twenty-First North Carolina Infantry - 900. Military records show that his name was J R DUGGINS.
108) DUGGINS, ROBERT - Co. F, Ninth Virginia Infantry - 3052.
109) DULLINS, P. E. L. - Co. L, First South Carolina Infantry - 2712.
110) DUNLAP, J. S. - Co. ER, Twelfth South Carolina Infantry - 841.
111) DURISCOE, C. L. - Co. D, Fourteenth South Carolina Infantry - 664.
112) DURN, PERRY - Co. F. First South Carolina Heavy Artillery - 3089.
113) EARLY, H. F. - Co. D, Eleventh Georgia Infantry - 673.
114) EARLY, S. D. - Co. E, Fourth Virginia Heavy Artillery - 3031.
115) ECKARD, CYRUS - Co. C, Twenty-Eighth North Carolina Infantry - no number given. Military records show that his name also appeared as Cyrus Eckart, Cyrus Eckhardt, and C Eckard on various rolls.
116) EDWARDS, J. H. - Co. F, Sixteenth North Carolina Infantry - 2950. Military records show that his name was JOHN H EDWARDS.
117) EDWARDS, T. D. - C. S. A. - 1643.
118) ELDRIDGE, D, - Co. H, Thirty-Seventh North Carolina Infantry - 182. His name appears as David Eldreth on a small number of rolls.

119) ELLIOTT, JOSEPH T. - Co. B, Twenty-Second North Carolina Infantry - 2845.
120) ELLIS, JOHN - Co. H, Fourth Texas Infantry - 703. His name appears as J W Ellis and J M Ellis on a small number of military records.
121) ELLMORE, JONAS - Co. C, Fifty-Fifth North Carolina Infantry - 3066. Military records show that his name was JONAS ELMORE.
122) EMERSON, JOHN R - Co. E, Twenty-Sixth North Carolina Infantry - 773. His name appears as J R Emerson and J B Emerson on a number of military records.
123) ENSTER, SAMUEL - Co. M, Twenty-Third North Carolina Infantry - 2784.
124) ESTIS, J. M. - Co. A, Twenty-Second North Carolina Infantry - 2785.
125) EVANS, JAY - Co. G, Twenty-First South Carolina Infantry - 1841.
126) FARMER, J L - Co. D, First South Carolina Infantry - 2941. Military records show that he served in the First (Regular) South Carolina Infantry.
127) FARMER, WILLIAM M - Co. H, Twenty-Fourth Georgia Infantry - 1838.
128) FERGUSON, G. N. - C. S. A. - 210.
129) FEW, M. D. - Co. E, Twenty-Fifth North Carolina Infantry - 2616.
130) FISHER, ULYSSES - Co. C, Sixth Louisiana Infantry - 843. His name also appears on various unit rolls as V W Fisher, U W Fisher, W W Fisher, V W Fischer, W A Fisher, and W W Fischer.
131) FLEMMING, JOHN E - Co. I, Fifty-Ninth Alabama Infantry - 2960. A small number of records show his name as John E Fleming.
132) FLETCHER, CHARLES - Co. K, Eighth Virginia Infantry - 3083.
133) FLOWERS, FRANKLIN - Co. A, First Tennessee Heavy Artillery - 2125. Military records show that his name was Benjamin Franklin Flowers.
134) FOUST, JACOB - Co. B, Twenty-Seventh North Carolina Infantry - 2612.
135) FOWLER, S. B. - Co. E. Fifty-Seventh Virginia Infantry - 2703.
136) FOWLER, T. - Co. D, Fifty-Third Virginia Infantry - no number given.

137) FOX, JAMES F. - Co. F, Fourteenth North Carolina Infantry - 704.

138) FRANKLIN, R L. - Co. K, Thirteenth South Carolina Infantry - 3051.

139) FREEMAN, JOHN - Co. K, Third South Carolina Artillery - 2952. Military records show that he served in the First South Carolina (Regular) Infantry. There was no such unit as the Third South Carolina Artillery.

140) FULK, JOHN W - Co. I, Twenty-Second North Carolina Infantry - 2772. Military records show that his name was JOHN W. FULKE.

141) GAMMON, H. J. - Co. H, Thirty-Eighth Virginia Infantry - 2961.

142) GARDNER, F. M. - Co., E, Twelfth South Carolina Infantry - 668. Military records show that his name was FRANCIS MARION GARDNER.

143) GARRETT, JAMES - Co. C, Fifty-Ninth Georgia Infantry - 683.

144) GAY, N. - C. S. A. - 3044. Military records show that his name was NATHANIEL GAY. He served in Co. B, Forty-Seventh North Carolina Infantry.

145) GEISLER, JAMES W - Co. K, Twenty-Sixth Tennessee Infantry - 3071. Military records show that his name was JAMES H. GEISLER.

146) GIBBS, GEORGE F. - Pegram's Virginia Battery - 2504.

147) GICE, C. M. - Co. M, First Alabama Cavalry - 2542.

148) GILDER, J. A. - Co. B, Fourteenth South Carolina Infantry - 731. Military records show that his name was GILFORD A GILDER. His name appears as G A Gilder and J A Gilden on a small number of unit rolls.

149) GILES, RICHARD - Co. C, First Virginia Infantry - 815.

150) GILLILAND, ABNER - Co. C, Eighteenth South Carolina Infantry - 3042.

151) GILMORE, HENRY J. - Co. H, Fourth Virginia Infantry - no number given. His name appears as Henry G Gilmore on a small number of records. His remains were removed to some unnamed location.

152) GLASGOW, J. N. - Co. G, Fourteenth South Carolina Infantry - 2998. Military records show that his name was JAMES N GLASGOW.

153) GLOVER, JOHN R. - Co. C, First South Carolina Infantry - 2838. He served in the First (Provisional Army) South Carolina Infantry.

154) GOOD, A. H. - Co. I, Seventh Virginia Infantry - 1114. Military records show that his name was ALBERT H. GOOD.
155) GOODING, THOMAS - Co. D, Eleventh South Carolina Infantry - 2589. His name also appears on a small number of records as T. GOODING.
156) GORDON, J HARVEY - Co. F, Thirty-Fifth North Carolina Infantry - 2796.
157) GOTTE, JACOB - C. S. A. - 3064. Military records show that he was a member of Co. D, First South Carolina Artillery. His name is also shown on regimental rolls as Jacob Gotti and Jacob Gottie.
158) GOUCH, CHARLES A. - Third Battalion Washington Louisiana Artillery - 700. He was a member of the Third Company, Washington Louisiana Artillery Battalion. His name appears on a small number of rolls as S. G. Gouch and S A Gouch.
159) GRADY, C. M. - Co. C. Twenty-First South Carolina Infantry - 3021.
160) GRADY, W. S. - Co. I, First North Carolina Cavalry - 2480.
161) GREEN, B. M. - Co. G, Fifth Texas Infantry - 1933.
162) GREEN, MASTON - Co. H, Forty-Fourth North Carolina Infantry - 2737.
163) GREGORY, _____ - C. S. A. - no number given.
164) GRIFFIN, D. T. - Co. C, Fifty-Fifth North Carolina Infantry - 990. Military records show that his name was DAVID T GRIFFIN.
165) GRIFFIN, SILAS - Co. A, Fourteenth South Carolina Militia - 2935. Military records show that his name was WILLIAM B GRIFFIN.
166) GRIFFIN, WILLIAM B. - Co. H, Seventh North Carolina Infantry - no number given. Military records show that he served in the Seventeenth North Carolina Infantry..
167) GRIFFITHS, F. O. - Co. A, Sixty-Third Georgia Infantry - 802.
168) GRIGG, WILLIAM - Co. F, Thirty-Eighth North Carolina Infantry - 656.
169) GRUMBLES, PERRY B. - Co. B, Fourth Texas Infantry - 803.
170) HAIR, W. J. - Co. I, First South Carolina Infantry - 858. He served in the First (Provisional Army) South Carolina Infantry.
171) HALL, JOSEPH T. - Co. A, Forty-Seventh North Carolina Infantry - 2899.
172) HALL, P. P. - Co. K, Twelfth South Carolina Infantry - 745.
173) HAMILL, A. - Co. H, Eleventh North Carolina Infantry - 829 Military records show that his name was A. R. HAMEL. His name appears on a small number of regimental records as A Harmel, A.

Hamel, and A. Hammel.

174) HAMMOCK,. J. H. - Co. B, Fifty-Ninth Virginia Infantry - 2995. Military records show that his name was JOSEPH H HAMMOCK. His name appears on a small number of records as J. H. Hammocks and J. H. Hamocks.

175) HANNAH, E. B. - Co. G, Forty-Fifth Georgia Infantry - 680.

176) HARMON, DAVID - Co. D, Twenty-Sixth North Carolina Infantry - 3007.

177) HARRIS, E. J. - Co. D, Sixth South Carolina Reserves - 2936.

178) HARTFORD, JOHN - Co. __, Florida Home Guards - 2303.

179) HARVEY, A. J. - Co. G, Seventeenth South Carolina Infantry - 2411. Military records show that his name was A JEFFERS HERVEY. A small number of records show his name as A G Harvey and Jefferson Harvey.

180) HARVILLE, WILLIAM - Co. I, Thirty-Third North Carolina Infantry - 3128.

181) HASSEL, _____ - C. S. A. - no number given.

182) HASSELL, JOHN W - Co. I, Thirty-Eighth North Carolina Infantry - 2927.

183) HAZLEGROVE, A. S. - Co. I, Fifteenth Virginia Infantry - no number given. Military records show that his name was A. S. HAZELGROVE.

184) HELM, A. J. - Co. F, Forty-Eighth North Carolina Infantry - 3033.

185) HELTON, ALFRED - Co. A, Twenty-Third North Carolina Infantry - 2901. Military records show that his name was ALFRED F. HELTON.

186) HENSON, W. B. - Co. E, Fifty-Second North Carolina Infantry - 699. Miscellaneous Confederate records show that he served in Co. I, Sixty-Second North Carolina Infantry.

187) HILL, J. H. - Co. C, First South Carolina Rifles - 2647

188) HILL, JESSE - Co., G, Thirty-Second North Carolina Infantry - 2876.

189) HODGES, ALEXANDER - Co. E, Thirty-Eighth North Carolina Infantry - 3124.

190) HOFFMAN, _____ - C. S. A. - 156.

191) HOGAN, W. P. - Co. A, Fifty-Third Virginia Infantry - no number given. Military records show that his name was WALKER P HOGAN.

192) HOLLERFIELD, JACOB - Co. G, First South Carolina Infantry - 2735. Military records show that his name was JACOB HOLLINGIELD. He served in the First (Regular) South Carolina Infantry.

193) HOLLIBINTON, A. J. - Co. M, Eighth South Carolina Infantry - 842. Military records show that his name was J J HOLLIBURTON.
194) HOLLINGSWORTH, WILLIAM J. - Co. I, Fifteenth Georgia Infantry - 712.
195) HORTON, NOAH C - Co. C, First Alabama Artillery Battalion - 2254.
196) HOWARD, J. C. - Co. H, Sixth North Carolina Senior Reserves - 2709.
197) HOWELL, HARVEY - Unassigned - 2602.
198) HOWELL, KODER - Co. F, First North Carolina Artillery - 3100.
199) HUDSPETH, JAMES J. - Co. I, Forty-Second Mississippi Infantry - 705. His name also appears on a small number of unit records as J. J. Hogpeth.
200) HUFHAM, WILLIAM F. - Co. E, Eighteenth North Carolina Infantry - 2670. His name appears on small number of unit records as William F. Huffham.
201) HUGHES, JOHN - Co. I, First South Carolina Infantry - 2898. The unit is which he served was the First (Provisional Army) South Carolina Infantry.
202) HULSEY, HENRY - Co. E, Eleventh Georgia Infantry - 681.
203) HUMPHREYS, J. J. - Co. C, Fifty-Eighth Virginia Infantry - 2529.
204) HURLEY, C. C. - Co. C, Fourteenth South Carolina Infantry - 3029.
205) HUTTO, CHARLES - Co. F, Seventeenth South Carolina Infantry - 3041.
206) HUTTO, JOHN - Co. K, Thirteenth South Carolina Infantry - 2620.
207) INGRAHAM, JAMES - Co. I, Fifty-Ninth Alabama Infantry - no number given.
208) IRBINET, ARCHIBALD - Co. A, First South Carolina Militia - 2918.
209) IRVING, A - Co. D, Thirty-Ninth North Carolina Infantry - 3319.
210) IVEY, W G - Co. G, Eleventh North Carolina Infantry - 756 Military records show that his name was WILLIAM G IVEY.
211) JENKINS, CHARLES - Co. D, Sixteenth North Carolina Infantry - 2826. Military records show that his name was CRAVEN JENKINS.
212) JENNINGS, _____ - no unit given - 4451.

213) JENNINGS, M - Co. I, Twenty-Eighth North Carolina Infantry - 147. Military records show that his name was S W JENNINGS but he was also carried on military records as W JENNINGS, J W JENNINGS, and G W JENNINGS.

214) JOHNSON, FLEET - Co. D, Second North Carolina Infantry Battalion - 2914.

215) JOHNSON, M D - Co. A, First South Carolina Infantry - 2873. Military records show that his name was MURDOCK D JOHNSON. He served in the First (Butler's) South Carolina Infantry regiment.

216) JOHNSON, STEPHEN - Co. G, Twenty-Sixth North Carolina Infantry - 2973.

217) JOHNSON, T A - Co. E, Ninth Virginia Infantry - 2907.

218) JOHNSTON, JOHN B - Co. A, First Alabama Artillery Battalion - 2207.

219) JOLLY, _____ - C. S. A. - no number given.

220) JONES, F M - Co. C, Seventeenth South Carolina Infantry - 2510.

221) JONES, J W - Co. H, Forty-Third North Carolina Infantry - 860. Military records show that his name was WESLEY JOWERS. His name appears also as J W Jowers.

222) JONES, MURDOCK - Co. D, Sixty-Fourth Georgia Infantry - 1216.

223) JONES, WILSON - Co. B, Thirty-Eighth North Carolina Infantry - 2662. A number of records show his name as Wesley Jones.

224) JORDAN, J J - Co. ___, First Georgia Infantry - 164. Military records show his name as JOHN S JORDAN. He served in the First (Olmstead's) Georgia Infantry.

225) JOWERS, J W - Co. A, Twenty-Third South Carolina Infantry - 2897.

226) JOYCE, SULLIVAN - Co. A, Forty-Fifth North Carolina Infantry - 708.

227) KAY, ROBERT M - Co. K, First South Carolina Rifles - 2836.

228) KEENEY, SIMPSON - Co. E, Fifty-Eighth North Carolina Infantry - 2569. Military records show that his name was SIMPSON KINEY.

229) KEEP, ERWIN H - Pegram's Virginia Battery - 2966.

230) KEGLEY, W. - Co. K, First Virginia Infantry - 3032. Military records show that his name was WILLIAM KEGLEY.

231) KEISLER, G A - Co. K, Thirteenth South Carolina Infantry - 694.

232) KELLY, JOHN J - Co. D, Fifth Florida Infantry - 2951 His name also appears on a number of military records as J J Kelly, John J Kelley and John Kelly
233) KENNEDY, PATRICK - Co. C, Fifty-Ninth Georgia Infantry - 821.
234) KENNEDY, ROBERT C - Citizen - no number given. Military records show that he served in the First Louisiana (Regular) Infantry and then served in the Confederate Secret Service.
235) KEYSER, W L - C. S. A. - 201.
236) KING, JOHN C - Co. C, Thirty-Eighth North Carolina Infantry - 787.
237) KING, M - Co. G, Forty-Fourth Georgia Infantry - 814.
238) KING, THOMAS J - Co. A, First Alabama Artillery Battalion - 2142.
239) KITE, STEPHEN - Co. G, Seventh North Carolina Infantry - 4447. Military records show that he served in the Seventeenth North Carolina Infantry.
240) KNIGHT, T H - Co.. E, Thirtieth North Carolina Infantry - 2947.
241) KORN, J A - Co. E, Fourteenth South Carolina Militia - 2640 Military records show that his name was J A HORN.
242) LAMBRA, PAUL - Co. B, Fifty-Third Georgia Infantry - 648. Military records show that his name was J A LUMMIUS.
243) LANCASTER, L L - Co. B, Fourteenth South Carolina Cavalry - 2543. Military records show that he served in the Fourteenth South Carolina Militia.
244) LANGDEN, J L - Co. F, First Alabama Artillery Battalion - 1463. Military records show that his name was J L LANSDEN.
245) LAWLESS, J J - Co. L, First Georgia Infantry - 2940.
246) LAWRENCE, IRA L. - Co. I, Thirty-Fifth Georgia Infantry - 819. His name also appears on a number of records as J L Lawrence.
247) LEDFORD, WILLIAM - Co. B, Fifty-Eighth North Carolina Infantry - 2726. Military records show his name as WILLIAM B LEDFORD but his name appears on a number of records as W B Ledford.
248) LEONARD, J D - Co. B, Thirteenth South Carolina Infantry - 670
249) LEONARD, LEVI - Co. I, Thirty-Fifth North Carolina Infantry - 2837. His name also appears on a numbers of records as Levi Leonart.
250) LEROACH, WILLIAM T - Co. A, First South Carolina Infantry - 2903. Military records show his name as WILLIAM

LAROCHE but a number of records show his name as William LaRoche. He served in the First (Regular) South Carolina Infantry.

251) LIGHT, CHARLES - Co. F, Thirty-Eighth Virginia Infantry - 710.

252) LITTEN, GEORGE W - Co. G, Twenty-Ninth Virginia Infantry - 2860.

253) LITTLE, JAMES - Co. B, Twenty-Second Georgia Battalion - 2425. Military records show that his name was JOHN B LITTLE. He originally served in the Cobb Guards Georgia Infantry Battalion and subsequently in the Twenty-Second Georgia Artillery Battalion.

254) LIVINGSTON, JOHN - Co. F, Thirty-Seventh North Carolina Infantry - 146.

255) LOGAN, J M - Co., B, Twenty-Eighth North Carolina Infantry - 762. His name is also shown as G M Logan on a number of records.

256) LOGAN, T C - Co. I, Eighteenth Mississippi Infantry - 849. Military records show that his name was THOMAS C LOGAN.

257) LONG, REUBEN - Co. H, Twenty-Fourth North Carolina Infantry - 3427,

258) LONG, RICHARD - Co. E, Twenty-Second North Carolina Infantry - 2931.

259) LONG, SIMON A - Co. K, Fifth Louisiana Infantry - 854

260) LUNDY, JAMES - Co. C, First South Carolina Artillery - 3006.

261) LYLE, SAMUEL A - Co. E, Fourteenth Virginia Infantry - 3036.

262) LYNCH, GEORGE - Co. D, Tenth Virginia Artillery - 2883

263) MACKLENERY, B C - Co. B, Twenty-Second North Carolina Infantry - 2749. Military records show that his name was B H MC GLAMERY.

264) MARTIN, BRICE A - Co. F, Fifty-Seventh Virginia Infantry - 2530.

265) MARTIN, R M N - C. S. A. - 213.

266) MASSEY, R R - Co. B, Forty-Ninth North Carolina Infantry - 2885. Military records show that his name was R R MASSIE.

267) MASSINGALE, R H - Co. K, Thirty-Eighth North Carolina Infantry - 2815. Military records show that his name was R H MASSINGILL.

268) MATHIS, THOMAS - Co. G, Fourteenth South Carolina Infantry - 2803.

269) MATTHEWS, E - Co. A, First South Carolina Infantry - 691

Records show that he served in the First South Carolina (Provisional Army) Infantry.
270) MATTHEWS, JAMES- Co. E, Thirteenth North Carolina Infantry - 747. Military records show that his name was JAMES MATHEWS. A number of records also refer to him as James M Mathis and James M Mathes.
271) MATTOX, R F - Co. E, Eighteenth Virginia Infantry - 2821 Military records show that his name was RICHARD T MATTOCKS. A number of rolls give his name as K Mattocks, R T Mattocks, and R F Mattoc.
272) MAY, JOHN D - Co. F, Second North Carolina Infantry - 735
273) MAY, WILLIAM H - Co. I, Fifty-Seventh Virginia Infantry - 2988.
274) MC CANN, AUSTIN - Co. E, Fifty-Ninth Virginia Infantry - 2893.
275) MC CARLEY, GREEN - Co. B, Second Mississippi Infantry - 899.
276) MC CARTY, MICHAEL - Co. C, First Virginia Infantry Battalion - 2810.
277) MC CLELLAN, _____ - C. S. A. - no number given.
278) MC CONIEL, R T - Co. G, Eleventh Georgia Infantry - 709. A number of records also give his name as R T McConniel.
279) MC CURLEY, DAVID - Co. E, Forty-Seventh Alabama Infantry - 851.
280) MC CURRY, JOHN S - Co. I, Fourteenth South Carolina Infantry - 855.
281) MC DERMITH, ALEXANDER H - Co. C, First Alabama Artillery Battalion - 1999. Military records show his name as ALEXANDER H MC DERMITH.
282) MC DONALD, CHRISTOPHER - Co. K, Thirty-Eighth North Carolina Infantry - 2685.
283) MC DONNELL, WILLIAM - Co. C, Sixth North Carolina Infantry - 696.
284) MC DOWELL, D C - Co. K, Twenty-Fourth Virginia Infantry - 707. Military records show that his name was DAVID E MC DANIEL. His name is also given on a number of records as D E MC DANIEL and D C MC DANIEL.
285) MC GILL, JOHN - Co. K, Thirty-Eighth North Carolina Infantry - 667.
286) MC HENRY, ALCANA - Co. B, Eleventh Mississippi Infantry - 820. Military records show his name as ALKANA MC HENRY. A small number of records also give his name as A McHenry.

287) MC KENZIE, H T - Co. B, Twenty-Second Georgia Battalion - 2862. Military records show his name as T H MC KENZIE

288) MC KETHAN, J A - Co. L, First South Carolina Infantry - 734. A small number of records also show his name as J A McKeathan. He served in the First South Carolina (Regular Army) Infantry.

289) MC RILEY, SAMUEL - Co. F, Fifty-Fifth North Carolina Infantry - 730. Military records show that his name was SAMUEL MC NEILLY.

290) MC VIKER, WILLIAM - Co. K, Thirty-Eighth North Carolina Infantry - 3057.

291) MEDLIN, F M - Co. I, Forty-Seventh North Carolina Infantry - 2554.

292) MEYER, J H - Co. F, First South Carolina Artillery - 2682.

293) MICHAEL, J W - Co. A, Third North Carolina Infantry - 3022. Military records show that he served in the Third North Carolina Reserve Infantry.

294) MIDDLETON, H P - Co. G, Forty-Fourth Alabama Infantry - 675.

295) MILBANK, W J - Co. K, Twelfth South Carolina Infantry - 2560.

296) MILLARD, JOHN J - Co. K, Sixty-Sixth North Carolina Cavalry - 2582. The unit in which he served was the Sixty-Sixth North Carolina Infantry.

297) MILLS, GILBERT - Co. K,. Fifty-Sixth North Carolina Infantry - 2614. A small number of records also show his name as Gilbert Miles.

298) MITCHELL, WILLIAM L - Co. D, Eleventh Georgia Infantry - 749. A small number of records show his name as WILLIAM MITCHAEL.

299) MIXON, RICHARD - Co. H, Fifty-First Georgia Infantry - 665.

300) MODLIN, ALPHA - Co. F, Seventh North Carolina Infantry - 4450.

301) MONTGOMERY, W - C. S. A. - 214.

302) MOORE, G E - Co. G, First Tennessee Infantry - 852. Military records show that his name was GEORGE E MOORE. He served in the First (Field's) Tennessee Infantry regiment.

303) MOORE, M P - Co. H, Second North Carolina Infantry - 935.

304) MORAN, J A - Co. G, Twenty-Sixth North Carolina Infantry - 811. Military records show that his name was JOHN A MORAN. A small number of records also give his name as John T Moran.

305) MORRIS, D C - Co. C, Thirty-Fifth North Carolina Infantry - 2526. Military records show that his name was DAVID C MORRIS.
306) MORRIS, JAMES - Co. H, Fourteenth North Carolina Infantry - 2769.
307) MORRIS, JOHN S - Co. A, Fourteenth South Carolina Cavalry - 2588. He served in the Fourteenth South Carolina Militia.
308) MORRISON, ANGUS - Co. A, First South Carolina infantry - 2774. He served in the First (Regular) South Carolina Infantry.
309) MOSES, MARTIN F - Co. A, First North Carolina Infantry - 216. Military records show that his name was Martin F Moser.
310) MULL, J H - Co. F, Eleventh Georgia Infantry - 718. Military records show that his name was JACOB M F MULL. His name also appears on a small number of records as J M F Marl and J H Mail.
311) MUNN, C D - Co. K, Thirty-Fourth North Carolina Infantry - 2896. Military records show that his name was CALVIN D MUNN.
312) MURDOCK, J G - Co. F, Fifty-Eighth North Carolina Infantry - 2926.
313) MURPHY, E E - Co. E, Fifteenth South Carolina Infantry - 863. Military records show that his name was ENOCH E MURPHY.
314) MURRAY, JOHN - Co. C, Tenth Louisiana Infantry - 273
315) MURRAY, MICHAEL - Co. H, Fifth Virginia Infantry - 2985.
316) NAKEEP, DANIEL - Co. K, Fifty-Seventh North Carolina Infantry - 812. Military records show that his name was DANIEL KANUP. A small number of records give his name as A P Kanup.
317) NIX, JACOB - C. S. A. - 3050.
318) NORWOOD, JOSEPH J - Co. E - Forty-Seventh North Carolina Infantry - 2892.
319) NOWELL, J HENRY - Co. F, Forty-Seventh North Carolina Infantry - 2843.
320) O'CONNER, PATRICK - Co. C, First South Carolina Artillery - 2613. A small number of records give his name as Patrick O'Connell and Patrick Connell.
321) OLIVIA, P D - Co. E, Fourth Louisiana Infantry 2164. Military records show that his name was P OLIVE.
322) OTIS, MARTIN - Co. ___, First South Carolina Militia - 2978. Military records show that he served in the Third South Carolina Reserve Infantry.
323) OVERFELT, R - Co. F, Fifty-Seventh Virginia Infantry - 3016.

324) OWENS, A P - Co. E, First South Carolina Infantry - 717. Military records show that his name was ALBERT P OWENS. He served in the First (Regular) South Carolina Infantry.
325) OWENS, W H - Co. E, Fiftieth North Carolina Infantry - 2771. Military records show his name was WILLIAM H OWENS.
326) PARKER, JAMES - Co. F, Third South Carolina Artillery - 2797.
327) PARRISH, JAMES M - Co. C, Forty-Eighth Alabama Infantry - 684.
328) PARTON, JAMES W - Co. H, Forty-Seventh North Carolina Infantry - 2872.
329) PATTERSON, NEAL - Co. ___, McDougald's North Carolina Infantry - 2818. Military records show that his name was NEILL PATTERSON.
330) PEASE, JOHN - C. S. A. - 689.
331) PEGRAM, JOSEPH E - Co. K, Fifty-Second North Carolina Infantry - 727.
332) PERRY, H H - Co. E, Sixteenth Georgia Infantry - 944.
333) PERRY, ROBERT - Co. B, Forty-Seventh North Carolina Infantry - 2462.
334) PERSIL, L - Co. A, Thirty-Eighth North Carolina Infantry - 985.
335) PETTY, WILLIAM E - Co. B, First Tennessee Artillery - no number given. A note indicates that his body was removed to Paducah, Kentucky.
336) PHELPS, DAVID - Co. A, First Alabama Artillery Battalion, 2074.
337) PHILLIPS, E W - Co. B, Thirty-Ninth Virginia Infantry - 3065. Military records show that his name was E W Phillippi..
338) PHILLIPS, RICHMOND - Co. B, Forty-Seventh North Carolina Infantry - 3069.
339) PHIPPS, JOHN - Co. F, Twenty-Second North Carolina Infantry - 3019. Military records show that his name was Joseph Phipps.
340) PLEMMONS, W C - Co. F, Eleventh Georgia Infantry - 746.
341) POLLARD, J W - Co. B, First Virginia Artillery - 3056.
342) POOR, JOHN W - Co. G, First South Carolina Artillery - 3024. Military records show that his name was JAMES M POOR.
343) PORTER, JOHN E - Co. ___, Second Texas Cavalry - 217
344) POWELL, H A - Co. F, Thirty-Fourth North Carolina Infantry - 732. Military records show that his name was ANDREW J POWELL. His name also appears on a number of records as A Jackson Powell and Jackson Powell.

345) POWELL, THOMAS - Co. __, Second Georgia Infantry - 2808. Military records show that his name was JAMES M POWELL. A number of records also show his name as J W Powell and S W Powell.
346) POWER, T B - Co. A, Orr's South Carolina Rifles - no number given. Unit officially the First South Carolina Rifles.
347) PRATT, THOMAS - Co. K, Forty-Fifth North Carolina Infantry - 682.
348) PRESTWOOD, E - Co. F, Twenty-Sixth North Carolina Infantry - 2994. Military records show his name as ERVAND PRESWOOD. A number of records show his name as E Presswood.
349) PRIDGEN, JOHN O - Co. __, Wilmington Railroad Guards - 2943. Military records show that he served in McDugald's North Carolina Infantry Company.
350) PROCTOR, THOMAS D - Co. A, Forty-Fifth North Carolina Infantry - .792
351) PUGH, ELI - Co. D, Fiftieth Virginia Infantry - 758.
352) QUACKENBUSH, J G - Co. E, Twenty-Second North Carolina Infantry - 2780.
353) RAINEY, JAMES - Co. D, Fourteenth Georgia Infantry - 2917.
354) RANDLEMAN, A T - Co. F, Twenty-Eight North Carolina Infantry - 677. Military records show that his name was AUGUST T RANDLEMAN.
355) RANSOM, JOHN H - Co. E, Twentieth Georgia Infantry - 822.
356) RAPE, S M - Co. D, Thirty-Seventh North Carolina Infantry - 163.
357) RAST, WILLIAM R - Fourteenth South Carolina Militia - 2781
358) RAY, A J - Co. D, Thirty-Fourth North Carolina Infantry - 711. Military records show that his name was JOSEPH A RAY.
359) REDDIX, JAMES - Co. A, Fifty-Eighth North Carolina Infantry - 2962.
360) REDMAN, T O - Co. C, Fortieth Virginia Infantry - no number given Military records show his name as THOMAS C REDMAN.
361) REESE, SAMUEL W - Co. B, Third Virginia Infantry - 2968.
362) REEVES, SANDERS - Co. K, Second North Carolina Infantry - 2745.
363) RESNER, HENRY - Coit's Virginia Battery - 2993. Military records show that he served in Wright's Virginia Heavy Artillery Company.

364) RICHARDSON, ROBERT N - Co. K, Fifty-Third Georgia Infantry - 753.
365) RIGGS, AUGUSTUS L - Co. K, Second Mississippi Infantry - 952.
366) RIGGS, GEORGE W - Co. C, Forty-Second Mississippi Infantry - 886.
367) ROBERSON, MC G - Co. F, Seventh North Carolina Infantry - 4446. The unit in which he served was the Seventeenth North Carolina Infantry.
368) ROBERTS, JOHN W - Co. G, Eleventh Georgia Infantry - 857. Military records show that his name was JOHN A W ROBERTS.
369) ROBERTS, JOHN M - Co. A, Forty-Fifth Georgia Infantry - 2841.
370) ROBERTS, WILLIAM D - Co. D, Fifty-Third Tennessee Infantry - 3254.
371) ROBERTSON, T C - Co. I, Eighteenth Mississippi Infantry - 865. Military records show that his name was THOMAS C ROBERTSON.
372) ROBINETT, L G - Co. G, Thirty-Seventh North Carolina Infantry - 766. Military records show that his name was LAWSON G ROBINETT.
373) ROBINSON, JAMES - Co. D, Sixteenth North Carolina Infantry - 2925. Military records show his name as JAMES L ROBERTSON.. He also appears in a number of records as J L Robberson.
374) ROGERS, J B - Co. D, Thirteenth North Carolina Infantry - 2657. Military records show that his name was JOHN B ROGERS. He also appears in a number of records as John B Rodgers and J B Rodgers.
375) ROGERSON, DAVID L - Co. F, Seventh North Carolina Infantry - 4445. The unit in which he served was the Seventeenth North Carolina Infantry.
376) ROLADES, J G - Co. K, Forty-Eighth Alabama Infantry - 695.
377) ROLAND, CHARLES - Co. K, Thirty-Eighth North Carolina Infantry - 2915.
378) ROLLINS, THOMAS - Co. C, First South Carolina Infantry - 3048. Records show that he served in the First (Regular) South Carolina Infantry regiment.
379) RONNINGER, J - Co. G, Second North Carolina Infantry - 741.

380) ROYAL, WILLIAM H - Co. B, Thirty-Eighth North Carolina Infantry - 2939. A small number of records show his name as William B Royal.
381) RUSSELL, A - Co. K, Fifty-Third North Carolina Infantry - 862. Military records show his name as ABEDNAGO RUSSELL.
382) RYLE, A J - Co. B, Fourteenth Georgia Infantry - 767. Military records show his name as ADAM J RYLE.
383) SALE, WILLIAM AUGUSTUS - Co. G, First South Carolina Infantry - 902. Military records show that he served in the First (Provisional Army) South Carolina Infantry.
384) SAPP, F M - Co. F, Eighth Alabama Infantry - 828.
385) SAVAGE, BRAXTON - Co. B, Fifty-Third Georgia Infantry - 671.
386) SAWYER, ROBINSON A - Co. H, Thirty-Third North Carolina Infantry - 145.
387) SAWYER, WILLIAM B - Co. B, Thirty-Second North Carolina Infantry - 243.
388) SCHRADER, SAMUEL E - Co. K, Twenty-Fifth Virginia Infantry - 759.
389) SCOTT, HENRY - Co. A, Fifty-Fifth North Carolina Infantry - 723.
390) SEARS, ROBERT - Co., B, Thirty-Fifth North Carolina Infantry - 3053. His name appears on a small number of records as Barb Sears.
391) SHARP, JOHN W - Co. A, Thirty-Fourth North Carolina Infantry - 3034. Military records show his name as JAMES W SHARP.
392) SHAVER, WILLIAM - Co. ___, Fifteenth South Carolina Infantry - 2782.
393) SHAW, HUGH - Co. E, Forty-Seventh North Carolina Infantry - 2991.
394) SHORE, WILLIAM L - Co. D, Twenty-First North Carolina Infantry - 2955.
395) SHORT, ROBERT - Pegram's Virginia Battery - 2963. Military records show his name as BENJAMIN F SHORTT.
396) SHULER, DANIEL M - Co. C, Fourteenth South Carolina Militia - 2707.
397) SHUTTLESWORTH, SAMUEL - Co. C, First Alabama Artillery Battalion - 2030.
398) SIEGEL, N M - Co. A, Twenty-Third North Carolina Infantry - 3321. Military records show his name as NOAH W SEAGLE. His name also appears on some records as N W Seagel.
399) SIMON, W - Co. K, Fifty-Seventh Virginia Infantry - 823.

400) SIMPSON, _____ - C. S. A. - 4449.
401) SIMPSON, RICHARD - Co. C, Thirty-Eighth North Carolina Infantry - 3093.
402) SKELTON, ALEX - Co. A, Fifty-Third Virginia Infantry - 953.
403) SLAUGHTER, SELIM - Co. D, Fifty-Third Virginia Infantry - 2572.
404) SMITH, A M - Co. B, First Tennessee Heavy Artillery - 2427. Military records show that his name was ALONZO M SMITH. He also appears on a number of records as A H Smith, A Smith, A W Smith, and Alonzo H Smith.
405) SMITH, GEORGE A - Co. H, Twentieth North Carolina Infantry - 776.
406) SMITH, HENRY - Co. H, Forty-Fifth Georgia Infantry - 1042.
407) SMITH, J A - Co. D, Fifty-Seventh Georgia Infantry - 777.
408) SMITH, J H - Co. D, Twelfth South Carolina Infantry - 733.
409) SMITH, MAJOR - C. S. A. - 234.
410) SMITH, WILLIAM A - Co. B, Eleventh North Carolina Infantry - 875.
411) SMITH, WILLIAM B - Co. A, First Alabama Artillery Battalion - 2092.
412) SMITH, ZEMERICK N - Co. E, Sixteenth North Carolina Cavalry - 2701. Records show that he served in the Sixteenth North Carolina Cavalry Battalion.
413) SNOW, JESSE L - Co. L, First South Carolina Infantry - 2770 He served in the First (Provisional Army) South Carolina Infantry.
414) SOLLER, R E A - Co. K, Eighteenth North Carolina Infantry - 864.
415) SPROULES, F J - Co. A, First South Carolina Infantry - 685. Military records show that his name was F J SPROULE. A number of records also identify him as F J SPRAWLS and J SPRAWLS. He served in the First (McCreary's) South Carolina Infantry regiment.
416) STATON, MALACHI - Co. D, Thirty-Seventh North Carolina Infantry - 791.
417) STEELEY, S - Co. K. Seventh North Carolina Infantry - 674. Military records show that his name was THOMAS STALEY.
418) STELLING, HASSAN - Co. F, Twenty-Sixth North Carolina Infantry - 827.
419) STEPHENS, C A T - Co. K, Ninth Georgia Infantry - 726.
420) STEVENSON, JAMES M - Thirty-Sixth North Carolina Infantry - removed. His remains were removed to Wilmington, North Carolina.

421) STILL, ISAAC, - Co. A, Fourteenth South Carolina Militia - 2805.
422) STILL, THOMAS E - Co. B, Fourteenth South Carolina Militia - 2637.
423) STOKES, B B - Co. B, First Tennessee Artillery - 1630.
424) STONE, GREEN P - Co. I, Nineteenth Mississippi Infantry - 2934.
425) STOWE, J N - Co. H, Twenty-Third North Carolina Infantry - 735.
426) STREET, P S - Co. I, Eleventh North Carolina Infantry - 797. Military records show that his name was PINCKNEY S STRUIT.
427) STRICKLAND, HENRY - Co. D, Twenty-Sixth North Carolina Infantry - 3005.
428) STROMAN, A - Co. E, Fourteenth South Carolina Infantry - 2665. Records show that he served in the Fourteenth South Carolina Militia.
429) STRUM, G B - Co. D, Fourteenth South Carolina Infantry - 2809. Military records show that his name was GEORGE B STROM.
430) SULLIVAN, JAMES V - Co. H, Tenth Alabama Infantry - 2953.
431) SUTHARD, WILLIAM R - Co. I, Fifty-Seventh Virginia Infantry - 2811.
432) SWALT, SIMEON O - Co. C, Fifteenth South Carolina Infantry - 706. Military records show that his name was SIMPSON OSWALT. A number of records also show his name as Simon Oswalt.
433) SWEETSER, THEODORE - Co. ___, First South Carolina Infantry - 937.
434) TEMPLETON, H B - Co. B, Fourteenth South Carolina Militia - 2929.
435) TEYSON, _____ - C. S. A. - no number given.
436) THOMAS, J M - Co. A, Eighteenth North Carolina Infantry - 2842.
437) THOMAS, WILLIAM - Co. I, Twenty-Seventh Alabama Infantry - 2767.
438) THOMPSON, H F - Co. B, Forty-Eighth Virginia Infantry - 798. Military records show his name as H F THOMSON.
439) THOMPSON, S M - Twelfth Texas Cavalry - 1817. Military records show his name as SAMUEL M THOMPSON.
440) TIDWELL, CLARK - Gist Guard South Carolina Heavy Artillery Company - 2748. A small number of records show his name as J S Tidwell and J S A Tidwell.

441) TILLY, WILLIAM - Co. D, Fourteenth South Carolina Militia - 2953. Military records show his name as WILLIAM TILLEY.
442) TIMBERLAKE, G W - Co. A, Third North Carolina Infantry - 754. Military records show his name as GEORGE W TIMBERLAKE. His name also appears as J W Timberlake on a small number of records.
443) TINDALL, H F - Co. I, Fifth South Carolina Cavalry - 2679.
444) TISON, WILLIAM L - Co. H, Ninth Georgia Infantry. - 764.
445) TITTERTON, SAMUEL D - Co. F, Seventh North Carolina Infantry - 4448.
446) TOLAN, S D - Co. E, Fifty-Ninth Virginia Infantry - no number given. Military records show his names as SAMUEL D TOLER. His name is also shown as Samuel D Towler, Samuel D Tolen, and Samuel D Tolar on a small number of records.
447) TORRINGTON, J - Fourth Maryland Light Artillery Company - 2971. Military records show his name as JOHN TORRINGTON
448) TOWLER, J E - Co. I, Forty-First Alabama Infantry - 2703.
449) TOWNSEND, GEORGE - Co. E, Thirty-Seventh North Carolina Infantry - 4153.
450) TRAITOR, WILLIAM - Co. I, Twentieth Georgia Infantry - 936. His name also appears on records as William Traytor, W Traitor, W F Traitor, and W W T Traitor.
451) TREXLER, J J - Co. A, Eighteenth South Carolina Militia - 2680.
452) TROUT, JOHN O - Co. C, Fifth Virginia Infantry - removed.
453) TURNER, JOHN - Co. A, First Alabama Artillery Battalion - 2172.
454) TURNHAM, THOMAS J - Co. C, Fifty-Ninth Alabama Infantry - 1786.
455) TUTT, JOHN - Co. A, Jeff Davis Mississippi Cavalry Legion - no number given.
456) TYRE, W B - Co. G, Thirteenth Virginia Cavalry - 2987. Military records show that his name was WILLIAM B TRYE.
457) TYSON, W T - Co. E, Thirty-Eighth North Carolina Infantry - 687.
458) UNKNOWN - C.S.A. - 66.
459) UNKNOWN - C.S.A - 68.
460) UNKNOWN - C.S.A. - 666.
461) UNKNOWN - C.S.A. - 672.
462) UNKNOWN - C.S.A. - 4432.
463) VANDERGRIFF, JOSEPH - Co. C, Tenth Louisiana Infantry - 721.

464) VARN, HANGFORD D - Co. K, Fourteenth South Carolina Militia - 2753.
465) VAUGHN, A G - Co. B, Tenth Georgia Cavalry - 2638. Military records show his name as G A VAUGHN.
466) VAUGHN, WILLIAM L - Co. F, Thirty-Fourth North Carolina Infantry - 3023.
467) VENDRICK, J A - Co. H, Twenty-Seventh North Carolina Infantry - 2652. A small number of records also show his name as J A Vendricke.
468) VENSON, W J - Co. E, First Alabama Artillery - 2187. Military records show his name as WILLIAM J VENSON.
469) WADSWORTH, E W - Co. I, Thirty-Fifth North Carolina Infantry - 2621. Military records show his name as ELI W WADSWORTH
470) WALKER, J C L - Co. G, Twenty-Eighth Georgia Siege Artillery Battalion - 2676. Records show that he served in the Twenty-Seventh Georgia Artillery Battalion.
471) WALKER, LEE - C. S. A. - 167
472) WALLACE, WILLIAM - Co. A, Forty-Sixth North Carolina Infantry - 3011.
473) WARD, W H - Co. H, Forty-Seventh North Carolina Infantry - 2970.
474) WARRICK, W P - Co. C, Twelfth South Carolina Infantry - 678.
475) WATKINS, WILLIAM H - Co. G, Forty-Seventh North Carolina Infantry - 3105.
476) WATSON, T J - Co. C, First Alabama Artillery Battalion - 1607. A small number o records refer to him as J J Watson.
477) WAYNE, FRANCIS A - Co. L, First South Carolina Infantry - 2747. Records show that he served in the First (Provisional Army) South Carolina Infantry regiment.
478) WEATHEBY, J M - Co. A, First South Carolina Infantry - 774. Military records show that he served in the First (McCreary's) South Carolina Infantry and that his name was J M WEATHERBEE.
479) WEBB, JOHN H - Co. D, Tenth Georgia Cavalry - 2916. Military records show that his name was JOHN N WEBB.
480) WEBB, LEVI - Co. K, Eighth Florida Infantry - 2992.
481) WHEEY, J A - Co. H, Twelfth South Carolina Infantry - 669. Military records show his name as J A WHERRY.
482) WHITE, E - Co. E, Thirteenth South Carolina Infantry - 654.
483) WHITE, FRANKLIN - Co. G, Sixty-Seventh North Carolina Infantry - 2875.

484) WHITEHURST, _____ - C. S. A. - no number given. Miscellaneous records show that his name was L WHITEHURST.

485) WHITING, WILLIAM H C - Major-General, C. S. A. - removed. Records show that his body was removed to Wilmington, North Carolina.

486) WILKINSON, GEORGE - Co. D, Fourteenth Virginia infantry - 2570.

487) WILLIAMS, _____ - C. S. A. - 839.

488) WILLIAMS, C D - Co. E, Thirty-Fifth North Carolina Infantry - 3389. Military records show his name as D C WILLIAMS.

489) WILLIAMS, R F - Co. K, Thirty-Seventh North Carolina Infantry - 801. Military records show his name as KILLIS F WILLIAMS.

490) WILLIAMS, S - C. S. A. - 200.

491) WILLIS, BILLY - Co. D, Deneal's Choctaw Indian Regiment - 2758.

492) WILLIS, JAMES P - Co. A, Eight Tennessee Infantry - 2758.

493) WILSON, DAVID - Co. D, Eleventh Georgia infantry - 831.

494) WILSON, G S - Co. K, Twenty-Second North Carolina Infantry - 2813. Military records show that his name was GEORGE S WILSON.

495) WILSON, J E - Co. K, Twenty-Second North Carolina Infantry - 2804. Military records show that his name was JAMES E WILSON.

496) WILSON, JOHN W - Co. E, Fifty-Fifth North Carolina Infantry - 2798.

497) WILSON, NATHANIEL - Co. ___, Eighth Tennessee Infantry - 2789.

498) WINN, WILLIAM D - Chisholm's Florida Home Guards - 785. Records show that he served in Norwood's Florida Home Guard Company. A small number of records refer to him as William D Wynn.

499) WINSTON, HENRY M - Co. F, Forty-Fifth North Carolina Infantry - 785. Military records show that his name was HENRY M WINSOR.

500) WOLF, HENRY F - Co. B, Thirteenth North Carolina Infantry - 658. A small number of records identify him as Henry Wolfe.

501) WOOD, D C C - Co. C, Twenty-Sixth Tennessee Infantry - 2786. He is also referred to as D C Wood in a small number of records.

502) WOOD, WILLIAM - Co. D, Eleventh North Carolina Infantry - 838.
503) WOOD, WILLIAM H - Co. B, Forty-Seventh North Carolina Infantry - 2768.
504) WOODALL, A G - Co. D, Twenty-Fourth North Carolina Infantry - 848.
505) WOODS, JOHN B - Co. F, Twenty-Fifth Virginia Infantry - 765.
506) WRIGHT, H C - Co. A, First Texas Infantry - 800. Military records show his name as HENRY CLAY WRIGHT.
507) YEDDER, STEPHEN - Co. G, Third South Carolina Infantry - 2760.
508) YORK, C P - Co. E, Twenty-Fourth Georgia Infantry - 793.
509) YOUNG, BEVERLY D - Co. I, Eleventh Mississippi Infantry - removed. A small number of records refer to him as Bev Young and B D Young.
510) YOUNG, JOHN - C. S. A. - 3043. Miscellaneous records identify him as an unassigned Conscript from South Carolina.
511) YOUNGINGER. J - Co. H, Fifteenth South Carolina Infantry - 264
512) YOW, JOHN W - Co. H, Forty-Fourth North Carolina Infantry - 3004.
513) ZWEIGLER, GEORGE - Co. E, Tenth Louisiana Infantry - 775. A small number of records identify him as J Zweigler.

APPENDIX II

Mortality rates for all prisoners of war during the Civil were regrettably very high. There were a number of causes for this, ranging from lack of proper sanitation or housing through the spread of contagious diseases to downright disregard for the well being of the prisoners. A review of the records of the five hundred and thirteen men identified here, shows no fewer than thirty-four causes of death. As can be seen all manner of illness and injuries causes death to those who were held or were in transit through New York City. The largest cause of death according to the records found in Unknown. A review of the causes of death follows. In some cases an individual's death was from more than one cause. Those cases are noted below.

Abscess of Hip:
1) Logan, T C

Amputation:
1) Coffey, J G
3) Good, A H
5) Jones, W B
7) King, Reuben
9) McCurry, John D
11) Mitchell, William L

2) Duriscoe, C L
4) Hannah, E B
6) Kennedy, Patrick
8) McCurley, David
10) McHenry, Alcana

Cerebral Abscess:
1) Robert, John W

Chronic Bronchitis:
1) Bryan, John J

2) Fletcher, Charles[28]

Chronic Diarrhea:
1) Allen, Robert H
3) Attleberry, Charles
5) Bozeman, M
7) Brown, Henry
9) Burnes, Patrick
11) Campbell, Robert
13) Clark, Joseph W

2) Archibald, E N
4) Bouldin, N H
6) Brown, Elisha
8) Brown, J J
10) Campbell, E
12) Carroll, John
14) Clark, W F

---

[28] a second report in his file lists his cause of death as Chronic Diarrhea

15) Cook, Samuel F
16) Cousins, James
17) Covington, Elijah
18) Coward, N M
19) Cubbage, J
20) Davis, A
21) Davis, J R
22) Davis, Sampson
23) Dixon, J J
24) Drummon, James
25) Duggins, Robert
26) Ellmore, James
27) Enster, Samuel
28) Estis, J M
29) Farmer, William H
30) Flemming, John E
31) Flowers, Franklin
32) Fowler, S B
33) Franklin, R L
34) Freeman, John
35) Fulk, J W
36) Gammon, H J
37) Glasgow, J N
38) Green, Maston
39) Griffin, Silas
40) Hair, W J
41) Hamill, A
42) Harris, E J
43) Hodges. Alexander
44) Hollerfield, Jacob
45) Howell, Harvey A
46) Jenkins, Charles
47) Jones, Wesley
48) Jowers, J W
49) Korn, J A
50) Lansdon, J L
51) Lawless, J J
52) Leonard, Levi
53) Lundy, James
54) Macklenery, B C
55) Massie, R R
56) May, William H
57) McDermith, Alex
58) McDonald, Chris
59) Michael, J W
60) Morris, John S
61) Morrison, Angus
62) Murdock, J G
63) Nakeep, Daniel
64) Olivia, P D
65) Otis, Martin
66) Overfelt, R
67) Patterson Neal
68) Pegram, Joseph E
69) Perry, Robert
70) Phelps, David[29]
71) Phillips, Richmond
72) Phipps, John
73) Poor, J W
74) Porter, John E
75) Power, T B
76) Resner, Henry
77) Robinson, James L
78) Rogers, J B
79) Shaw, Hugh
80) Shore, William L
81) Shuler, Denial
82) Simpson, Richard
83) Smith, A H[30]
84) Southard, William R
85) Still, Isaac
86) Still, Thomas
87) Strum, G B
88) Sullivan, J V
89) Templeton, H B
90) Thomas, J M
91) Thompson, S M
92) Tilly, William

---

[29] Cause of death as Chronic Diarrhea and variola
[30] cause of death reported as Chronic Diarrhea and Mumps

93) Tindall, H F
95) Torrington, J
97) Tyre, W B
99) Wadsworth, E E[31]
101) Watkins, William
103) Webb, John H

94) Tolan, S D
96) Trexlor, J J
98) Varn, Hangford
100) Walker, J C L[32]
102) Watson, J K

Consumption:
1) Hammock, J H
3) Hazelgrove, A S
     5) Leroach, William

2) Hogan, W P
4) Howell, Koder

Dropsy:
1) Crawford, E P.

Dysentery/Chronic Dysentery:
1) Duff, B R
3) Strickland, Henry
     5) Wilkinson, George

2) Gooding, Thomas
4) Vaughn, A G

Erysipelas:
1) Harville, William

Execution:
1) Beall, John Yates

2) Kennedy, Robert

Fever:
1) Jennings, W.

Gunshot Wound:
1) Adams, A B
3) Bullis, Simeon
5) Cash, Peter
7) Davidson, Lewis
9) Ellis, John
11) Gardner, F M
13) Gilder, J A
15) Gilmer, Henry J
17) Grumles, Perry B
19) Hudspeth, James K
21) Jones, J W
23) Lawrence, Ira J
25) Light, Charles
27) May, John D
29) McGill, John

2) Bird, W L
4) Camden, J S
6) Darrold, J L
8) Early, H F
10) Fisher, Ulysses W
12) Garrett, James
14) Giles, Richard [33]
16) Green, B M
18) Holliburton, A K
20) Ivey, W G
22) Lambra, Paul
24) Leonard, J D
26) Matthews, E
28) McDonnell, William
30) McKeoithan, J A

---

[31] cause of death reported as Chronic Diarrhea and Typhoid Fever
[32] cause of death reported as Diarrhea and Pleuritis
[33] cause of death reported as Shell Wound

31) McRiley, Samuel
33) Mixon, Richard
35) Owens, A P
37) Powell, Thomas
39) Pugh, Eli
41) Robertson, T C
43) Scott, Henry
45) Skelton, Alex [35]
47) Sprules, F J
49) Stephens, C A T
51) Timberlake, G W
53) Vandergraff, John
55) White, E
57) Williams, W F
59) Wolf, Henry
61) Woodall, A G
63) York, C P
32) Middleton, Samuel
34) Moore, M P
36) Parrish, James M
38) Pratt, Thomas
40) Riggs, George W
42) Rolades, J G
44) Siegel, N M[34]
46) Smith, William A
48) Staton, Malachi
50) Stowe, J W
52) Trout, John O
54) Wheey, J A
56) Whiting, William H C[36]
58) Winston, Henry M
60) Wood, William
62) Woods, John B
64) Young, Beverly

Hemorrhage/Secondary Hemorrhage:
1) Barker, Killis
3) Keisler, G A
5) Randleman, A T [39]
2) Evans, Jay [37]
4) Pease, John [38]
6) Zweigler, George

Inflammation of Bowels:
1) Martin, Brice

Inflammation of Brain:
1) Kegley, W
2) McCann, Austin
3) Tidwell, Clark

Inflammation of Lungs:
1) Allen, R F

Irritative Fever:
1) Moses, Martin

Meningitis:
1) Johnson, Fleet
2) Murray, John

Nostalgia:
1) Pridgen, John O

Old Age:

---

[34] cause of death reported as gun shot wound followed by gangrene
[35] cause of death reported as gunshot wound compounded by Chronic Diarrhea
[36] cause of death reported as wounds
[37] cause of death reported as Secondary Hemorrhage from gunshot wound on left side
[38] cause of death reported as hemorrhage of bladder
[39] cause of death reported as Hemorrhage of lungs

1) Early, S D
Pericarditis:
1) Dee, Patrick
Peritonitis:
1) Richardson, Robert N   2) Sapp, F M
Phlebitis:
1) Farmer, J L
Phthisis:
1) Bass, Jethro   2) Champion, William
3) Riggs, Augustus L   4) Roberts, William D
5) Traitor, William
Phthisis Pulmanarius:
1) Chambers, George W   2) Davenport, M C
3), Jordan, J J   4) Williams, _____
Pneumonia/Double Pneumonia:
1) Anderson, Joseph R   2) Bartley, Smith
3) Boughman, H L   4) Burdick, E W C
5) Coleman, Hazel   6) Crouder, William
7) DeBar, L W   8) Duff, James A
9) Eldridge, D [40]   10) Glover, John A
11) Hassel, John W   12) Hill, Jesse
13) Johnson, Stephen   14) Kenney, Simpson
15) Kelly, John J   16) King, Thomas S
17) Norwood, Joseph J   18) Nowell, J Henry
19) Owens, W H   20) Rainey, James
21) Roberts, John M   22) Short, Robert
23) Slaughter, Selim   24) Snow, Jesse L
25) Stevenson, James M   26) Turner, John
27) Wayne, Francis A   28) Wilson, G S
29) Wilson, John W   30) Yow, John W
Pyaemia:
1) Anderson, Leroy   2) Benson, Jesse W
3) Blake, A P   4) Blood, L W
5) Blunt, T H   6) Bradshaw, J P
7) Burmingham, John   8) Carroll, Robert
9) Duggans, J R   10) Emerson, John R
11) Fox, James F   12) Grigg, William
13) King, John C   14) Logan, J M
15) Long, Simon   16) McCarley, Green

---

[40] cause of death reported as Pneumonia and Diarrhea

17) Mull, J H
18) Murdoch, E E
19) Powell, H A
20) Proctor, Thomas D
21) Redman, T O
22) Russell, Abednego
23) Ryle, A J
24) Sale, William
25) Schrader, Samuel
26) Smith, George A
27) Smith, Henry
28) Smith, J H
29) Street, P A
30) Tison, William L
31) Tyson, W T
32) Warrick, W P
33) Weatherby, J M
34) Wright, H C

Remittent Fever:
1) Lyle, Samuel
2) Rolades, George
3) Stone, Green P

Scurvy:
1) Knight, T H

Smallpox:
1) Boggs, John D

Typhoid Fever/Fibris Typhoides:
1) Abernathy, William R D
2) Barbury, J E
3) Bird, Joshua
4) Branham, W
5) Brown, _____
6) Burnett, William T
7) Clifton, George
8) Collins, James
9) Cox, Leander
10) Davidson, William
11) Eckard, Cyrus
12) Edwards, J H
13) Edwards, T D
14) Few, M D
15) Foust, Jacob
16) Gordon, J Hervey
17) Gough, Charles A
18) Grady, W S
19) Gregory, _____
20) Griffin, D T
21) Hall, Joseph [41]
22) Hassell, _____
23) Helm, A J
24) Huffman, William
25) Hughes, John
26) Jennings, _____
27) Jolly, _____
28) Lancaster, J L
29) Litten, George
30) Long, Richard
31) Mathis, Thomas
32) Matthews, James
33) McClellan, _____
34) McVicker, Samuel
35) Medlin, F M
36) Millard, John J
37) Mills, Gilbert
38) Morris, James
39) Murray, Michael
40) O'Connor, Patrick
41) Parker, James
42) Quackenbusch, J G
43) Rape, S M
44) Reeves, Sanders
45) Robinett, L G
46) Savage, Braxton

---

[41] cause of death reported at Typhoid Fever and Pneumonia

47) Sawyer, Robinson A
49) Smith, Zemmerick[42]
51) Teyson, _____
53) Vaughn, William L
55) White, Franklin
57) Wood, William H

48) Sears, Robert
50) Swalt, Simeon
52) Townsend, George
54) Vendrick, J A
56) Whitehurst, _____
58) Younginger, J [43]

Typhoid Pneumonia:
1) Boyle, Stephen
3) Carter, Timothy
5) Humphreys, J J
7) McKenzie, H T
9) Sharp, John W
11) Tuit, John

2) Brown, John
4) Elliott, Joseph T
6) Massingale, R H
8) Morris, D C
10) Thompson, H F
12) Wilson, J E

13) Wood, D C C

Variola:
1) Amos, David
3) Petty, William L
5) Smith, William B[44]

2) Horton, Noah C
4) Simpson, _____
6) Stokes, B B

7) Venson, W J

Unknown:
1) Anderson, James
3) Baker, G D
5) Beard, James O
7) Bellshaw, John
9) Blankenship, J T
11) Blount, Hosea
13) Bradbury, Wiley
15) Brown, H E
17) Bushing, _____
19) Camp, James
21) Cannon, John
23) Cartland, Francis
25) Casey, A M
27) Chambers, Harvey R
29) Conetrain, James
31) Costelle, Lewis
33) Dudley, J

2) Bailey, W
4) Barnes, James
6) Beckman, W H
8) Bennett, A W
10) Block, C
12) Bowine, James
14) Bradley, _____
16) Bullis, David W
18) Camhill, Charles
20) Campbell, R K
22) Carlton, James
24) Carver, Lewis
26) Chambers, G W
28) Coindrey, Jefferson
30) Cosart, Lewis
32) DeBrady, DeYoung
34) Duppins, P E L

---

[42] cause of death reported as Typhoid Fever and Measles
[43] cause of death reported at "Confederate Typhoid Fever"
[44] cause of death reported as Variola and Chronic Diarrhea

35) Dunlap, J S
37) Ferguson, G N
39) Gay, N
41) Gibbs, George F
43) Gilliland, Abner
45) Grady, C M
47) Griffiths, F O
49) Harmon, David
51) Harvey, A J
53) Henson, W B
55) Hoffman, _____
57) Howard, J C
59) Hurley, C C
61) Hutto, John
63) Irbinet, Archibald
65) Johnson, M D
67) Johnston, John B
69) Jones, Murdock
71) Kay, Robert M
73) King, M
75) Ledford, William
77) Livingston, John
79) Martin, R M V
81) Maxwell, Hudson
83) McConniell, R T
85) Meyer, J H
87) Modlin, Alpha
89) Moore, G E
91) Munn, C D
93) Owens, A P
95) Perry, H H
97) Plemmons, W C
99) Prestwood, E
101) Rast, William R
103) Reese, Samuel
105) Rogerson, David L
107) Ronninger, J
109) Sawyer, William B
111) Shuttlesworth, Samuel
113) Smith, J A
115) Soller, R E A
117) Steelling, Hassan
119) Suthard, William R

36) Edwards, T N
38) Fowler, T
40) Feisler, James
42) Gice, C N
44) Gotte, Jacob
46) Griffin, William B
48) Hall, P P
50) Hartford, John
52) Helton, Alfred
54) Hill, J H
56) Hollingshead, William
58) Hulsey, Henry
60) Hutton, Charles
62) Ingraham, John
64) Irving, A
66) Johnston, T A
68) Jones, F M
70) Joyce, Sullivan
72) Kyeser, W L
74) Kite, Stephen
76) Little, James
78) Lynch, George
80) Mattox, R F
82) McCarter, Michael
84) McDowell, D C
86) Milbank, W J
88) Montgomery, W
90) Moran, J A
92) Nix, Jacob
94) Persil, L
96) Phillips, E W
98) Pollard, J W
100) Ranson, John H
102) Reddix, James
104) Roberson, David L
106) Rollins, Thomas
108) Royal, William H
110) Shaver, Wiliam
112) Simon, W
114) Smith, Major
116) Steeley, S
118) Stroman, A
120) Sweetser, Theodore

121) Thomas, William
123) Towler, J E
125) Unknown
127) Unknown
129) Unknown
131) Wallace, William
133) Webb, Levi
135) Willis, James P
137) Wilson, Nathaniel
139) Yedder, Stephen

122) Titterton, Samuel D
124) Turnham, Thomas J
126) Unknown
128) Unknown
130) Walker, Lee
132) Ward, W H
134) Williams, C D
136) Wilson, David
138) Winn, William D
140) Young, John

APPENDIX III

More than one hundred and eighty units are represented by those found on the cemetery burial list. The list below shows these units with the names of the members. In cases where research has identified or clarified the unit listed, this information is footnoted.

FIRST ALABAMA ARTILLERY BATTALION
1) Barnes, John
2) Davis, Sampson
3) Horton, Noah C
4) Johnston, John B
5) King, Thomas J
6) Langdon, J L
7) McDermith, Alexander
8) Phelps, David
9) Shuttlesworth, Samuel
10) Smith, William B
11) Turner, John
12) Venson, W J
13) Watson, J J

FIRST ALABAMA CAVALRY
1) Gice, C M

SEVENTH ALABAMA CAVALRY
1) Archibald, E N

NINTH ALABAMA CAVALRY
1) Davidson, William T

THIRD ALABAMA INFANTRY
1) Carroll, Robert A

EIGHTH ALABAMA INFANTRY
1) Sapp, F M

TENTH ALABAMA INFANTRY
1) Bennett, A W
2) Sullivan, James V

TWENTY-SEVENTH ALABAMA INFANTRY
1) Thomas, William

FORTY-FIRST ALABAMA INFANTRY
1) Towler, J E

FORTY-FOURTH ALABAMA INFANTRY
1) Middleton, H P

FORTY-SEVENTH ALABAMA INFANTRY
1) McCurley, David

FORTY-EIGHTH ALABAMA INFANTRY
1) Cash, Peter
2) Chambers, Harvey
3) Parrish, James M
4) Rolades, J G

FIFTY-NINTH ALABAMA INFANTRY
1) Flemming, John E
2) Ingraham, James
3) Turnham, Thomas J

CONFEDERATE STATES PROVISIONAL ARMY
1) Whiting, William H C
CONFEDERATE STATES NAVY
1) Beall, John Y[45]
CONFEDERATE STATES SECRET SERVICE
1) Kennedy, Robert[46]
FIFTH FLORIDA INFANTRY
1) Kelly. John J
EIGHTH FLORIDA INFANTRY
1) Webb. Levi
NINTH FLORIDA INFANTRY
1) Cannon, John   2) Carlton, James
CHRISHOLM'S FLORIDA HOME GUARD COMPANY
1) Winn, William D[47]
NORWOOD'S FLORIDA HOME GUARD COMPANY
1) Dixon, J J
TWENTY-SECOND GEORGIA HEAVY ARTILLERY BATTALION
1) Bozeman, M   2) Little, James
                        3) McKenzie, H T
TWENTY-EIGHTH GEORGIA HEAVY ARTILLERY BATTALION
1) Cook, Samuel F   2) Walker, J C L[48]
TENTH GEORGIA CAVALRY
1) Vaughn, A G   2) Webb, John H
FIRST GEORGIA INFANTRY
1) Bailey, W [49]   2) Jordan, J J[50]
                        3) Lawless, J J[51]
SECOND GEORGIA INFANTRY
1) Blunt, T H   2) Powell, Thomas
NINTH GEORGIA INFANTRY
1) Stephens, C A T   2) Tison, William L

ELEVENTH GEORGIA INFANTRY
1) Early, H F   2) Hulsey, Henry

---

[45] originally served in the Second Virginia Infantry
[46] originally served in the First Louisiana Infantry
[47] actually served in Norwood's Florida Home Guard Company
[48] served in Twenty-Seventh Georgia Artillery Battalion
[49] served in First (Lawton's/Mercer's/Olmstead's) Georgia Infantry
[50] ibid.
[51] not found in any of the units designated the First Georgia Infantry. however

3) McConiel, R T
4) Mitchell, William L
5) Mull, J H
6) Plemmons, W C
7) Roberts, John W
8) Wilson, David
FOURTEENTH GEORGIA INFANTRY
1) Rainey, James
2) Ryle, A J
FIFTEENTH GEORGIA INFANTRY
1) Hollingsworth, William J
SIXTEENTH GEORGIA INFANTRY
1) Perry, H H
TWENTIETH GEORGIA INFANTRY
1) Ransom, John H
2) Traitor, William
TWENTY-FOURTH GEORGIA INFANTRY
1(Farmer, William M
2) York, C P
THIRTY-FIFTH GEORGIA INFANTRY
1) Lawrence, Ira J
FORTY-FIRST GEORGIA INFANTRY
1) Bradbury, Wiley
FORTY-FOURTH GEORGIA INFANTRY
1) King, M
FORTY-FIFTH GEORGIA INFANTRY
1) Hannah, E B
2) Roberts, John M
3) Smith, Henry
FIFTY-FIRST GEORGIA INFANTRY
1) Mixon, Richard
FIFTY-THIRD GEORGIA INFANTRY
1) Lambra, Paul
2) Richardson, Robert
3) Savage, Braxton
FIFTY-SEVENTH GEORGIA INFANTRY
1) Smith, J A
FIFTY-NINTH GEORGIA INFANTRY
1) Garrett, James
2) Kennedy, Patrick
SIXTY-THIRD GEORGIA INFANTRY
1) Griffiths, F)
SIXTY-FOURTH GEORGIA INFANTRY
1) Jones, Murdock
DENEAL'S CHOCTAW INDIAN REGIMENT
1) Willis, Billy
BURDSALL'S LOUISIANA ARTILLERY COMPANY
1) Brown, Henry
WASHINGTON LOUISIANA ARTILLERY BATTALION
1) Gouch, Charles A
FOURTH LOUISIANA INFANTRY
1) Olivia, P D

FIFTH LOUISIANA INFANTRY
10 Long, Simon, A
SIXTH LOUISIANA INFANTRY
1) Fisher, Ulysses
TENTH LOUISIANA INFANTRY
1) Murray, Thomas   2) Vandergriff, Joseph
       3) Zweigler, George
FOURTH MARYLAND LIGHT ARTILLERY COMPANY
1) Torrington, J
FIRST MARYLAND INFANTRY
1) Anderson, Leroy[52]
JEFF DAVIS MISSISSIPPI CAVALRY LEGION
1) Tuitt, John
SECOND MISSISSIPPI INFANTRY
1) McCarley, Green   2) Riggs, Augustus L
ELEVENTH MISSISSIPPI INFANTRY
1) Burmingham, John   2) McHenry, Alcana
       3) Young, Beverly D
THIRTEENTH MISSISSIPPI INFANTRY
1) Barker, Killis C
EIGHTEENTH MISSISSIPPI INFANTRY
1) Logan, T C   2) Robertson, T C
NINETEENTH MISSISSIPPI INFANTRY
10 Stone, Green P
FORTY-SECOND MISSISSIPPI INFANTRY
1) Hudspeth, James J   2) Riggs, George W
FORTY-EIGHTH MISSISSIPPI INFANTRY
1) Bryan, John J
FIRST NORTH CAROLINA ARTILLERY
1) Cartland, Francis   2) Davis, A[53]
       3) Howell, Koder
THIRD NORTH CAROLINA ARTILLERY
1) Bird, Josiah [54]
FIRST NORTH CAROLINA CAVALRY
1) Grady, W S
SIXTEENTH NORTH CAROLINA CAVALRY
1) Smith, Zemerick N[55]

---

[52] First Maryland Infantry Battalion
[53] First North Carolina Artillery Battalion
[54] Third North Carolina Heavy Artillery
[55] Sixteenth North Carolina Cavalry Battalion

SIXTY-SIXTH NORTH CAROLINA CAVALRY
1) Millard, John J[56]

FIRST NORTH CAROLINA INFANTRY
1) Moses, Martin F

SECOND NORTH CAROLINA INFANTRY
1) Bass, Jethro
2) Champion, William
3) Johnson, Fleet
4) May, John D
5) Moore, M P
6) Reeves, Sanders
7) Ronninger, J

THIRD NORTH CAROLINA INFANTRY
1) Michael, J W[57]
2) Timberlake, G W

FOURTH NORTH CAROLINA INFANTRY
1) Crawford, E P

SIXTH NORTH CAROLINA INFANTRY
1) McDonnel, William

SIXTH NORTH CAROLINA SENIOR RESERVE INFANTRY
1) Howard, J C

SEVENTH NORTH CAROLINA INFANTRY
1) Blount, Hosea[58]
2) Griffin, William B[59]
3) Kite, Stephen[60]
4) Modlin, Alpha
5) Roberson, Mc G[61]
6) Rogerson, David[62]
7) Steeley, S
8) Titterton, Samuel D

ELEVENTH NORTH CAROLINA INFANTRY
1) Davidson, Lewis
2) Hamill, A
3) Ivey, W G
4) Smith, Wiliam A
5) Street, P S
6) Wood, William

THIRTEENTH NORTH CAROLINA INFANTRY
1) Blood, L W
2) Bradshaw, J P
3) Rogers, J B
4) Wolf, Henry F

FOURTEENTH NORTH CAROLINA INFANTRY
1) Carroll, John
2) Fox, James F
3) Morris, James

FIFTEENTH NORTH CAROLINA INFANTRY
1) Brown, Elisha

SIXTEENTH NORTH CAROLINA INFANTRY

---

[56] Sixty-Sixth North Carolina Infantry
[57] Third North Carolina Reserve Infantry
[58] Seventeenth North Carolina Infantry
[59] ibid.
[60] ibid.
[61] ibid.
[62] ibid.

10 Edwards, J H   2) Jenkins, Charles
            3) Robinson, James

EIGHTEENTH NORTH CAROLINA INFANTRY
1) Hoffman, William F   2) Soller, R E A
            3) Thomas, J M

TWENTIETH NORTH CAROLINA INFANTRY
1) Smith, George A

TWENTY-FIRST NORTH CAROLINA INFANTRY
1) Duggans, J R   2) Shore, William L

TWENTY-SECOND NORTH CAROLINA INFANTRY
1) Dee, Patrick   2) Elliott, Joseph T
3) Estis, J M   4) Fulk, John W
5) Long, Richard   6) Macklenery, B C
7) Phipps, John   8) Quackenbush, J G
9) Wilson, G S   10) Wilson, J E

TWENTY-THIRD NORTH CAROLINA INFANTRY
1) Enster, Samuel   2) Helton, Alfred
3) Siegel, N M   4) Stowe, J N

TWENTY-FOURTH NORTH CAROLINA INFANTRY
1) Long, Reuben   2) Woodall, A G

TWENTY-FIFTH NORTH CAROLINA INFANTRY
10 Few, M D

TWENTY-SIXTH NORTH CAROLINA INFANTRY
1) Bullis, Simeon   2) Coffey, J G
3) Emerson, John R   4) Harmon, David
5) Johnson, Stephen   6) Moran, J A
7) Prestwood, E   8) Stelling, Hassan
            9) Strickland, Henry

TWENTY-SEVENTH NORTH CAROLINA INFANTRY
1) Faust, Jacob   2) Rape, S M
            3) Vendrick, J A

TWENTY-EIGHTH NORTH CAROLINA INFANTRY
1) Barbury, J E   2) Eckard, Cyrus
3) Jennings, M   4) Logan, T C
            5) Randleman, A T

THIRTIETH NORTH CAROLINA INFANTRY
1) Knight, T H

THIRTY-SECOND NORTH CAROLINA INFANTRY
1) Hill, Jesse   2) Sawyer, William B

THIRTY-THIRD NORTH CAROLINA INFANTRY
1) Beckman, W H   2) Chambers, G W
3) Coleman, Hazel   4) Harville, William
            5) Sawyer, Robinson

THIRTY-FOURTH NORTH CAROLINA INFANTRY
1) Brown, John
2) Munn, C D
3) Powell, H A
4) Ray, A J
5) Sharp, John W
6) Vaughn, William L

THIRTY-FIFTH NORTH CAROLINA INFANTRY
1) Cosart, Lewis
2) Gordon, J Harvey
3) Leonard, Levi
4) Morris, D C
5) Sears, Robert
6) Wadsworth, E W
7) Williams, C D

THIRTY-SIXTH NORTH CAROLINA INFANTRY
1) Stevenson, James M

THIRTY-SEVENTH NORTH CAROLINA INFANTRY
1) Abernathy, William R D
2) Blankenship, J T
3) Cox, Leander
4) Elkdridge, D
5) Livingston, John
6) Robinett, L G
7) Staton, Malachi
8) Townsend, George
9) Williams, R F

THIRTY-EIGHT NORTH CAROLINA INFANTRY
1) Allen, R F
2) Block, C
3) Grigg, William
4) Hasselll, John W
5) Hodges, Alexander
6) Jones, Wilson
7) King, john C
8) Massingale, R H
9) McDonald, Christopher
10) McGill, John
11) McViker, William
12) Persil, L
13) Roland, Charles
14) Royal, William H
15) Simpson, Richard
16) Tyson, W T

THIRTY-NINTH INFANTRY
1) Irving, A

FORTY-THIRD NORTH CAROLINA INFANTRY
1) Allen, Robert h
2) Jones, J W

FORTY-FOURTH NORTH CAROLINA INFANTRY
1) Green, Maston
2) Yew, John W

FORTY-FIFTH NORTH CAROLINA INFANTRY
1) Benson, Jesse W
2) Joyce, Sullivan
3) Pratt, Thomas
40 Proctor, Thomas D

FORTY-SIXTH NORTH CAROLINA INFANTRY
1) Wallace, William

FORTY-SEVENTH NORTH CAROLINA INFANTRY
1) Clifton, George
2) Hall, Joseph T
3) Medlin, F M
4) Nowell, J Henry
5) Parton, James W
6) Perry, Robert
7) Phillips, Richmond
8) Shaw, Hugh

9) Ward, W H 10) Watkins, William H
11) Wood, William H

FORTY-EIGHTH NORTH CAROLINA INFANTRY
10 Helm, A J 2) Winston, Henry M

FORTY-NINTH NORTH CAROLINA INFANTRY
1) Massey, R R

FIFTIETH NORTH CAROLINA INFANTRY
1) Owens, W H

FIFTY-SECOND NORTH CAROLINA INFANTRY
1) Bullis, David W 2) Henson, W B[63]
3) Pegram, Joseph E

FIFTY-THIRD NORTH CAROLINA INFANTRY
1) Russell, A

FIFTY-FOURTH NORTH CAROLINA INFANTRY
1) Griffin, D T

FIFTY-FIFTH NORTH CAROLINA INFANTRY
1) Boggs, John D 2) Boyle, Stephen
3) Ellmore, James 4) McRiley, Samuel
5) Scott, Henry

FIFTY-SIXTH NORTH CAROLINA INFANTRY
1) Mills, Gilbert

FIFTY-SEVENTH NORTH CAROLINA INFANTRY
1) Nakeep, Daniel

FIFTY-EIGHTH NORTH CAROLINA INFANTRY
1) Keeney, Simpson 2) Ledford, William
3) Murdock, J G 4) Reddix, James
5) Wilson, John W

SIXTY-SEVENTH NORTH CAROLINA INFANTRY
1) White, Franklin

MC DUGALD'S NORTH CAROLINA INFANTRY
1) Patterson, Neal

WILMINGTON NORTH CAROLINA RAILROAD GUARDS
1) Pridge, John O[64]

FIRST SOUTH CAROLINA ARTILLERY
1) Meyer, J H 20 O'Conner, Patrick
3) Poor, John W

FIRST SOUTH CAROLINA HEAVY ARTILLERY
1) Durn, Perry 2) Gotte, Jacob
3) Lundy, James

---

[63] served in Sixty-Second North Carolina Infantry
[64] McDugald's North Carolina Infantry

THIRD SOUTH CAROLINA ARTILLERY
1) Freeman, John [65]   2) Parker, Thomas

FOURTH SOUTH CAROLINA ARTILLERY
1) Campbell, R J [66]

GIST GUARD SOUTH CAROLINA HEAVY ARTILLERY COMPANY
1) Tidwell, Clark

MARION SOUTH CAROLINA ARTILLERY COMPANY
1) Casey, A M

FIRST SOUTH CAROLINA CAVALRY
1) Tindall, H F

SIXTH SOUTH CAROLINA CAVALRY
1) Brown, J J   2) Camp, James

SEVENTH SOUTH CAROLINA CAVALRY
1) Davis, J R

FOURTEENTH SOUTH CAROLINA CAVALRY
1) Lancaster, L L [67]

FIRST SOUTH CAROLINA INFANTRY [68]
1) Boughman, H L   2) Camhill, Charles
3) Campbell, Robert   4) Carter, Timothy
5) Covington, Elijah   6) Dullins, P E L
7) Farmer, J L   8) Glover, John R
9) Hair, W J   10) Hollerfield, Jacob
11) Hughes, John   12) Johnson, M D
13) Leroach, William T   14) Matthews, A
15) McKithan, J A   16) Morrison Angus
17) Owens, A P   18) Rollins, Thomas
19) Sale, William Augustus 20) Snow, Jesse L
21) Sproules, F J   22) Sweetser, Theodore
23) Wayne, Francis A   24) Weatherby, J M

FIRST SOUTH CAROLINA MILITIA
1) Irbinet, Archibald   2) Otis, Martin [69]

FIRST SOUTH CAROLINA RIFLES

---

[65] First (Regular) South Carolina Infantry
[66] Pee Dee South Carolina Artillery Company
[67] First South Carolina Militia
[68] Boughman, Campbell, Glover, Hair, Hughes, Matthews, Sale, Snow, and Wayne served in the First (Provisional Army) South Carolina Infantry; Carter, Farmer, Hollerfield, Johnson, Leroach, McKithan, Morrison, Owens and Rollins served in the First (Regular) South Carolina Infantry; Sprules and Weatherby served in the First (Volunteers) South Carolina Infantry; Covington served in the First South Carolina Heavy Artillery; it is not known which unit Camhill, Dullins, and Sweetser served in.
[69] served in the Third South Carolina Reserve Infantry

1) Beard, James O   2) Hill, J H
3) Kay, Robert M   4) Power, T B
SECOND SOUTH CAROLINA INFANTRY
1) Bard, W L
THIRD SOUTH CAROLINA INFANTRY
1) Yedder, Stephen
SIXTH SOUTH CAROLINA RESERVES
10) Harris, E J
EIGHTH SOUTH CAROLINA INFANTRY
1) Hollibinton, A J
ELEVENTH SOUTH CAROLINA INFANTRY
1) Gooding, Thomas
TWELFTH SOUTH CAROLINA INFANTRY
1) Dunlap, J S   2) Garner, F M
3) Hall, P P   4) Milbank, W J
5) Smith, J H   6) Warrick, W P
            7) Wheey, J A
THIRTEENTH SOUTH CAROLINA INFANTRY
1) Brown, H E   2) Burnett, William T
3) Franklin, R L   4) Hutton, John
5) Keisler, G A   6) Leonard, J D
            7) White, E
FOURTEENTH SOUTH CAROLINA INFANTRY
1) Adams, A B   2) Burdick, E W C
3) DeBar, L W   4) Drummon, James
5) Duriscoe, C L   6) Gilder, J A
7) Glasgow, J N   8) Hurley, C C
9) Mathis, Thomas   10) McCurry, John S
11) Morris, John S[70]   12) Stroman, A[71]
            13) Strum, G B
FOURTEENTH SOUTH CAROLINA MILITIA
1) Coward, N M   2) Griffin, Silas
3) Korn, J A   4) Rast, William R
5) Shuler, Daniel   6) Still, Isaac
7) Templeton, H B   8) Tilly, William
9) Tilly, William   10) Varn, Hangford D
FIFTEENTH SOUTH CAROLINA INFANTRY
1) Murphy, E E   2) Shaver, William
3) Swalt, Simeon   4) Youninger, J

---

[70] Fourteenth South Carolina Militia
[71] ibid.

SIXTEENTH SOUTH CAROLINA INFANTRY
1) Campbell, A[72]
SEVENTEENTH SOUTH CAROLINA INFANTRY
1) Harvey, A J   2) Hutto, Charles
        3) Jones, F M
EIGHTEENTH SOUTH CAROLINA INFANTRY
1) Gilliland, Abner
EIGHTEENTH SOUTH CAROLINA MILITIA
1) Trexler, J J
TWENTY-FIRST SOUTH CAROLINA INFANTRY
1) Evans, Jay   2) Grady, C M
TWENTY-THIRD SOUTH CAROLINA INFANTRY
1) Jowers, J W
UNASSIGNED SOUTH CAROLINA CONSCRIPT
1) Young, John C
FIRST TENNESSEE HEAVY ARTILLERY
1) Amos, David   2) Flowers, Franklin
3) Petty, William E   4) Smith, A M
        5) Stokes, B B
FIRST TENNESSEE INFANTRY
1) Moore, G E[73]
EIGHTH TENNESSEE INFANTRY
1) Willis, James P   2) Wilson, Nathaniel
TWENTY-SIXTH TENNESSEE INFANTRY
1) Geisler, James W   2) Wood, D C C
FIFTY-THIRD TENNESSEE INFANTRY
1) Roberts, William D
SECOND TEXAS CAVALRY
1) Attleberry, Charles   2) Porter, John E
TWELFTH TEXAS CAVALRY
1) Thompson, S M
FIRST TEXAS INFANTRY
1) Wright, H C
FOURTH TEXAS INFANTRY
1) Ellis, John   2) Grumbles, Perry B
FIFTH TEXAS INFANTRY
1) Green, B M
FIFTEENTH TEXAS INFANTRY
1) Burnes, Patrick

---

[72] served in the Fifteenth South Carolina Infantry
[73] First (Field's) Tennessee Infantry

FIRST VIRGINIA ARTILLERY
1) Pollard, J W
FOURTH VIRGINIA ARTILLERY
1) Duff, James A   2) Early, S D
TENTH VIRGINIA ARTILLERY
1) Lynch, George A
SIXTEENTH VIRGINIA HEAVY ARTILLERY
1) Carver, Louis C[74]
CARPENTER'S VIRGINIA ARTILLERY BATTALION
1) Blake, A P[75]
COIT'S VIRGINIA BATTERY
1) Clark, W F[76]   2) Resner, Henry[77]
LEE'S VIRGINIA ARTILLERY COMPANY
1) Costelle, Patrick
LUCAS VIRGINIA ARTILLERY BATTALION
1) Crouder, William [78]
PEGRAM'S VIRGINIA BATTERY
1) Gibbs, George E   2) Keep, Erwin H
           3) Short, Robert
STURDIVANT'S VIRGINIA ARTILLERY COMPANY
1) Duff, B R
THIRTEENTH VIRGINIA CAVALRY
1) Tyre, W B
FIRST VIRGINIA INFANTRY
1) Giles, Richard   2) Kegley, W
FIRST VIRGINIA INFANTRY BATTALION
1) McCarty, Michael
THIRD VIRGINIA INFANTRY
1) Reese, Samuel W
FOURTH VIRGINIA INFANTRY
1) Gilmore, Henry J
FIFTH VIRGINIA INFANTRY
1) Murray, Michael   2) Trout, John O
SEVENTH VIRGINIA INFANTRY
1) Good, A H
EIGHTH VIRGINIA INFANTRY
1) Anderson, Joseph R   2) Fletcher, Charles

---

[74] served in the Twelfth Virginia Artillery Battalion
[75] served in Crenshaw's Virginia Artillery Company
[76] served in Pegram's Virginia Battery
[77] served in Wright's Virginia Heavy Artillery Company
[78] served in the Fifteenth South Carolina Artillery Battalion

NINTH VIRGINIA INFANTRY
1) Duggins, Robert   2) Johnson, T A

FOURTEENTH VIRGINIA INFANTRY
1) Condrey, Jefferson   2) Lyle, Samuel A
3) Wilkinson, George

FIFTEENTH VIRGINIA INFANTRY
1) Hazelgrove, A S

EIGHTEENTH VIRGINIA INFANTRY
1) Mattox, R F

TWENTY-FOURTH VIRGINIA INFANTRY
1) McDowell, D C

TWENTY-FIFTH VIRGINIA INFANTRY
1) Schrader, Samuel   2) Woods, John B

TWENTY-SEVENTH VIRGINIA INFANTRY
1) Camdon, J S

TWENTY-NINTH VIRGINIA INFANTRY
1) Litten, George W

THIRTY-EIGHTH VIRGINIA INFANTRY
1) Gammon, H J   2) Light, Charles

THIRTY-NINTH VIRGINIA INFANTRY
1) Phillips, E W

FORTIETH VIRGINIA INFANTRY
1) Redman, T O

FORTY-FIRST VIRGINIA INFANTRY
1) Cousins, James

FORTY-SIXTH VIRGINIA INFANTRY
1) Branham, W

FORTY-EIGHTH VIRGINIA INFANTRY
1) Thompson, H F

FIFTIETH VIRGINIA INFANTRY
1) Pugh, Eli

FIFTY-THIRD VIRGINIA INFANTRY
1) Clark, Joseph W   2) Cubbage, J
3) Fowler, T   4) Hogan, W F
5) Skelton, Alex   6) Slaughter, Selim

FIFTY-SEVENTH VIRGINIA INFANTRY
1) Bouldin, N H   2) Fowler, S B
3) Martin, Brice A   4) Nay, William F
5) Overfelt, R   6) Simon, W
7) Suthard, William R

FIFTY-EIGHTH VIRGINIA INFANTRY
1) Humphreys, J J

FIFTY-NINTH VIRGINIA INFANTRY

1) Hammock, J H   2) McCann, Austin
           3) Tolan, S D
UNKNOWN
1) Anderson, James   2) Baker, G D
3) Bartley, Smith[79]   4) Bellshaw, John[80]
5) Bowine, James[81]   6) Bradley, _____
7) Brown, _____   8) Bushing, _____
9) Cushing, James   10) Conetrain, J
11) DeBrady, DeYoung   12) Dudley, J
13) Edwards, T D   14) Ferguson, G N
15) Gay, N[82]   16) Gregory, _____
17) Hartford, John [83]   18) Hassel, _____
19) Hoffman, _____   20) Howell, Harvey[84]
21) Jennings, _____   22) Jolly, _____
23) Keyser, W L   24) Martin, R M N
25) McClellan, _____   26) Montgomery, W
27) Nix, Jacob   28) Pease, John
29) Simpson, _____   30) Smith, Major
31) Teysor. _____   32) Walker, Lee
33) Whitehurst, L   34) Williams, _____

---

[79] Company __, Montgomery Guards
[80] Company E, __ Virginia Militia
[81] Thirteenth Florida Infantry
[82] Forty-Seventh North Carolina Infantry
[83] Company __, Florida Home Guards
[84] Unassigned

BIBLIOGRAPHY

Books:
Confederate P.O.W.'s (1984), Nacogdoches, Tex.: Ericson Books (Reprint of U S War Dept.'s *Register of Confederate Soldiers and Sailors Who Died in Federal Prisons and Military Hospitals* (1914), Washington, D.C.: U S War Dept.

Hewett, Janet B (Ed.) (1995), *The Roster of Confederate Soldiers, 1861-185* (Vols. 1 - 16). Wilmington, N.C.: Broadfoot Publishing Co.

Horan, James D. (1954), *Confederate Agent: A Discovery in History*. New York: Crown Publisher

Lucas, Daniel B. (Ed.) (1865), *Memoir of John Yates Beall: His Life, Trial, Correspondence; Diary and Private Manuscript Found Among His Papers, Including His own Account of the Raid on Lake Erie*. Montreal: John Lovell, Publisher.

Steiner, Paul E, Ph.D., M.D. (1968), *Disease in the Civil War*. Springfield, Ill., Charles C Thomas, Publisher.

War of the Rebellion, The: A Compilation of the Official Records of the Union and Confederate Armies (1890), Washington: Government Printing Office

Warner, Ezra J (1959), *Generals in Gray*. Baton Rouge: Louisiana State University Press.

Microfilm:
National Archives, Record Group 94.
- Consolidated Index to Compiled Service Records of Confederate Soldiers, M253.
- Compiled Service Records of Confederate Soldiers Who Served in Organizations From the State of Alabama. M311.
- Compiled Service Records of Confederate Soldiers Who Served in Organizations From the State of Florida. M251,
- Compiled Service Records of Confederate Soldiers Who Served in Organizations From the State of Georgia. M266.
- Compiled Service Records of Confederate Soldiers Who Served in Organizations From the State of Louisiana. M320.

Compiled Service Records of Confederate Soldiers Who Served in Organizations From the State of Maryland. M321.
Compiled Service Records of Confederate Soldiers Who Served in Organizations From the State of Mississippi. M269.
Compiled Service Records of Confederate Soldiers Who Served in Organizations From the State of North Carolina. M270.
Compiled Service Records of Confederate Soldiers Who Served in Organizations From the State of South Carolina. M392.
Compiled Service Records of Confederate Soldiers Who Served in Organizations From the State of Tennessee. M268.
Compiled Service Records of Confederate Soldiers Who Served in Organizations From the State of Texas. M323.
Compiled Service Records of Confederate Soldiers Who Served in Organizations From the State of Virginia. M324.
Compiled Service Records of Confederate Soldiers Who Served in Organizations Raised Directly by the Confederate Government. M258.
Unfiled Paper and Slips Belonging to Confederate Compiled Service Records. M347.

Newspapers:
New York Times

Periodicals:
America's Civil War
Civil War Times Illustrated
Confederate Veteran Magazine

INDEX

The names shown on the following index are of those individuals for whom biographies do not exist. For information of those for whom a biography does exist, see the alphabetic listings in Chapter 3 and Appendix I.

Alvord, Benjamin - 31, 138
Asboth, Alexander - 50
Atkinson, S - 51
Barbee, Joseph - 19
Beauregard, Pierre G T - 76
Boiles, John A - 90
Bouldin, Sally Ann - 28
Brown, May B - 31
Byrd, Nancy E - 24
Canby, E R S - 148
Case, A J - 85
Cobb, Howell - 89
Davenport, Randolph - 48
Day, H - 22, 90
Dix, John A - 90
Dula, T P - 43
Dunlap, Nancy - 52
Eckard, David 54
Edmundsen, James K - 36
Elliott, Stephen, Jr - 67
Erwin, E A - 77
Eubank, Warren - 125
Frost, F L - 49
Gilder, Martha A - 64
Hill, Daniel H - 24
Hollingfield, Preston - 76
Howe, M S - 22, 90
Ivey, Eliza - 82
Jennings, Elizabeth G - 83
Jordan, Mary J - 87
Jordan, Thomas - 76
Keisler, Martha A D - 88
Kirkland, William W - 130
Lancaster, May - 92
Lee, Robert E - 46
Levering, A K - 16

Lincoln, Abraham - 22, 90
Lyons, Charles - 162
Mallory, Stephen - 21
McDonald, Ballamb - 103
McGill, Neill - 104
Merwin, J B - 10, 85
Millard, Chairy - 106
Morris, William H - 22, 90
Murphy, John - 111
O'Beirne, R F - 90
Parker, Joseph G A - 129
Parrish, John - 115
Powell, J W - 120
Rape, Sarah A - 123
Ratlife, Thomas - 104
Savage, Louise - 132
Seagle, George - 135
Sickles, Daniel - 139
Struit, Rhoda - 145
Thompson, Charles W - 12, 148
Tilley, Martha - 148
Turnham, Frances - 153
Vendrick, Nice - 155
Walton, William A - 62
Warren, Fitz Henry - 22, 90
Watkins, Charlotte - 157

ABOUT THE AUTHOR

JOHN WALTER has been interested in the Civil War since his 8th grade teacher made history come alive for him more than fifty years ago. He specializes in small unit histories and the lives and activities of individual soldiers. In 1994 John turned his Civil War hobby and avocation into a full time profession as a genealogist and historical researcher. He and his wife Peg have four children and two grandchildren. He has lived in Middle Village, Queens County, New York, his entire life.

www.ingramcontent.com/pod-product-compliance
Lightning Source LLC
Chambersburg PA
CBHW051048160426
43193CB00010B/1112